A Nicaraguan Exceptionalism?

Debating the Legacy of the Sandinista Revolution

edited by Hilary Francis

Institute of Latin American Studies, School of Advanced Study,
University of London, 2020

British Library Cataloguing-in-Publication Data
A catalogue record for this book is available from the British Library

This book is published under a Creative Commons Attribution-NonCommercial-NoDerivatives 4.0 International (CC BY-NC-ND 4.0) license. More information regarding CC licenses is available at https://creativecommons.org/licenses/.

This book is also available online at http://humanities-digital-library.org.

ISBN:
978-1-908857-57-6 (paperback edition)
978-1-908857-78-1 (.epub edition)
978-1-908857-79-8 (.mobi edition)
978-1-908857-77-4 (PDF edition)

DOI: 10.14296/220.9781908857774 (PDF edition)

Institute of Latin American Studies
School of Advanced Study
University of London
Senate House
London WC1E 7HU

Telephone: 020 7862 8844

Email: ilas@sas.ac.uk
Web: http://ilas.sas.ac.uk

Typesetting by Thomas Bohm, User Design, Illustration and Typesetting.

Cover image © Franklin Villavicencio.

Contents

	List of illustrations	v
	Notes on contributors	vii
	Introduction: exceptionalism and agency in Nicaragua's revolutionary heritage *Hilary Francis*	1
1.	'We didn't want to be like Somoza's Guardia': policing, crime and Nicaraguan exceptionalism *Robert Sierakowski*	21
2.	'The revolution was so many things' *Fernanda Soto*	45
3.	Nicaraguan food policy: between self-sufficiency and dependency *Christiane Berth*	61
4.	On Sandinista ideas of past connections to the Soviet Union and Nicaraguan exceptionalism *Johannes Wilm*	87
5.	Agrarian reform in Nicaragua in the 1980s: lights and shadows of its legacy *José Luis Rocha*	103
6.	The difference the revolution made: decision-making in Liberal and Sandinista communities *Hilary Francis*	127
7.	Grassroots verticalism? A Comunidad Eclesial de Base in rural Nicaragua *David Cooper*	145
8.	Nicaraguan legacies: advances and setbacks in feminist and LGBTQ activism *Florence E. Babb*	165
9.	Conclusion: exceptionalism and Nicaragua's many revolutions *Justin Wolfe*	179
	Index	185

List of illustrations

Figure
1.1 'Courtesy and respect for the law are inseparable'. 'A man who does not respect a woman is a coward. A man who does not respect a young female police officer (una muchacha policía) and does not follow her instructions is twice as cowardly and also an enemy of the law.' (Tomás Borge). 29
3.1 Basic grain production, 1977–90 (in t). 67
5.1 Evolution in the size of farms by range (in percentages of land used for agriculture). 120

Notes on contributors

Florence Babb is Harrington Distinguished Professor in Anthropology at the University of North Carolina at Chapel Hill. She specializes in gender and sexuality as well as race and class in changing contexts in Latin America. Her publications include *After Revolution: Mapping Gender and Cultural Politics in Neoliberal Nicaragua* (University of Texas Press, 2001), *The Tourism Encounter: Fashioning Latin American Nations and Histories* (Stanford University Press, 2011), and *Women's Place in the Andes: Engaging Decolonial Feminist Anthropology* (University of California Press, 2018).

Christiane Berth is Wilhelm and Alexander von Humboldt Chair in Humanities and Social Sciences at the University of Costa Rica. A historian of food politics and consumer history in global perspective, with a particular focus on Mexico and Central America, Dr Berth has published widely on the history of food politics in Nicaragua. Other recent works include a book on the history of the coffee trade between Germany and Central America; a chapter on Sandinista comics for the University of Pittsburgh Press; and an edited volume on the culture of Sandinismo in Nicaragua.

David Cooper is a social anthropologist, and received his PhD from the department of anthropology at UCL in 2015. He has since held several postdoctoral positions, most recently the ESRC-funded 'Politicised provision: development and welfare under Latin America's new left'. His publications include 'Grounding rights: populist and peasant conceptions of entitlement in rural Nicaragua' (Social Analysis) and 'Pentecostalism and the peasantry: domestic and spiritual economies in rural Nicaragua' (Ethnos). He is currently teaching at the University of Bristol.

Hilary Francis is a Vice-Chancellor's Research Fellow at the University of Northumbria. Her doctoral research – on Nicaragua's Contra War – drew on extensive oral history research with ex-combatants in Nicaragua. She is currently working on two postdoctoral projects: a history of the relationship between US aid and pesticide use in Nicaragua; and a collaborative study of the environmental and health impacts of the Masaya volcano from 1850 to the present.

José Luis Rocha is Senior Researcher at the Universidad Rafael Landívar in Guatemala and Universidad Centroamericana "José Simeón Cañas" in El Salvador, and associate Researcher with the Brooks World Poverty Institute at the University of Manchester. He holds a PhD in Sociology from the Philipps-Universität Marburg, Germany. His work focuses on issues relating to youth gangs, social movements, political analysis, and migration. He is a member of the editorial committee of the academic journal Anuario de Estudios Centroamericanos (Costa Rica) and the magazine Envío. His last publications include the books *Autoconvocados y conectados. Los universitarios en la revuelta de abril en Nicaragua* (UCA publicaciones y UCA editores, 2019), *El debate sobre la justica maya. Encuentros y desencuentros del pluralismo jurídico en la Guatemala del siglo XXI* (EDUSAC, 2019), *La desobediencia de las masas. La migración no autorizada de centroamericanos a Estados Unidos como desobediencia civil* (UCA editores, 2018), and *Expulsados de la globalización* (IHNCA, 2011).

Robert Sierakowski received his PhD in history from UCLA. His book *Sandinistas: A Moral History* is forthcoming from the University of Notre Dame Press. Dr Sierakowski is a history teacher and advisor in the Department of History, Trevor Day School. He is a former lecturer in the Department of History and Archaeology at the University of the West Indies.

Fernanda Soto (PhD, University of Texas at Austin) is the author of *Ventanas en la Memoria: recuerdos de la Revolución en la Frontera Agrícola* (UCA, 2011). Dr Soto is Projects Coordinator at the NGO Winds of Peace and a researcher at the Center for Global Education and Experience, Ausgburg University, USA.

Johannes Wilm obtained his PhD from Goldsmiths College in 2013. His book *Nicaragua, Back from the Dead? An Anthropological View of the Sandinista Movement in the Early 21st Century* was published by New Left Notes in 2011. Wilm is currently affiliated with the Historical Studies section at the Department of Society, Culture and Identity at the University of Malmö.

Justin Wolfe is a William Arceneaux Professor of Latin American History and Suzanne and Stephen Weiss Presidential Fellow. He specializes in Central America, particularly post-colonial social and cultural history. His research interest include nation-formation, race and ethnicity, and the African Diaspora. His publications include *Blacks and Blackness in Central America: Between Race and Place* (Duke University Press, 2010) and *The Everyday Nation-State: Community and Ethnicity in Nineteenth-Century Nicaragua* (University of Nebraska Press, 2007).

Introduction: exceptionalism and agency in Nicaragua's revolutionary heritage

Hilary Francis

On 10 January 2017, ten days before Donald Trump took his oath of office, Daniel Ortega was sworn in as President of Nicaragua for the fourth time. These two very different presidents both gave inauguration speeches suffused with nationalism, but only one of them claimed that his country was exceptional. In his remarks to scattered crowds on Pennsylvania Avenue, Donald Trump promised to make America great again (again), but in spite of his inflated jingoistic rhetoric, Trump is not, in fact, an American exceptionalist. He does not believe that his country is innately different, nor that accidents of geography or history have conspired to set the United States apart as a nation with a particular role in the world. It was Ortega, not Trump, who used his inauguration speech to emphasise, once more, his belief in Nicaragua's exceptionalism, calling this small Central American country of six million people a 'blessed' nation.[1]

The contrast between the two indicates something fundamental about the nature of exceptionalism: it relies on a sense of a particular moral purpose. Trump rejects the concept because he rejects morality. For him, international politics is a zero sum game in pursuit of material resources. Therefore, the United States cannot be exceptional as long as other countries 'are eating our lunch'.[2] This logic leads him to conclude that the Iraq War was a bad idea because Americans did not 'take the oil' before getting out.[3] Daniel Ortega, in contrast, asserts that Nicaragua is exceptional precisely because, in spite of an acute lack of material resources, the particular moral character of Nicaraguans allows them to overcome great odds. Claiming that Nicaragua has 'the lowest crime rate in Latin America and one of the lowest on the planet', Ortega argues that 'These goals have been reached with limited material resources, because we have infinite moral

---

1 'Toma de posesion e investidura de Daniel Ortega en 2017', YouTube video, available at https://www.youtube.com/watch?v=qAKUaAWvX9k (accessed 15 Apr. 2019); S. Wertheim, 'Trump and American Exceptionalism' (2017).

2 Wertheim, 'Trump and American exceptionalism'.

3 Ibid.

H. Francis, 'Introduction: exceptionalism and agency in Nicaragua's revolutionary heritage', in H. Francis (ed.), *A Nicaraguan Exceptionalism? Debating the Legacy of the Sandinista Revolution* (London: University of London Press, 2019), pp. 1–19. License: CC-BY-NC-ND.

resources, that is our strength.'⁴ Rosario Murillo, who is both vice-president and first lady, claims that Nicaragua is a peaceful country in the midst of a 'world full of conflict' because 'Nicaraguans have accumulated within themselves a heritage of respect, moral strength, and admiration which is unbreakable, unyielding, hard-working and heroic, qualities which are recognised around the world.'⁵

This collection is, in part, a reaction to this government rhetoric. Its chapters began life as a set of papers presented at a conference at the Institute of Latin American Studies at the University of London in March 2015. At that time, several of us were thinking independently about the idea of Nicaraguan exceptionalism. The FSLN (Sandinista National Liberation Front) government's claims were always clearly overblown, but they belied a range of phenomena which suggested that Nicaragua really was different. Nicaragua was not wracked with violence in the same way as her Central American neighbours: homicide rates and levels of emigration to the United States were both substantially lower. Furthermore, beyond the rhetoric, it was clear that many Nicaraguans outside of the party of government – and vehemently opposed to it – also considered Nicaragua's heritage to be unique. They believed that their country's history bestowed on Nicaragua's citizens a particular set of strengths and traits, even as it imposed a particular – sometimes unbearable – burden upon them.

Nicaraguan exceptionalism is unique among exceptionalisms for the emphasis it places on the moral duty of the individual. Many cultures of exceptionalism rely upon a belief in the particular moral virtues of a nation's citizens, but most combine this with a conviction that certain material factors have contributed to this cultural exceptionalism. The United States, it is argued, is exceptional because of the vast resources that were mobilised by westward expansion. Venezuela is exceptional because of its oil reserves. Cuba is exceptional because its strategic importance meant that independence came late and, once the revolution had triumphed, the island's topography ensured ease of control.⁶ In the Nicaraguan case a similar retreat to the concrete is impossible. Before the revolution in 1979 nobody had suggested that Nicaragua was exceptional nor that the nation possessed any intrinsic assets that made the revolution more likely. Nicaraguan exceptionalism is seen as the result of human endeavour, achieved by sheer force of will.

The lens of exceptionalism gives us a new way to consider an old question, much discussed in scholarship on Nicaragua: what remains of the revolution?⁷

4   *La Voz del Sandinismo*, 'Daniel: Policía Nacional tiene resultados excepcionales', 9 Dec. 2014.
5   Y. Prado Reyes, 'Compañera Rosario', 12 Dec. 2016.
6   I. Tyrrell, 'American exceptionalism in an age of international history', 96 (4) (1991); S. Ellner and M. Tinker Salas, 'The Venezuelan exceptionalism thesis: separating myth from reality' (2007); L. Whitehead, 'On Cuban political exceptionalism', (2007).
7   D. Rodgers, 'Searching for the time of beautiful madness (2009); F. Babb, *After revolution* (2001); R. Montoya, *Gendered Scenarios of Revolution* (2012). The idea of Nicaraguan exceptionalism is addressed explicitly in S. Martí i Puig and D. Close, 'La excepción Nicaragüense?' (2009); and J.M. Cruz, 'Democratization under assault: criminal violence in post-transition Central America', PhD diss., Vanderbilt University, 2010.

Were the sacrifices that brought the Sandinistas to power in 1979 entirely in vain? What tangible (and not so tangible) changes survived the upheaval of the revolutionary decade? It was clear to us that any credible answer to this question required scholarship that was fully grounded in both the past and the present, and which gave a detailed account of the connections between the two. As a group of historians, sociologists and anthropologists, that task forced all of us out of our immediate comfort zones. It demanded that the social scientists think in more detail about the historical antecedents for the phenomena they described, and it required the historians to write all the way up to the present. At the time of writing, the historians especially have reason to curse the hubris that pushed us into this endeavour. The present is always a moving target, but in 2018 Nicaragua experienced the most intense period of political upheaval since the revolution of 1979. The verdict of the *Envío* editorial team in the month after the violence began cannot be disputed: 'There is a clear dividing line between the Nicaragua that existed before these unexpected days of rebellion and the Nicaragua of today. We still don't know how this new country, born of this outburst of unrest, will take shape. But we know that nothing will be in the same place as it was before.'[8]

The violence of 2018 ripped Nicaraguan society open in ways that may never be repaired. But it also exposed continuities that were a surprise to many. In 2007, when Daniel Ortega first returned to power, former vice-president and leading dissident Sergio Ramírez spoke of a Nicaragua that was divided into three: the deluded who chose to believe Ortega's promises about a second stage of the revolution; the betrayed, who felt that their revolutionary-era sacrifices had come to nothing; and the young, who viewed 'what has come down to them from history as a cacophony so confused as to induce only oblivion'.[9] In fact, events of recent months have shown that young Nicaraguans are not the apathetic, self-involved consumerist types that their elders had hitherto perceived them to be.[10] Young Nicaraguans have led the current protest movement – and they have done so by drawing widely and creatively on Nicaragua's revolutionary traditions. In their actions and analysis they have made it clear that they are keenly aware of their country's recent past. They have shown that they are heirs to a particular sense of agency and duty, a particular moral imperative, which we call Nicaraguan exceptionalism. This introduction has three sections. The first discusses the evolution of exceptionalist ideas from 1979 until 2017. The second looks at the ways in which these same ideas have played out during the protest

---

8   *Envío*, 'Abril 2018: La insurrección de la conciencia', no. 434, May 2018, http://www.envio.org.ni/articulo/5479 (accessed 15 Apr. 2019).

9   S. Ramírez, 'Nicaragua: through the abyss', 3 Sept. 2007.

10 M. Córdoba, 'La apática generación post-revolución sale a las calles y hace tambalear al gobierno de Daniel Ortega', *Infobae*, 22 Apr. 2018. There is substantial survey data and other research which suggest that most young people are not interested in politics. See, e.g., F. Maradiaga, 'Youth analysis for strategic planning', 28 Nov. 2017.

movement and government crackdown of 2018. The last explores in more detail each chapter's particular contribution to this volume.

Exceptionalism in the 'first' and 'second' stages of the revolution: 1979–2017

In 1979 the FSLN led a broad-based popular movement which overthrew the dictatorship of the Somoza dynasty. The Somozas had ruled Nicaragua for 43 years, relying on US support and increasingly brutal repression to remain in power. When Ronald Reagan's administration began an undeclared war on Nicaragua, the country's plight became an international cause célèbre. International supporters of the Sandinistas were drawn by the conflict's stark injustice – with the might of the United States ranged against a tiny, impoverished Central American nation – but they were also attracted by the Sandinistas' policies. A mixed economy, the county's first free elections in 1984, and a commitment to grassroots democracy, via a series of mass organisations, all suggested that Nicaragua might be the first example of viable, democratic socialism, succeeding where so many others failed before. At the time, academics frequently referred to the Nicaraguan experience as a 'unique experiment'.[11]

In 1990, with the economy in crisis and the country struggling with the impact of a decade of war, Nicaraguans voted the Sandinistas out of office, opting instead for a coalition of mainly right-wing parties backed by the United States. Sixteen years of right-wing neoliberal government ensued, until Daniel Ortega was elected to the presidency in November 2006, and then won further elections in 2011 and 2016. He has held office continuously for more than a decade, overturning Nicaragua's constitutional prohibition on re-election in order to do so. Ortega's new period in office has been characterised by an acute intolerance for any threat to his hold on power, however slight. In 1990, Ortega had agreed to bring elections forward as part of the Central American peace process, because he and the FSLN assumed that they would win comfortably. The shock of that defeat, and the fact that it took the FSLN 16 years to return to office, created the conditions for the paranoia and increasing authoritarianism that have characterised the FSLN's attitude to power since 2007.[12]

From the beginning, there were clear irregularities in the way that elections were run. In the 2008 municipal elections – the first held with the FSLN as national incumbent – the number of votes cast exceeded the number of voters

---

11 The phrase 'unique experiment' is used, to give just a few examples, in R.S. Garfield and G. Williams, *Health and Revolution: The Nicaraguan Experience* (1989), 197; C. Robinson, *Nicaragua: Against All Odds* (1989), 12; D. Faber, *Environment under Fire: Imperialism and the Ecological Crisis in Central America* (1993), 189; T. Walker, *Nicaragua: The Land of Sandino* (1986), 120; H.E. Vanden and G. Prevost, *Democracy and Socialism in Sandinista Nicaragua* (1996), 75.

12 For a visceral account of the Sandinista experience of the 1990 electoral defeat, see S. Ramírez, *Confesión de amor* (1991).

on the electoral roll in multiple districts in 40 different municipalities.[13] In 2011, there were widespread irregularities in the electoral process, even though opinion poll data suggest that the government could have won comfortably without fraud: the FSLN's goal was not just to win, but to win an absolute majority in the National Assembly. IPADE, a respected Nicaraguan NGO with a long history of election monitoring, was denied accreditation. International observers from the European Union and the Organisation of American States (OAS) were accredited in 2011, but their work was significantly undermined: 20 per cent of the OAS observers were prevented from observing election-day preparations at the polling stations to which they had been assigned, which meant that they could not verify that the ballot boxes were empty when they were sealed.[14] No independent election observers, national or international, were accredited for the 2016 presidential elections. In any event, the contest was a foregone conclusion because Eduardo Montealegre, leader of the main opposition party, was removed from office by Nicaragua's Supreme Court less than five months before the vote.[15]

This need for absolute control is also clear in the Ortega administration's attitude to peaceful protest. Orteguista officials clearly subscribe to the notion that 'whoever has the streets has the power' and in the years since 2007 they have acted accordingly.[16] In 2013 a group of elderly protestors and their student supporters staged a sit-in demonstration at the Institute of Social Security (INSS) to demand pension reform. They were beaten, threatened and robbed by an organised group of assailants who had been transported to the scene in vehicles belonging to the Managua mayor's office. The attacks took place in full view of the Nicaraguan police, who did not intervene as the violence unfolded.[17] Since 2013 anti-canal protestors have fiercely resisted the government's transoceanic canal project. Their protests have repeatedly been thwarted by Nicaraguan police and groups of pro-government supporters: in 2014 a demonstrator lost an eye after police shot him with a rubber bullet, and in 2016 a bridge was destroyed to prevent peasant protesters taking part in a march.[18]

---

13 Such discrepancies were not apparent in subsequent elections because the government stopped releasing district-by-district statistics. Consorcio Panorama Electoral, 'Informe preliminar elecciones 2016', 4.

14 *Envío*, 'Elecciones 2011: Perdió Nicaragua', no. 356, Nov. 2011; The Carter Center, 'The 2011 Elections in Nicaragua', Study Mission Report, 7.

15 N. Lakhani, 'Nicaragua suppresses opposition to ensure one-party election, critics say', *Guardian*, 26 June 2016.

16 G. Rothschuh, 'Observatorio de los medios', *Confidencial*, 17 Apr. 2018.

17 *Envío*, 'The challenge of the others', no. 384, July 2013; Centro Nicaraguense de Derechos Humanos (CENIDH), 'Violaciones de derechos humanos en el contexto de la protesta de los adultos mayores por su derecho a una pensión reducida de vejez', 27 June 2013; C. Salinas, 'El gobierno de Ortega reprime la protesta de los "viejitos" en Nicaragua', *El País*, 23 June 2013.

18 CENIDH, *Derechos humanos en Nicaragua: Informe 2013* (2014), 39; CENIDH, *Derechos humanos en Nicaragua: Informe 2015* (2016), 42–4; M. Aguilera, 'Destrozan puente para impidir marcha campesina', *Hoy*, 30 Nov. 2016; V. Vásquez, 'Perdió un ojo en marcha anticanal, pero continúa en la protesta', *Confidencial*, 18 June 2017.

A pattern of state violence has also been reported in the north of Nicaragua, where former Contra combatants have rearmed in opposition to the FSLN government. Press and human rights reports indicate that between 2011 and 2017 the Nicaraguan army killed at least 31 people in at least 14 attacks on suspected Contra groups, suggesting a widespread practice of extrajudicial execution of armed opponents of the government.[19]

Nonetheless, in the 11 years before April 2018 the Ortega government was able to broadcast its version of Nicaraguan exceptionalism with some success, partly because of economic progress. In 2015 IMF executive director Otaviano Canuto described Nicaragua as 'a success story in the making' and by 2017 the country had the third highest growth rate in Latin America. The 'buoyant' economic growth was partly the result of aid from Venezuela, but it was also built upon the firm pact established between Ortega's government and the Nicaraguan private sector.[20] This economic growth was closely linked to the central thread in the government's claims to exceptionalism: the idea that Nicaragua was the safest country in Central America. And while some have questioned the claim, the statistics certainly supported it: in 2017 murders in Nicaragua totalled 431, or 7 per 100,000 people, a fraction of the 60 per 100,000 reported in nearby El Salvador. Huge numbers of migrant children have arrived in the United States from Central America in recent years, but hardly any come from Nicaragua, even though it is the poorest country in the region.[21] The crudest explanations for this difference suggest that Nicaraguans have no need to flee violence and high crime rates because 'Nicaragua has good cops', an approach that has aged extremely poorly since April 2018.[22] Nonetheless, even if we discount the

19 L.E. Martínez M., 'Ejército enfrentó a un solo hombre en Ayapal', *La Prensa*, 9 Mar. 2017; A. Cerda, 'Ejército letal contra "armados"', *Confidencial*, 7 Feb. 2017; CENIDH, 'Informe del CENIDH sobre violaciones de derechos humanos en Las Magdalenas, Ciudad Antigua, Nueva Segovia', 17 Nov. 2016; E. Romero, 'Muere el armado Enrique Aguinaga en enfrentamiento con Ejército de Nicaragua', *La Prensa*, 30 Apr. 2016; E. Chamorro Mendieta, 'Cerrato fue torturado con saña antes de su asesinato', *La Prensa*, 24 Apr. 2016; E. Romero, 'Seis muertos en combate entre Ejército y armados en Ayapal', *La Prensa*, 30 Mar. 2016; 'Dos muertos tras enfrentamiento con la Policía en Jinotega', *La Prensa*, 21 Aug. 2015; CENIDH, 'Informe del CENIDH concluye: "Fue una acción militar"', 9 Feb. 2015; W. Aragón, 'Sepultan a ex Contra "Triple H"', *La Prensa*, 15 Sept. 2014; 'Nicaragua: La Contra conmemora desmovilizacion mientras siguen asesinando a sus dirigentes', *Nicaragua Hoy*, 27 June 2014; E. Romero, 'Ejército confirma muerte de "Cascabel"', *La Prensa*, 16 Apr. 2014; A. Lorío, 'Asesinan al "flaco Midence"', *La Prensa*, 22 Dec. 2013; E. Romero, 'Repudio en pantasma por muertes', *La Prensa*, 12 Oct. 2013.

20 O. Canuto, 'Nicaragua: a success story in the making', *Huffington Post*, 11 Sept. 2015; Economic Commission for Latin America and the Caribbean, *Preliminary Overview of the Economies of Latin America and the Caribbean 2018: Briefing Paper*; IMF, 'IMF concludes staff visit to Nicaragua', 5 Dec. 2016.

21 T. Clavel, '2017 homicide rates in Latin America and the Caribbean', *Insight Crime*, 19 Jan. 2018; D. Rodgers, 'Living in the shadow of death: gangs, violence and social order in urban Nicaragua, 1996–2002' (May 2006), 267–92.

22 J. Replogle, 'Why Nicaraguan kids aren't fleeing to U.S.', *KPB2*, 29 Jul. 2014; National Public Radio, 'Why Nicaragua's not in the conversation about Central American migrants', 1 Aug, 2014; I. Castro, 'Migration outlier: how Nicaragua escaped neighbors' deadly spiral',

Nicaraguan government's boasts of the country's 'infinite moral resources', it is clear that Nicaragua's recent history follows a distinctive path that requires further explanation.

Before April 2018 talk of Nicaraguan exceptionalism was not confined to Ortega and his allies; nevertheless, other versions of the discourse carried nothing of the confidence and triumphalism expressed by the government. Rather, Sandinistas from all walks of life felt a pervading sense of guilt and betrayal. The belief that Nicaragua was – and should be – unique led them to feel that they had failed, because so many of the dreams of the revolution had come to nothing. José Luis Rocha, who discusses agrarian reform in this volume, has written elsewhere about his experience as a *brigadista* in the 1980 literacy crusade, giving a lucid account of this pernicious sense of guilt and anger over a dream betrayed:

> We have journeyed from frankness to dissembling, from a straightforward and direct way of doing things to one involving a thousand twists and turns. From taking pride in being able to walk for hours, tame a horse, rope a mule and milk a cow, we now boast about our new cars, our credit cards and the clubs and graduate degrees we are accumulating. What we have is what we are. The Miami way of life won out over the revolutionary culture. We lost that battle … and it was the most decisive one.[23]

This same sense of guilt is shared by some of the poorest Nicaraguans, those without access to the 'Miami way of life'. In her 20-year study of the Sandinista community of Tule, Rosario Montoya argues that the expectations created by revolutionary discourse left the citizens of Tule with a crippling sense of guilt for having 'failed' to fulfil an impossible dream of the utopian 'new man' and 'new woman' of the revolution.[24]

The burden of this strain of exceptionalism led many dissident Sandinistas to blame themselves for Ortega's increasing authoritarianism. In an article written in 2016, Henry Ruiz, a member of the Sandinistas' governing junta in the 1980s, asked, 'How did we get here?' He found his answer in searing self-criticism. 'We are the people most responsible for the fact that Daniel Ortega is where he is, all of us who fought against the Somoza dictatorship, all of us of the generation that fought against the dictatorship and then little by little allowed this man to ensconce himself in power … Yes, we are guilty, some more than others.'[25]

In the months since April 2018 that sense of guilt has turned to anger and defiance. The impact of the violence itself is shocking enough, but the events of 2018 also forced many Nicaraguans to relive the buried traumas of the past. The period of silent resentment is over, and this new outpouring of grief and

---

Reuters, 28 Aug. 2014; R. Lovato, 'What explains Nicaragua's surprisingly low murder rate?', *Boston Globe*, 12 Jan. 2018.

23 J.L. Rocha, 'A passionate memory in times of disillusion', *Envío*, no. 230, Sept. 2000.
24 Montoya, *Gendered Scenarios of Revolution*.
25 H. Ruiz, 'Daniel Ortega es un tránsfuga político y la tarea hoy es evitar que consolide su dictadura familiar', *Envío*, no. 414, Sept. 2016.

anger has made the discourses of exceptionalism more obvious and more explicit: fervent patriotism and ideas about duty to country form the backbone of the current opposition movement.

Exceptionalism and the martyrs of April: April–December 2018

The violence began on 18 April 2018. Two days earlier, the government had finalised reforms to the Nicaraguan Institute of Social Security (INSS). The INSS had been struggling for some time and Nicaraguan journalists have discovered a range of issues relating to mismanagement and financial impropriety.[26] The government's implementation of the INSS reforms was a response to pressure from the IMF, but it was poorly timed. In the weeks before, hundreds of students had protested against the government's mismanagement of a forest fire in the Indio Maíz reserve in the south of the country. These protests were the most significant student mobilisation since the INSS protests of 2013. It is difficult to understand, therefore, why the government chose to press ahead with the INSS reforms – a known flashpoint – when the momentum of student protests had already begun to build.

On 18 April government supporters used familiar tactics, roughing up demonstrators and journalists in Managua and León. Photographs of bloodied protesters, including pensioners, led to larger demonstrations the next day. At this point, for reasons which are still unclear, the state responded with unprecedented, lethal force. According to Ligia Gómez, a former Sandinista official at Nicaragua's Central Bank, a meeting of party officials was convened at midday on 19 April. '*Vamos con todo*', they were told. 'We're going to give it everything we've got. We're not going to let them steal the revolution from us.'[27] Later that day, two protestors and a policeman were killed, but the escalation only served to increase dissent. Demonstrations took place across the country on the following day, and agents of the state across the country responded with lethal force. On 20 April eight people were killed in Managua, two in Ciudad Sandino, one in Tipitapa, two in Estelí, three in León, four in Masaya and one in Sébaco.[28]

In the next few months more than 325 Nicaraguans were killed, most at the hands of agents of the state.[29] Hundreds of thousands of people, particularly the young, participated in marches, roadblocks and university occupations. The

26 'El mal manejo de los fondos del INSS', *La Prensa*, 3 Jul. 2017; J.A. Silva et al., 'Se siembra alarma entre pensionados', *El Nuevo Diario*, 3 June 2008.
27 W. Miranda Aburto, '"Vamos con todo": filtración desvela que Rosario Murillo ordenó aplastar las protestas en Nicaragua', *Univisión*, 21 Nov. 2018; C.F. Chamorro, 'Habla exsecretaria política FSLN en el Banco Central', *Confidencial*, 18 Nov. 2018.
28 Grupo Interdisciplinario de Expertos Independientes (GIEI) Nicaragua, 'Informe sobre los hechos de violencia occurridos entre el 18 de abril y el 30 de mayo 2018'.
29 OAS, IACHR, 'IACHR warns of new wave of repression in Nicaragua', 18 Oct. 2018; Amnesty International, 'Shoot to kill', 18 Oct., 2018, 5.

assumption that had prevailed for so long – that most young people had little interest in politics – was proved wrong. In many cases, the most intense resistance came from traditionally Sandinista working-class neighbourhoods: Monimbó in Masaya, the eastern barrios of Managua, Barrio Sandino in Jinotega.[30] Foreign journalists came to Nicaragua in a trickle rather than the flood seen in the 1980s. But they did come. And they saw a rebellion that looked like the mirror image of the Sandinistas' struggle to overthrow Somoza. Multiple articles asked how Ortega had become a copy of the dictator he had helped to overthrow, and many noted the obvious echoes of the past: the use of *adoquines* (hexagonal paving stones) to make barricades; the ubiquity of the rallying cry '*que se rinda tu madre*' ('Tell your mother to surrender', the last words of Sandinista poet and revolutionary Leonel Rugama).[31] In the *New Yorker*, Jon Lee Anderson traced the historical roots still further, linking Masaya's trenchant resistance to a century of rebellion stretching back to the war of 1912.[32]

Nicaraguans themselves were clear that this tradition of rebellion made them unique. When Evo Morales tweeted in defence of Ortega, suggesting that, just as in Venezuela, the Nicaraguan government was the victim of a US-backed coup, Nicaraguan journalist Tifani Roberts derided the possibility of any comparison with Venezuela. 'No one can tame Nicaraguans,' she said, 'They don't bow their heads, they won't allow it, they're brave, they defend themselves, they do not surrender.'[33] Here, we suggest that Nicaraguan ideas of exceptionalism stem from the experience of the revolutionary decade, but Nicaraguans themselves offered a range of theories in their responses to Roberts' comment. For some, Nicaraguans' defiance came from Sandino; for others, it was the legacy of rebellious, indigenous blood. Exceptionalism was no longer confined to those who still called themselves Sandinistas.

In the months after the violence began, the discursive tradition of exceptionalism meant that many Nicaraguans did not just hope that they might overthrow a dictatorship once again – they knew that they must, and would. The sense of a duty and moral imperative imposed by the sacrifices of those who came before them was palpable and inescapable. In the week after the violence began, Nicaraguan poet and revolutionary Gioconda Belli wrote of a 'judgement day' for Nicaragua's rulers, and a struggle suffused with the presence the country's heroes and martyrs:

> The blood of those who fought for a free country: those who fell in the struggle against Somoza and those who have fallen in the last 11 years and

---

30 *La Prensa*, 'Barrio Sandino, el pequeño Monimbó de Jinotega', 18 June 2018; E. Reyes, 'Sitios que fueron resistencia del sandinismo y hoy se levantaron en contra', *Maje*, 13 June 2018.

31 C. Lane, 'Ortega is becoming the sort of autocrat he once despised', *Washington Post*, 16 July 2018; J. Webber, 'A rebel no more, Ortega comes to resemble the dictator he replaced', *Irish Times*, 22 Aug. 2018; J. Bauluz, 'Viewpoint: Ortega's Nicaragua crisis evokes memories of past', BBC, 1 Sept. 2018.

32 J.L. Anderson, '"Fake news" and unrest in Nicaragua', *New Yorker*, 27 Aug. 2018.

33 T. Roberts, Tweet, https://twitter.com/TifaniRoberts/status/994793874873901057?s=19 (accessed 16 Apr. 2019).

above all in this brave week, that blood has returned to live again in this new generation of Nicaraguans who are ready to revive the dream of a free fatherland. Those exemplary, generous men and women who wanted to light up the darkness did not exist in vain. Their ghosts are with us, their legacy is with us. Sandino lives.

The principle that sacrifice denotes political authority has also been passed on to this new generation of protestors. In May, 20-year-old student Lesther Alemán challenged Ortega on the first day of the national dialogue, which was broadcast live. Alemán asserted his right, as a representative of the students, to demand Ortega's departure, because '*nosotros hemos puesto los muertos*' ('We have provided the dead').[34] His phrasing echoed a dark joke in the 1980s about the power of Conservative elites from the city of Granada which suggested that 'León provided the dead, Granada provided the ministers'.[35]

Leonel Delgado has expressed concern about this 'sacrificial narrative', and many within the protest movement are aware of the dangers of such an approach.[36] For this reason, one of the most popular slogans of the movement has been 'Free fatherland and life!', a reformulation, favoured by Sandinista poet Ernesto Cardenal in the early 1980s, of the standard revolutionary slogan 'Free fatherland or death!'[37] But despite this obvious self-awareness, there is still a real danger that the exceptionalism which drives the movement will also be its downfall. Exceptionalism lends itself to Manichean versions of history, it pits pantheons of heroes against pantheons of villains. The current movement has claimed for its own the revolutionary heroes who died before 1979 and consigned to the scrapheap anyone who has collaborated with Ortega in recent years.[38] But in order to avoid repeating the mistakes of the past, this new generation will need a much deeper understanding of the exact nature of those mistakes. Many of the most reflective, critical voices in Nicaraguan civil society are fully aware that the only way forward is to seek a much deeper engagement with more nuanced accounts of the past. This book hopes to contribute to that search.

---

34 *El Nuevo Diario*, 'Primer día del diálogo nacional en Nicaragua'.
35 C.M. Vilas, 'Family affairs: class, lineage and politics in contemporary Nicaragua' (1992): 309–41, 324.
36 L. Delgado, 'Fin de Época', *Situación de Nicaragua*, 22 Apr. 2018.
37 *El País*, 'Ernesto Cardenal inaugurará en Madrid una exposición de arte', 4 Dec. 1981.
38 See, e.g., the photo of a mural in Rivas, taken by Tom Phillips, in which the faces of Tomás Borge and Daniel Ortega have been defaced, but that of Carlos Fonseca has been left untouched. 'Ghost resorts: Nicaragua crisis ravages nascent tourism industry', *Guardian*, 6 Aug. 2018.

Debating Nicaraguan exceptionalism

Aside from Robert Sierakowski's contribution, these chapters were finalised just before the violence of 2018 began. They take varying approaches to the subject: some are concerned with the question of whether the concrete gains of the revolution really were exceptional, others explore Nicaraguans' own exceptionalist beliefs. Throughout, there is a clear connecting thread: a sense of agency. Our findings echo the work of Rosario Montoya in the village of Tule, where local citizens displayed 'a commitment to active participation in their own lives' as well as a 'belief in their capacity to affect the forces that shape their lives and society' which, she suggests, may be the most durable legacy of the Sandinista Revolution.[39]

If asked in March 2018, I would not have said that our approach to this legacy was romanticised. Most of the scholars involved in this volume were born around the time of the revolution. We began our professional lives long after the electoral defeat of 1990, and the scholarship in which we immersed ourselves was preoccupied with the failure of the Sandinista project and the reasons for that failure.[40] Much of what follows conveys the bleak sense of disappointment that has characterised many people's relationship with the Sandinista Revolution for many years.

Nonetheless, there is no doubt that rereading this work in the light of recent events brings different things to the fore. In his account of the Nicaraguan police, Robert Sierakowski draws on Seymour Martin Lipset's concept of exceptionalism as a double-edged sword. In Sierakowski's version, exceptionalist beliefs in Nicaragua inculcated the unswerving loyalty and dedication that produced the successes of the National Police in the 1980s and '90s, but also prepared the ground for the violence of 2018. Similarly, Johannes Wilm writes of the confidence and self-belief that led the FSLN to act as if it were a much larger power on the international stage. A year ago, this posturing was an interesting anomaly that sometimes yielded results. Now, it helps to explain a far more maladjusted and damaging set of behaviours. In December 2018, for example, it looked as though the OAS would invoke its democratic charter against Nicaragua. The FSLN government had precipitated this by closing NGOs and arresting journalists, seemingly oblivious to the inevitable international reaction. Former ambassador José Luis Velásquez noted that the regime 'was unable to

---

39 Montoya, *Gendered Scenarios of Revolution*, 202.
40 This literature includes, but is not limited to: A. Bendaña, *Una tragedia campesina: testimonios de la resistencia* (1991); Rodgers, 'Searching for the time of beautiful madness'; Babb, *After Revolution*; J.L. Gould, *To Lead as Equals: Rural Protest and Political Consciousness in Chinandega, Nicaragua, 1912–1979* (1990); O. Núñez Soto and G. Cardenal, *La Guerra en Nicaragua* (1991); F. Soto Joya, *Ventanas en la memoria: recuerdos de la revolución en la frontera agrícola* (2011).

recognise' the climate of international opinion and the predictable consequences of their actions.[41]

It would be a serious mistake, however, to read what follows as nothing more than a cautionary tale about the dangers of fanaticism. My own chapter compares decision-making in two rural communities, one fiercely Sandinista and the other a former bastion of support for the Contras. Both communities exercise considerable agency in different ways, but the Sandinista community, here called El Junco, has developed a profound tradition of community participation and consultation which is clearly rooted in the community's experience of the revolutionary decade. Here as well, the double-edged sword of exceptionalism is clearly in play. In 2015, one interviewee in El Junco told me that his parents would 'never ever' change their support for Ortega, *'pase lo que pase'* ('Whatever happens'). He was not wrong. Some in the village, at great personal risk, have spoken out forcefully against the abuses that began in April 2018. But the majority of Junco residents still support Ortega. The supporters include some close friends who will not talk to me now. This is an experience shared by many Nicaraguans and others with close ties to the country. In a piece in *Confidencial*, Guadalupe Wallace Salinas describes the anguish caused by conflicts with friends and family members who are still complicit with or supportive of the FSLN regime. 'Along with the tears,' she writes, 'a part of me has gone.'[42]

It is not straightforward, therefore, to argue that we should listen to these voices. But it is crucial. In their May editorial, the *Envío* team declared, with not-at-all-concealed exasperation, that surely now the majority of Sandinistas would turn away from Daniel Ortega.[43] In fact, many have not, and the reasons for this require our close attention – now more than ever. This book shows clearly that the revolution failed because it could not deal with diversity. Whether it was confronted with young gay and lesbian revolutionaries or poor peasants who wanted their own land, the first FSLN government repeatedly imposed its own ideas of what was required, rather than engaging with the cacophony of voices, histories and ideas that it inherited in 1979.

There is a danger that this same pattern will repeat itself if Daniel Ortega ever steps down. Leading intellectuals and opposition figures in Nicaragua have been quick to condemn continuing support for the FSLN as the product of ignorance and lack of education. The similarity with pronouncements from the FSLN in the early 1980s is uncanny. When Félix Maradiaga suggests that the small percentage of the population which still supports Ortega needs to be 'rescued from the deceits to which poverty and oppression have condemned them' he sounds a lot like Tomás Borge in 1980, arguing that 'it was understandable' that peasants supported the Contras, because '400 years of exploitation and

---

41 J.I. Espinoza, '¿Cuáles son las consecuencias que sufriría Nicaragua con la Carta Democrática de la OEA?', *El Nuevo Diario*, 29 Dec. 2018.

42 G. Wallace Salinas, 'Nicaragua 2018: annus horribilis y annus mirabilis', *Confidencial*, 29 Dec. 2018.

43 *Envío*, 'Abril 2018: La insurrección de la conciencia', no. 434, May 2018.

misery which we inherited from Somocismo could not be wiped out in one year of revolution'.[44] In 2018 Sergio Ramírez went further. The basic problem, he suggested, was that Nicaragua continues to be a 'rural society' where a lack of progress and modernity allows dictatorships to flourish.[45]

The narrative of exceptionalism divides the world into enlightened fulfillers of moral destiny and ignorant types who hold up the march of progress. That approach obscures the infinite variety of ways in which Nicaraguans experience the present moment and the recent past. It complements and compounds an older set of discourses in which Nicaraguan intellectuals construct 'good peasants', who embody the change they want to see in the world, and 'bad peasants', who are the scapegoat for the failure to achieve that utopia.[46] It is these discourses, rather than rurality itself, which have no place in the 21st century.

Five of the eight chapters in this volume relate to the rural experience during and after the revolution. Alongside Rocha and Berth's chapters on food policy and agrarian reform come three chapters (from Soto, Cooper and myself) which draw on extensive fieldwork to give an account of the impact of changing relationships with the FSLN at the community level. There is no unity in our findings. Rather, the key contribution of this work is that it demonstrates the profound local and regional differences in the way that the revolution was experienced. A truly rich literature on experience of the revolution in the countryside, if we ever get one, might look something like the historiography of Shining Path and its antecedents in Peru: a complex mosaic of local and national power struggles which puts rural people's subjective experience of change at the centre of the story.[47]

This book is not only about the rural experience, although we cannot claim to provide a similarly comprehensive treatment of other aspects of the legacy of the revolution. Such an effort would require consideration of the experience of Nicaragua's Atlantic Coast, of the history of the army, and of the development of labour politics and trade unions, to name just a few of the most notable omissions. But the book's rural core is complemented by three chapters which

---

44 F. Maradiaga, Tweet, 30 July 2018, https://twitter.com/maradiaga/status/1023713856676290560 (accessed 16 Apr. 2019); 'Twenty-five peasants detained in Quilalí [sic] cleared', Radio Sandino, 4 Aug. 1980, Foreign Broadcast Information Service.

45 F.J. Larios, 'Sergio Ramírez: "Quiero transformar las cifras en rostros"', *El Nuevo Herald*, 28 Sept. 2018.

46 L. Delgado Aburto, 'Desplazamientos discursivos de la representación campesina en la Nicaragua pre y post-sandinista', *Latinoamérica: Revistas de estudios latinomericanos*, no. 58; L. Serra, 'El movimiento social nicaragüense por la defensa de la tierra, el agua y la soberanía' (2016), is a good example of the kind of homogenising, ahistorical approach which is common: a single rebellious peasant consciousness is attributed to an inheritance passed down from ancestors who fought the Spanish conquistadores and participated in Sandino's war against the US occupation in the 1920s and 1930s, among others.

47 See, e.g., S.J. Stern (ed.), *Shining and Other Paths: War and Society in Peru 1980–1995* (1998); K. Theidon, *Intimate Enemies: Violence and Reconciliation in Peru* (2012); J. Puente, 'La "massacre" de Ondores: reforma, comunidad y violencia en la Sierra Central (1969–1979)' (2016).

set the book within a wider context: Sierakowski's work on the police, Wilm's research with Sandinista activists in León and Babb's account of the LGBTQ (Lesbian, Gay, Bisexual, Trans and Queer Questioning) movement in Nicaragua since 1979. This combination helps us to think beyond an overly schematic separation of rural and urban experience. We show clearly that no homogenous rural world exists in Nicaragua: there is considerable variety between the rural case studies explored here. At the same time, crossovers and connections can be perceived between particular rural case studies and particular urban ones: we can see similarities between the single-minded devotion of Sierakowski's urban police recruits and the attitude of community activists noted by Wilm and myself in León and El Junco respectively. Babb's LGBTQ revolutionaries experience a tension between personal awakening and emotional investment in the revolution, tempered by a revolutionary state that coopts, manipulates and denies their true identity. There is much in that account which resonates with Soto's haunting, bleak rendition of the experience of Sandinista-supporting peasants on the agricultural frontier.

Robert Sierakowski's account of the Sandinista National Police, which opens the book, provides its starkest analysis of the dangers of exceptionalism. As elsewhere, there is an emphasis on the perception of power that the revolution brought, the changes wrought by a generation of young police cadets who saw themselves as 'the vanguard of the emerging socialist society ... [with] a transcendent mission that emphasised sacrifice, solidarity, humanism and human rights'. The case of the police service stands out, however: Sierakowski shows that this voluntaristic faith was translated into a tangible structural change in terms of a commitment to community policing and a strong institutional culture which scorned self-interest. This laid the foundations for a system of policing which successfully eradicated the endemic violence of the Somoza years. Ultimately, however, the success and sacrifice of the 1980s and '90s only serve to demonstrate the immensity of the police force's subsequent fall from grace. Sierakowski argues that the exceptionalist tradition made it easier for Ortega to use the police as a tool of state repression.

Fernanda Soto's account of Sandinista peasants in Mulukukú is equally preoccupied with the question of what has been lost, but she also turns her attention to what might still remain. Soto begins with the story of a recent murder, the alleged killing of a prominent landowner by a *mozo*, or labourer. Could it be, she asks, that it was because of the revolution that '*mozos* are not like they were before' – less deferential, less willing to suffer provocation in silence? Her answer to that question sets the tone for much of what follows: many of the achievements of the revolution proved to be ephemeral, partly because of the incalculable impact of the Contra War, but also because present and past interactions with the FSLN have reaped a harvest of inequality and corruption. However, she notes that, despite their wartime experiences, most of her informants continue to support the revolution, which 'opened a space for Nicaraguans to imagine themselves and their society in new ways'.

The sense that personal empowerment is the revolution's chief legacy is reinforced by Christiane Berth's chapter on the Sandinista food policy. Berth rejects the standard view, which attributes Nicaragua's nutritional crisis to the cuts of the neoliberal era after 1990. In fact, she argues, calorie intakes had already plummeted to the levels of the 1950s in the last years of the revolutionary decade. In the honeymoon years immediately after the revolution, the Sandinistas had sought to achieve self-sufficiency in basic foods, and the Nicaraguan programme was promoted by NGOs and international organisations as a model for food policy in the Global South. Ultimately though, this effort was unsuccessful, and Nicaragua's record regarding food policy cannot be regarded as exceptional. A number of factors, including the pressure of the Contra War and the economic blockade, as well as policy errors and increasing tensions between the Sandinista government and the peasantry, led to an increasingly severe subsistence crisis in the years after 1985. Berth argues that the present FSLN government's policies are a pale imitation of the programmes of the revolutionary era, because they do not include any attempt to make profound changes in economic structures or land distribution. Nonetheless, she suggests that civil society activism in Nicaragua, particularly the campaign for a food sovereignty law in the early 2000s, is evidence of the continuing existence of a vibrant network of peasant organisations, a direct legacy of the revolution itself.

In his chapter on Sandinista relations with the Eastern Bloc, Johannes Wilm seeks to define and explain the ways in which agency is understood within *Sandinismo*. Drawing on interviews with Sandinista activists in León and elsewhere, Wilm deploys the Nicaraguan term '*protagonismo*' to describe this set of ideas. He makes a direct link between Sandinista activists' *protagonismo* and their faith in Nicaraguan exceptionalism, and shows how activists' belief in Nicaraguans' superior political consciousness and organisational skills lead them to perceive their country as one that can act as the equal of any major power. In the eyes of these activists, Nicaragua is exceptional compared to the other countries of Central America, countries which are still bound to the United States by the chains of economic dependency. Wilm is careful to note that he is concerned with *perceptions* of exceptionalism, rather than the question of whether these beliefs reflect reality. Nonetheless, he suggests that the Sandinistas' enduring confidence on the world stage has had a tangible effect on the country's foreign relations: in recent years, just by insisting on its right to a strong alliance with Russia, Nicaragua has obtained something that seemed impossible.

In his account of Nicaragua's agrarian reform, José Luis Rocha suggests that the events of the revolutionary decade have left rural Nicaraguans with a particular sense of agency and capacity for organisation. But he takes pains to point out that this legacy is not the result of a deliberate plan executed by the FSLN government in the 1980s, but rather the product of a number of shifts in policy forced by opposition to the government in the countryside and the circumstances of the Contra War. The initially slow pace of agrarian reform, and a tendency to privilege large state farms over small-scale peasant production, created tensions between the government and landless peasants, which helped to accelerate support for the counter-revolution in rural Nicaragua. In later years, the distribution of small plots to peasant producers was emphasised, which helped to reduce rural support for the Contras. The piecemeal and contradictory nature of the reforms, combined with the pressures of war, meant that changes to land tenure were only partial. In many instances these were easily reversed after the Sandinistas' electoral defeat in 1990. Despite this, Rocha argues that agrarian reform did have lasting, tangible legacies which continue to make Nicaragua exceptional. A culture of cooperativism and the strength of peasant organisation have created particularly fruitful conditions for the development of fair-trade schemes in recent years. An existing knowledge of, and predisposition towards, 'democratic' cultivation has made Nicaragua a world leader in the fair-trade coffee market.

Rocha's overview of the revolution's legacy in the countryside is followed by two case studies which explore the impact of the revolution at the community level. My own chapter considers structures of decision-making in two rural communities: one is predominantly Sandinista and the other had strong ties to the Contras in the 1980s and has historically always voted for parties of the right. It suggests that the revolution allowed rural Sandinistas to develop a strong culture of local organisation and decision-making, a culture that persists to this day. However, it also points to the divisive effect of this legacy: communities that supported the Contras developed very different structures for decision-making, and these different legacies, in addition to the experience of the war itself, continue to set communities apart.

In his ethnography of the Segovian village of Gualiqueme, David Cooper argues that community members' sense of the legacy of the revolution is predicated upon a particular set of beliefs about what constitutes social change and how it is achieved. For Cooper, community residents are not primarily concerned with the wider social hierarchies that preoccupy NGOs and activists who work with the community. Rather, they think in terms of inclusion and exclusion, and hope to strengthen Gualiqueme's links with redistributive networks in the wider world. Seen in this light, Cooper suggests, the villagers' continuing support for Daniel Ortega's social programmes, and their continuing faith in the positive legacy of the revolution, make perfect sense. Villagers prize their ongoing relationship with Ortega and the FSLN because of the party's ability to bind the community more tightly with wider flows of material wealth.

In the book's final chapter, Florence Babb explores the revolution's equivocal record in relation to the LGBTQ movement. She argues that by the early 1990s Nicaragua was 'a regional leader in LGBTQ activism and cultural development', but she also notes the considerable difficulties that LGBTQ people continue to face in Nicaraguan society today. Babb suggests that this ambiguous outcome is rooted in the two faces of Nicaraguan exceptionalism. The revolution brought new encounters and freedoms that provided many with opportunities for self-discovery. The experience of organising in the revolution also allowed activists to develop 'the strategic tools necessary to develop a way of struggling for sexual rights'. At the same time, the heteronormative ethos of the revolution, and the emphasis on state-based development, placed restrictions on autonomous initiatives for change, restrictions which are also apparent in the actions of the current FSLN administration.

In his prescient conclusion to this volume, written before the outbreak of violence in 2018, Justin Wolfe notes the fragility of the apparent consensus forged by the FSLN. He wonders whether the legacies of the revolution will provide the necessary springboard for change when the status quo inevitably crumbles. At the time of writing, Nicaraguans are bitterly divided on that question. For every young protestor who claims the ideals and tactics of the revolution as their own, there is another Nicaraguan who regards the violence of 2018 as yet another reason to obliterate all traces of the Sandinista past once and for all. Future debates about the legacy of the revolution will be belligerent and near-impossible to resolve, but they are nonetheless preferable to the silence about the traumas of the 1970s and 80s that has prevailed for the last thirty years. Any new consensus will require a nuanced and unflinching attempt to reckon with Nicaragua's recent history. We hope that this book will contribute in some small way to that essential task.

Bibliography

Babb, F. (2001) *After Revolution: Mapping Gender and Cultural Politics in Neoliberal Nicaragua* (Austin, TX).

The Carter Center (n.d.) 'The 2011 Elections in Nicaragua', Study Mission Report, https://www.cartercenter.org/resources/pdfs/peace/americas/nicaragua_2011_report_post.pdf (accessed 15 Apr. 2019).

Chamorro, C.F. (2016) 'La reeleccion de Daniel Ortega, sin legitimidad', *El País*, 11 June, http://internacional.elpais.com/internacional/2016/06/11/actualidad/1465603218_994900.html (accessed 15 Apr. 2019).

Consorcio Panorama Electoral (n.d.) 'Informe Preliminar Elecciones 2016', www.eyt.org.ni/2016/INFORME%20PRELIMINAR%20PANORAMA%20ELECTORAL%202016%20Nov%206%20version%20final.pdf (accessed 15 Apr. 2019).

Cruz, J.M. (2010) 'Democratization under assault: criminal violence in post-transition Central America', Vanderbilt University PhD thesis.

Diario Las Americas (2016) 'Exguerrillera de Nicaragua llama "fascista" al gobierno de Ortega', 5 Feb., www.diariolasamericas.com/5051_portada-america-latina/3606266_exguerrillera-nicaragua-llama-fascista-gobierno-ortega.html (accessed 15 Apr. 2019).

Ellner, S. and M. Tinker Salas (2007) 'The Venezuelan exceptionalism thesis: separating myth from reality', in S. Ellner and M. Tinker Salas (eds.)

Venezuela: Hugo Chávez and the Decline of an 'Exceptional Democracy', (Lanham, MD).

Faber, D. (1993) *Environment under Fire: Imperialism and the Ecological Crisis in Central America* (New York).

Garfield, R.S. and G. Williams (1989) *Health and Revolution: The Nicaraguan Experience* (Oxford).

Jara, F. (2008) 'Comandante sandinista dice que Ortega imita a Somoza para gobernar Nicaragua', *Nacion*, 23 Nov., www.nacion.com/ln_ee/2008/noviembre/23/mundo1786278.html (accessed 15 Apr. 2019).

La Voz del Sandinismo (2014) 'Daniel: Policía Nacional tiene resultados excepcionales', 9 Dec., www.lavozdelsandinismo.com/nicaragua/2014-12-09/daniel-policia-nacional-tiene-resultados-excepcionales/ (accessed 15 Apr. 2019).

Lakhani, N. (2016) 'Nicaragua suppresses opposition to ensure one-party election, critics say', *Guardian*, 26 June.

Martí i Puig, S. and D. Close (2009) 'La excepción Nicaragüense?', in S. Martí i Puig and D. Close (eds.) *Nicaragua y el FSLN: Un analisis de la realidad politica desde 1979 hasta hoy* (Barcelona).

Montes, J. and J. de Córdoba (2016) 'Nicaragua's leftist Ortega embraces business – and authoritarianism', *Wall Street Journal*, 4 Nov.

Montoya, R. (2013) *Gendered Scenarios of Revolution: Making New Men and New Women in Nicaragua, 1975–2000* (Tucson, AZ).

Nowrasteh, A. (2014, updated 2016) 'Why aren't child migrants fleeing to the U.S. from Nicaragua?', *Huffington Post*, www.huffingtonpost.com/alex-nowrasteh/nicaragua-child-migrants-us_b_5592209.html (accessed 16 Apr. 2019).

Prado Reyes, Y. (2016) 'Compañera Rosario: nuestro pueblo privilegia la seguridad y la tranquilidad, por eso hay que seguirlas fortaleciendo', *El Pueblo Presidente*, 12 Dec., www.elpueblopresidente.com/noticias/ver/titulo:37548-companera-rosario-nuestro-pueblo-privilegia-la-seguridad-y-la-tranquilidad-por-eso-hay-que-seguirlas-fortaleciendo (accessed 16 Apr. 2019).

Robinson, C. (1989) *Nicaragua: Against All Odds* (Oxford).

Rocha, J.L. (2000) 'A passionate memory in times of disillusion', *Envío*, 230 (Sept.).

— (2006) 'Why are there no Maras in Nicaragua?', *Envío*, 301 (Aug.), www.envio.org.ni/articulo/3351 (accessed 15 Apr. 2019).

Rodgers, D. (2009) 'Searching for the time of beautiful madness: of ruins and revolution in post-Sandinista Nicaragua', in H.G. West and P. Raman (eds.), *Enduring Socialism: Explorations of Revolution and Transformation, Restoration and Continuation* (London).

Tyrrell, I. (1991) 'American exceptionalism in an age of international history', *American Historical Review*, 96 (4).

Vanden, H.E. and G. Prevost (1996) *Democracy and Socialism in Sandinista Nicaragua* (Boulder, CO).

Walker, T. (1986) *Nicaragua: The Land of Sandino* (Boulder, CO).

Wertheim, S. (2017) 'Trump and American exceptionalism: why a crippled America is something new', *Foreign Affairs*, 3 Jan.

Whitehead, L. (2007) 'On Cuban political exceptionalism', in L. Whitehead and B. Hoffman (eds.), *Debating Cuban Exceptionalism* (Basingstoke).

1. 'We didn't want to be like Somoza's Guardia': policing, crime and Nicaraguan exceptionalism

Robert Sierakowski

In late April 2018, for the first time since the end of the Cold War, political violence in Nicaragua made international headlines. Thanks to smartphones and social media, people all over the world could watch in real time as the country's police forces and armed paramilitaries worked together to crush a wave of popular protest against the Sandinista government of Daniel Ortega. Livestreamed videos showed killers with their faces covered by bandanas and balaclavas, firing weapons of war while storming neighbourhoods, universities and even a church. Often the masked groups were filmed riding aboard government-owned Toyota Hilux trucks which travelled in large convoys protected by police vehicles.

Peaceful student demonstrations, which began as protests against cuts to social security, soon expanded to calls for Ortega's resignation due to the government's heavy-handed response to the protests. With the police and paramilitaries firing live ammunition at barricades, outgunned youths fought back with the weapons at their disposal, largely rocks and homemade *morteros* (mortars), an artisanal 'weapon' traditionally used in Nicaraguan social movements. In this David and Goliath struggle, youthful demonstrators sometimes had only slingshots with which to respond to government bullets. Over the coming months, Sandinista agents – both police and allied civilian militias – killed hundreds of Nicaraguans, wounded thousands and chased thousands more into exile. Most of the victims were young men in their twenties, while others among the dead included teenagers and even young children shot down by the police and paramilitaries. In addition to an estimated 300 civilians murdered by Ortega loyalists, approximately 22 police officers were killed by violent elements of the opposition. The three months of repression marked the deadliest wave of mass killing outside of wartime in the history of the republic. For outside observers, the events fit comfortably in their view of Latin American instability and human rights violations. Many commented on the irony that history seemed to be repeating itself: a political party that had first come to power in a youth-led uprising against a repressive dictatorship was now carrying

---

R. Sierakowski, '"We didn't want to be like Somoza's Guardia': policing, crime and Nicaraguan exceptionalism', in H. Francis (ed.), *A Nicaraguan Exceptionalism? Debating the Legacy of the Sandinista Revolution* (London: University of London Press, 2019), pp. 21–44. License: CC-BY-NC-ND.

out eerily similar violence to keep itself in power. Ortega, it was repeated, had betrayed the 1979 Revolution.

For those familiar with Nicaraguan history, the widespread police violence and state backing for death squad attacks proved perhaps even more shocking. Until April 2018, Nicaragua was seen as an exceptional 'island of peace' in Central America, a region in which criminal violence carried out by street gangs and drug traffickers are an ever-present part of daily life. Nicaragua is the second poorest country in the western hemisphere, but its police force has consistently been recognised as a regional leader in the areas of public safety, human rights and community policing. Whereas the 'Northern Triangle' of Guatemala, El Salvador and Honduras registered homicide rates of 26.1, 60 and 42.8 murders per 100,000 people respectively in 2017, in Nicaragua, the figure dropped to a record-breaking low of 7 per 100,000. Even the far more economically developed Central American country of Costa Rica had a higher homicide rate at 12.1 per 100,000.[1] While the Nicaraguan police force was considered the 'most efficient and least corrupt' in the region, that of Guatemala, El Salvador and Honduras competed for first place in hemispheric rankings of corruption.[2] Opinion polls from 2014 suggest that crime was a distinctly secondary problem for the vast majority of Nicaraguans. Whereas 53.4 per cent of Salvadorans, 46.2 per cent of Hondurans, 37.6 per cent of Guatemalans and 18.7 per cent of Costa Ricans chose 'crime' as their most pressing concern, an infinitesimal 3.5 per cent of Nicaraguans did so.[3] In 2015, *The Economist* went so far as to write that Nicaragua's police force, with its community policing and success against organised crime and gangs, was 'in danger of giving socialism a good name'.[4]

In this chapter, I argue that the outrageous scale of repression in 2018, as well as the decades-long reputation for low levels of crime, can be traced to the emergence of the country's law enforcement structures in the aftermath of the 1979 Sandinista Revolution. After coming to power, the Sandinista National Liberation Front (FSLN) replaced the Somoza dictatorship's corrupt and repressive Guardia Nacional (National Guard, GN) with the country's first national police force, Policía Sandinista (Sandinista Police, PS). Former *guerrilleros* motivated by revolutionary enthusiasm – including, importantly, many young women – took on leadership positions in the new force. This pivotal moment, I argue, helped to establish a new *mística* (a self-sacrificing morale of service and voluntarism) within the police force, with a socialist vision of

---

1 T. Clavel. 'Insight Crime's 2017 homicide round-up', *InSight Crime*, 19 Jan. 2018. For earlier data, see World Bank, *Crime and Violence in Central America:* 1–2.
2 W. Grigsby, '¿Tenemos la Policía que nos merecemos?', *Envío*, no. 290, May 2006.
3 M.F.T. Malone, 'Why do the children flee? Public security and policing practices in Central America', 3. Drawing on AmericasBarometer data from 2014, Malone shows that trust in the police and belief that their rights will be respected is also greatest among Nicaraguans.
4 *The Economist*, 'A broken system: crime in Latin America', 12 July 2014.

community policing, as well as an aversion to bribery.[5] At the same time, the revolutionary police force was deeply politicised and drew on dense networks of informants for intelligence gathering and maintaining order, established on the model of Cuba and other communist countries. Today's Nicaraguan Policía Nacional (National Police, PN) is the direct institutional successor of the Sandinista Police of the 1980s and heir to its legacies.

Having lived through the dramatic violence and repression of the dictatorship against young people in the late 1970s, the Sandinista Police sought to become 'the antithesis of Somoza's Guardia'. While for many years the institution proved widely successful in this endeavour, the police's role in repression during the summer of 2018 revealed an organisation that closely mirrored Somoza's GN in its utter loyalty to a political party and a ruling family. Formerly a capable, professional body with a reputation for community policing, the PN degenerated into a personal police force willing to countenance the most heinous abuses in defence of Daniel Ortega and his government. Just as Ortega had transformed Sandinismo from its revolutionary roots into a corrupt, clientelistic and personalistic political machine, so the PN itself became an arm of the repressive regime.

Crime and policing before the revolution

Prior to the Sandinista Revolution, Nicaragua was dominated for more than four decades by the Somoza family's dictatorship. The ruling dynasty began under the regime of General Anastasio Somoza García, the head of the National Guard created by the United States during its last military occupation of the country (1927–33).[6] After the withdrawal of the United States, Somoza converted the National Guard into his own personal army, carried out a military coup and established a dictatorship. Following Somoza García's assassination in 1956, he was succeeded as president by his sons Luis and Anastasio Somoza Debayle. Over their many decades of rule, the Somoza family used extensive official corruption to gain control over much of the country's economy, accruing fabulous wealth.

The GN was not loyal to the Nicaraguan nation or people, instead it operated as the Somoza family's praetorian army. Given its reputation for violence, many foreign observers assumed that the GN 'maintained law and order' and effectively repressed crime through harsh policing.[7] However, such characterisations are profoundly inaccurate. One of the reasons for this substantial misinterpretation is the fact that, as one legal scholar put it, there has been 'remarkably little

---

5   As José Miguel Cruz puts it in his comparative study, Nicaragua 'insulated' its police force 'to some extent from criminal organisations and enabled it to construct a different relationship with the population': 'Criminal violence and democratization in Central America, 7.
6   R. Millett, *Guardians of the Dynasty*.
7   W.R. Duncan, *Latin American Politics*, 49.

written about criminal justice in pre-revolutionary Nicaragua, particularly in the decades of control by the Somoza family'.[8]

During those long years of dictatorship, Nicaragua was, in fact, exceptional for its high homicide rate. The country consistently ranked in the top three most violent nations in the world – alongside Colombia and Mexico – and, for several years during the 1960s, had the *single highest* homicide rate recorded by the United Nations. Between 1961 and 1967, the country's murder rate rose from 23.1 to 30.9 per 100,000 people.[9] Nearly all of this bloodshed was not political but 'social' in nature, often alcohol-fuelled and the result of fighting between young and middle-aged men, whether as individuals, family groups or members of *pandillas* (gangs).

Ironically, given its reputation for iron-fisted abuse of political opponents, Somoza's National Guard proved utterly ineffective at crime control. On the contrary, GN officers fostered an entire 'illegal' economy of vices run by regime loyalists, including prostitution, drug trafficking, gambling and bootlegging. The Guard tolerated these purportedly illegal activities, profiting greatly from kickbacks and netting thousands of córdobas in bribes each month.[10] Though officially 'apolitical' and prevented from voting in Somoza's faux elections, in practice all GN members were required to identify with Somocismo and support the dictator's Liberal Party.

Rather than imposing regimentation on Nicaraguan society, the Somoza regime fostered disorder by enabling regime loyalists to act with impunity, as the country's growing poverty, unemployment and inequality gave impetus to criminality. In 1965, the US ambassador identified an inability to control crime as the GN's greatest failing, writing that gangs 'operated with ease in Managua and some of the other larger towns'.[11] Another Embassy employee asserted two years later, 'Law and order is non-existent in Nicaragua … it is officially recommended that one carry a gun if one [goes] out of the city of Managua … the Guardia Nacional were never really trained for police work [and] are no good at all as policemen.'[12] American experts sent in 1970 to report on the situation of the GN were likewise shocked by the rising levels of violence:

> Murder and aggravated assault appear to be the major criminal threat in all parts of the country … There has been an increase in geometric proportions of common crime of an increasingly brutal character. Homes and persons have been violated and whole sections of Managua have become a no-man's land at

8   R.J. Wilson, 'Criminal justice in revolutionary Nicaragua, 317–18.
9   United Nations and Statistical Office, *Demographic Yearbook*, 1960, Table 19; 1966, Table 20; 1967, Table 24; S. Hunter Palmer, *The Violent Society*, 28–9; *La Prensa*, 'Atribuyen a Nicaragua primer lugar violento', 11 May 1968.
10 J. Pérez, *Semper fidelis: el secuestro de la Guardia Nacional de Nicaragua*, 46.
11 M.D. Gambone, *Capturing the Revolution: The United States, Central America, and Nicaragua, 1961–1972*, 140.
12 Patrick Nicholas Theros, interview by Robert J. Alexander, Managua, 26 June 1967, in *Robert J. Alexander Interview Collection, 1947–1994*. Microfilm (Leiden, Netherlands: IDC, 2002), Reel 10, Frame 841.

night ... The homicide ratio of 29.4 per 100,000 reported in 1967 was very high by Latin American standards and represented a 12% increase over 1964. A very large proportion of the population regularly go armed.[13]

Faced with this scourge of criminal violence and homicide, the military-based GN proved unable to respond.

Particularly in the wake of the 1959 Cuban Revolution, US interest in the GN was focused on the promotion of counter-insurgency tactics and Cold War anti-communist ideology. Rather than law and order, and criminal justice, police and intelligence efforts were targeted at the growing revolutionary threat posed by the FSLN, a left-wing guerrilla group seeking to topple Somoza. The FSLN formed only the tip of the iceberg of a mass movement for political and social change, encapsulated in a vision of moral regeneration and an end to extreme poverty. Leading protests against the Somoza regime were student groups, radical labour unions and Christian organisations inspired by Catholic liberation theology and its 'preferential option for the poor'. Among their proposals, the FSLN promised that, with the revolution, 'Organised Crime Will Disappear Forever: sex trafficking, prostitution, dice tables, "illegal" gaming, the red light districts and all those businesses controlled by the military and the accomplices of Somocismo ... will be swept away by the FRENTE SANDINISTA.'[14]

In the face of growing popular protests and clandestine guerrilla activity during the late 1970s, the GN responded with ever-increasing state-sponsored repression and violence, ranging from tear gas to bullets and bombs. In Managua, the highly repressive Colonel Alesio Gutiérrez served as chief of police and was responsible for the systematic torture of political prisoners. In the wake of the September 1978 armed insurrection led by the Sandinistas, the Guardia began carrying out large-scale massacres of the youth of the cities in so-called *Operaciones de Limpieza* (clean-up operations). As many who lived through this period recall, it soon became 'a crime to be young'.[15] In the countryside, the Guardia similarly committed mass killings in those areas where the FSLN was operating. This indiscriminate and chaotic terror, however, generated a countervailing force as the urban youth threw in their lot with the guerrilla army in an open civil war against the GN. Guardia units and paramilitary death squads murdered thousands of Nicaraguans over the coming months. On 17 July 1979, a cornered Anastasio Somoza Debayle finally fled the country. Without

---

13   D.R. Powell and K.B. Youngs, *Report of the Public Safety Program and the Nicaragua National Guard*, 20–1.
14   *Lucha Sandinista*, '¿Por qué lucha el FSLN junto al pueblo?', June 1978.
15   M. Solaún, 'Atrocity Summary', US Embassy Cable 4541, 22 Sept. 1978; M. Solaún, 'n/a', US Embassy Cable 5053, 13 Oct. 1978; M. Solaún 'Draft Nicaragua Human Rights Report', US Embassy Cable 5871, 15 Nov. 1978, Wikileaks PlusD Database; Inter-American Commission on Human Rights, *Report on the Situation of Human Rights in Nicaragua: Findings of the 'On-Site' Observation in the Republic of Nicaragua, October 3–12, 1978*, 43; G. Black, *Triumph of the People: The Sandinista Revolution in Nicaragua*, 132–3; J.A. Booth, *The End and the Beginning: The Nicaraguan Revolution*, 173.

the dictator at the helm, his Guardia collapsed, as members of its units fled for the borders to escape the FSLN and popular indignation.

'Guardians of the people's happiness': revolution and policing, 1979–1990

In the wake of the revolutionary upheaval, the Sandinistas took control of a country in great turmoil with an economy largely in ruins. During this early period, the triumphant guerrillas – mostly in their teens and early twenties – were incapable of stemming criminality and maintaining public order. Managua and other large towns were rocked by 'armed robberies of houses and businesses by those who took advantage of the material limitations and lack of experience in police work … in the wake of Somoza's departure'.[16] During 1980 alone, 38,781 crimes were recorded, a rate of 106 per day. The vast majority of these offences went unpunished.[17]

With the National Guard gone, the Sandinistas were uniquely positioned to start from scratch and completely reimagine what a Central American police force could be. To meet the threat of social chaos head-on, the FSLN established the new Sandinista Police mainly made up of former guerrilla fighters in September 1979. 'We didn't know how to be police,' national Chief Aminta Granera recalled two decades later. 'We only knew that we didn't want to be like the Somozan Guard.'[18] Importantly, the Sandinista leadership made an early decision to split the police and army into separate bodies – one military, one civilian – rather than continuing the constabulary model of the Somoza period. On 9 August 1980, Decree 485 officially instituted the Sandinista Police, declaring the institution responsible for the prevention, neutralisation and solution of crime.[19] Placed under the control of the Ministerio del Interior (interior ministry, MINT) and led by FSLN Comandante Tomás Borge, the PS created new divisions in areas such as traffic control, public safety, surveillance and prisons. Former guerrilla commander René Vivas Lugo was named the first national police chief.[20]

Given the GN's lack of efficacy at police work or controlling common crime, the PS found almost no material legacy on which to build. Digging through the paperwork of the GN's police stations across the country, they found few detailed police records, no systematic archives of criminals nor even a single study of basic crime statistics.[21] The PS needed to quickly educate a thousand women and men

16 *La Prensa*, 'Empeora la ola de delincuencia', 7 Dec. 1979.
17 V. Núñez de Escorcia, 'Justice and the control of crime in the Sandinista popular revolution', 11.
18 *Economist*, 'A surprising safe haven: crime in Nicaragua', 28 Jan. 2012.
19 Corte Suprema de Justica, Nicaragua, *La justicia en la revolución: memoria del seminario jurídico Silvio Mayorga*, May 1981,196–7.
20 *Barricada*, 'Reestructuran Policía Nacional Sandinista', 28 Oct. 1980.
21 *Barricada*, 'Batalla contra la delincuencia', 24 Dec. 1980.

in order to carry out these basic tasks. During its first months of existence, the new force was trained and equipped by the Panamanian government of General Omar Torrijos.[22] However, rather quickly the PS came under the influence of the FSLN's closest regional ally, Fidel Castro's Cuba. Since their own revolution two decades earlier, Cuba had established a model of community policing and surveillance that the Sandinistas now adopted in developing their new police academy.[23]

Though increasingly professional in orientation, the PS was highly politicised and inspired by the era's revolutionary fervour. Shortly after its foundation, Comandante Borge referred to the PS as the *centinelas de la felicidad del pueblo* (guardians of the people's happiness) and declared, 'love and good relations with the people is what should distinguish the Sandinista Police'.[24] Members were taught to see themselves as 'new men' and 'new women' who were to serve as the vanguard of the emerging socialist society. Police officers conceived of themselves as possessed of *la mística revolucionaria,* characterised as a transcendent mission that emphasised sacrifice, solidarity, humanism and human rights.[25] Police chief René Vivas declared in 1980, 'the fundamental work that we face is to politically and morally prepare each of our members and turn them into true servants of the Nicaraguan people'.[26] A remarkable institutional culture developed which celebrated service and scorned self-interest, from petty bribery to large-scale enrichment. The new PS, the ruling party proudly stated, 'will be an example for the world'.[27]

Most of those who joined the new force during the 1980s were enthusiastic young people who had participated in the struggle against Somoza and were passionate about achieving social transformation. Notably, a large number of young female revolutionaries now enlisted as police officers, while their male counterparts gravitated in larger numbers to the newly formed army (Ejército Popular Sandinista, EPS). By 1985, fully 45 per cent of PS members were female. Between 1985 and 1988, former FSLN guerrilla leader Doris Tijerino Haslam – who had been tortured by Somoza's GN – served as the first female national

---

22 *La Prensa*, 'Nueva Policía', 11 Aug. 1980; F.J. Bautista Lara, *Policía, seguridad ciudadana y violencia en Nicaragua: breves ensayos y un testimonio*, 19; Policía Nacional de Nicaragua, *Una historia que merece ser contada: Modernización institucional con equidad de género en la Policía Nacional de Nicaragua, 1996–2005*, 15–16.

23 Policía Nacional de Nicaragua, *Sistematización del Modelo Policial Comunitario Proactivo de Nicaragua*, 13–14. The Police Academy was later named after Walter Mendoza Martinez, a Sandinista guerrilla killed shortly before the fall of Somoza.

24 *La Prensa*, 'Nueva Policía', 11 Aug. 1979.

25 B. van de Velde, 'Revolutionary policing: a case study about the role of La Mística and El Espíritu in the Nicaraguan police institution and in the lives of its fundadores', Master's diss., Utrecht University, 2011.

26 *Patria Libre*, 'La Policía Sandinista cumple con la revolución: entrevista con el Comandante René Vivas', May 1980, 32.

27 *Barricada*, 'Policía Sandinista será un ejemplo para el mundo', 15 Aug. 1980.

police chief in the world.[28] With women representing a significant proportion of the new police force, the contrast with neighbouring nations, where the police corps continued to be almost universally male, was remarkable. Of course, for a society steeped in centuries of machismo and decades of military dictatorship under the GN, interacting with young female police officers was a paradigm shift. Visitors to Nicaragua after the revolution remarked on the 'night and day' change they found, with the police no longer being feared as threatening who expected bribes.[29] Police chief Doris Tijerino boasted in 1986 that, 'bribes have been completely eliminated whereas before, for example, no one was ever fined for a traffic infraction'.[30] The PS dramatically curtailed human rights abuses and the use of violence in everyday interactions with the public.

Neighbourhood watch groups known as Comités de Defensa Sandinista (Sandinista Defence Committees, CDS) participated actively in the fight against crime. These had emerged during the revolution itself, as neighbours organised to support the guerrillas with food, water, information and medical supplies. Now they began patrolling their communities 24 hours a day in *vigilancia revolucionaria* (revolutionary guard duty) to bring crime under control and keep a watch out for 'counterrevolutionary sabotage'.[31] In May 1980, the PS launched Operation Death to Criminality with the aim of eradicating gangs, closing illegal brothels and shuttering the cantinas that had been focal points of violence since the Somoza era. In Managua, 140 cantinas were shut down for 'constant scandals and not following liquor laws or standards of hygiene and morality'.[32] More than 30 brothels located in the Mercado Oriental, the city's primary market, were shut down and many were burnt to the ground.[33] 'El Palo de Gato', for instance, an infamous Managua brothel formerly controlled by the GN and a scene of violence for decades, was among those publicly demolished. The FSLN newspaper *Barricada* announced plans to use the remains of 'El Palo' to construct a school for literacy classes.[34] The government tackled prostitution

---

28 *Barricada*, 'Doris: primera jefa de policía del mundo', 3 Apr. 1985. She would pay particular attention to crimes of sexual violence, with the PS allegedly solving 23 out of 25 rape cases that took place between Sept. and Dec. 1985, *La Prensa*. 'Declaraciones de la Comandante Tijerino, acerca de abusos sexuales', 11 Dec. 1985.

29 L.A. Mansilla, 'Nicaragua: la insurrección y la guerra victoriosa. Entrevista a Octavio Cortés', 38. A 1,000 córdoba fine and a punishment were imposed on anyone who attempted to bribe a police officer. Those officers who did accept bribes faced removal from the force. *Barricada*, 'Multa y arresto a quien intente a sobornar policía', 16 Jan. 1980; *Barricada*, 'Policía ejemplar rechazó soborno', 1 Sept. 1980.

30 G. Beretta, 'Nicaragua: una mujer en un puesto de decisión. Entrevista a Doris Tijerino', 22.

31 W.G. West, 'Vigilancia revolucionaria: a Nicaraguan resolution to public and private policing', 147–71; *Barricada*, 'Fuerzas auxiliares ayudarán a la Policía', 17 Aug. 1980.

32 *Barricada*, 'Cierran 140 cantinas', 6 June 1980; *Barricada*, 'Cierran cantinas en un operativo', 5 Sept. 1980.

33 *La Prensa*, 'Policía desata guerra a la prostitución', 21 June 1980.

34 *Barricada*, 'De centros de vicios a locales escolares; se acabó el Palo de Gato', 14 May 1980.

*Figure 1.1. 'Courtesy and respect for the law are inseparable'. 'A man who does not respect a woman is a coward. A man who does not respect a young female police officer (*una muchacha policía*) and does not follow her instructions is twice as cowardly and also an enemy of the law.' (Tomás Borge) (Image:* Barricada, *14 Sept. 1980)*

and alcoholism as social ills and provided many former prostitutes with new training and employment opportunities.[35]

These community-based policing campaigns worked in tandem with the social reforms instigated to dramatically improve the crime situation. In 1981, there were 26,624 volunteer *vigilantes* in 84 different Managua neighbourhoods, helping to reduce crime by more than half compared to the previous year.[36] Between 1981 and 1982, the crime rate halved again, to a rate even lower than pre-revolutionary figures.[37] By November of the following year, according to the FSLN's official organ, the Defence Committees had more than 60,000 *vigilantes revolucionarios* in Managua volunteering to patrol the streets.[38] Between 1980 and 1983, the number of crimes committed per 100,000 people fell from 106 to just 29.[39] As part of these operations, *La Prensa* reported that the police had broken up powerful street gangs in the Managua barrios of San Judas

35 T. Borge, 'Intervención ante los CDS de Managua, 26 de febrero de 1981', in his *Los primeros pasos: la revolución popular sandinista* (Siglo XXI, 1988), 129.
36 *Barricada*, 'Las masas han reducido a la mitad a la delincuencia', 29 Nov. 1981.
37 *Barricada*, 'Disminuyeron delitos por la vigilancia revolucionaria', 7 Apr. 1981. *Barricada*, 'Recuento de la lucha contra la delincuencia', 3 Dec. 1982; Núñez de Escorcia, 'Justice and the control of crime in the Sandinista popular revolution', 11.
38 *Barricada*, 'Ya tenemos 60 mil vigilantes en Managua', 21 Nov. 1982.
39 A. Granera Sacasa and S. Cuarezma Terán, *Evolución del delito en Nicaragua, 1980–1995*, 24.

and Altagracia.[40] This success coincided with the FSLN's similar use of mass mobilisation to carry out improvements in healthcare and education for poor Nicaraguans, such as the 1980 National Literacy Crusade which considerably increased literacy rates in the country.

The darker side of this community-centred approach was the PS's adoption of illiberal surveillance and intelligence-gathering methods. Nicaraguan police officers were regularly sent to communist countries such as the Soviet Union, East Germany and Bulgaria to receive training.[41] The security forces of those governments, like that of Cuba, were infamous for heavy-handed monitoring and spying on their populations. These techniques included widespread tapping of phone lines, the opening of mail and the use of thousands of government loyalists and paid informants to spy for the state. While this approach was effective in controlling the activities of organised crime and counter-revolutionary groups in Nicaragua, the government regularly infringed the civil liberties and privacy of dissidents and other citizens. At times, the PS and Defence Committees worked hand-in-glove with the government's Dirección General de Seguridad del Estado (secret police, DGSE), operating as the 'eyes and ears' of the ruling party and targeting opposition activists for arrest.

As the decade proceeded, Nicaragua became a battleground in the Cold War. American President Ronald Reagan used the Central Intelligence Agency (CIA) to provide financial and military aid to the rebel Contras (or *contrarrevolucionarios*), many of whom were former GN soldiers, to destabilise Nicaragua. To beat back the invasion, the FSLN instituted a military draft for young men aged between 17 and 24 and dedicated more than half of its annual budget to military defence. With the economy under great strain due to the bloody civil war and a US embargo, the country saw spiralling inflation, rising poverty and the roll-out of rationing. Many Nicaraguans refused to attend CDS meetings or volunteer for *vigilancia*, accusing these institutions of abuses against their neighbours. Amid political polarisation, citizens denounced the Sandinista Police for harassing opposition protesters, while permitting riotous attacks by pro-government mobs.[42] During these years of economic crisis, the country witnessed a steady rise in crime and violence, as robberies, prostitution and drug use once again became ever more prevalent in the cities.[43] Boys and young men in Managua's shantytowns again formed gangs and clashed violently with youths from other barrios, although not on the scale of the Somoza period.[44] The

---

40   *La Prensa*, 'Cinco mil delitos comunes en primer semestre de 1982', 2 July 1982.
41   D. Kruijt, *Guerrillas: War and Peace in Central America*, 109; R. Vivas Lugo, 'Todos los gobiernos han instrumentalizado a la policía para sus intereses', *Envío*, no. 351, June 2011.
42   *La Prensa*, 'Policía sandinista culatea al pueblo', 11 July 1988; *Demokratizatsiya*, 'Tropical Chekists: the secret police legacy in Nicaragua', 429.
43   Sacasa and Terán, *Evolución del delito en Nicaragua*, 25–6; J.L. Rocha, 'Why no Maras in Nicaragua?', *Envío*, no. 301, Aug. 2006.
44   L. Grove, 'Rebels without a Cause in Managua', *Washington Post*, 10 Aug. 1986.

overstretched and underfunded PS appeared incapable of keeping up with the social and political consequences of external aggression and civil war.

Revolutionary police under neoliberal governments, 1990–2006

With continuing economic dislocation and the highly unpopular military draft still in place, the Sandinistas were voted from office in February 1990, effectively bringing Nicaragua's revolutionary period to an end. The victory of Violeta Chamorro, the candidate of a united opposition, over FSLN standard-bearer President Daniel Ortega, precipitated the enactment of a series of sweeping political and economic reforms. During the transition, the future of the Sandinista police and army became a critical bone of contention. For some, these arms of the party-state needed to be abolished and replaced by new, clean institutions. However, the FSLN assured the survival of the police and army in the post-revolutionary era by agreeing to 'depoliticise' and 'institutionalise' these one-time partisan bodies that were now under the civilian control of the newly elected government. Interestingly, creative tensions between the 'reformed' police and the conservative governments of the 1990s and 2000s helped to produce an internationally recognised model of public safety and efficient policing.

The Sandinista Police was now renamed the Nicaraguan National Police (PN) to emphasise its allegiance to the country as a whole rather than to a particular party. Police uniforms and insignia were changed and responsibility for law enforcement was transferred from the Ministerio del Interior to the Ministerio de Gobernación. Subsequent laws in 1992 and 1996 further solidified the police's new 'civilian, professional, apolitical, nonpartisan' character. The operations of the police force were constitutionally linked directly to the functioning of the judiciary, rather than state security.[45] Despite efforts to introduce non-partisan officers, the transition was limited as Sandinista officers continued to be hegemonic in both law enforcement and the military during the years of opposition rule. By retaining its control over these armed institutions, the Sandinistas continued to possess a power base within the state even after defeat at the ballot box.

The first significant test for the PN came in the early 1990s when Sandinista-led student and trade union protests exploded in response to neoliberal economic reforms. When some in the PN leadership refused to crack down on their former comrades-in-arms, the Chamorro government removed them from their positions. In 1992, under US pressure, 12 top Sandinista figures, including PN chief René Vivas, were purged from the police force and replaced by pliable officials more willing to use force.[46] In the violent strikes that took place

---

[45] R. Cajina, 'Reforma del sector seguridad ciudadana, transición política y construcción democrática. Ley 290 y Ley 228', 35–57; O.J. Pérez, *Civil-Military Relations in Post-Conflict Societies: Transforming the Role of the Military in Central America*, 74–5.

[46] *La Prensa*, 'Cambios en la Policía', 5 Sept. 1992; *La Prensa*, 'Estados Unidos elogia jefatura civil de la policía', 9 Sept. 1992.

between 1992 and 1995, at times the PN carried out harsh abuses in the course of their bloody clashes with left-wing protesters, which left a small number of demonstrators and police dead.[47] Still, Tomás Borge insisted in retrospect, 'the police survived the efforts of the ultra-right to make it a deadly force ... Its essence was unchanged; the police force remains good despite all the efforts to change it; it still has a Sandinista *mística*.'[48] Herein lay a contradiction that would have long-term consequences: the fact that the police were still opposed to Guardia-style repression against social protests was at least partially due to its latent loyalty to the political party leading the upheaval.

Some long-time members of the police, however, felt that significant budget cuts and the new political context had led to a decline in solidarity within the force. The PN shrank substantially in size and closed its academy between 1990 and 1994. Female police officers complained that amid the individualism and careerism of the period, they were passed over in favour of their male colleagues, while ambitious officers lacking the ideological commitment of the PS's founding generation ascended to leadership positions. The government slashed salaries further and there was a notable and much-commented-on rise in petty bribery by traffic cops. While some individual members of the police force engaged in drug trafficking and vice rackets, such corruption never reached the scale of neighbouring countries.[49]

The period following the FSLN's exit from power and the end of the civil war also saw rapidly increasing crime and homicide rates which, starting in 1993, began to spiral out of control.[50] Mass layoffs in the privatised state sector, as well as the abrupt demobilisation of thousands of young men from both the EPS and the Contra forces, helped to foster mass unemployment in the country. By 1995, the police were recording an average of at least one murder and one rape reported every 24 hours.[51] At the start of the decade, 47 youth gangs were operating in Managua, such as the *Comemuertos* (Eaters of the Dead), a well-armed and violent group active in the Reparto Schick neighbourhood. By 1999, there were more than a hundred gangs exceeding 6,000 members.[52]

---

47 *Barricada*, 'Presidenta ordena uso de la fuerza', 10 July 1990; *Barricada*, 'Matan a jefe policial', 22 Sept. 1993; *La Prensa*, 'Saúl Alvarez víctima de la violencia; cayó a los pies de un periodista', 22 Sept. 1993; *Barricada*, 'Informe de CENIDH es contundente', 2 June 1995.
48 Cajina, 'Security in Nicaragua: Central America's exception', 4–5.
49 *La Prensa*, 'Escándalo narco sacude al gobierno', 6 May 1998; Grigsby, '¿Tenemos la Policía que nos merecemos?'
50 *La Prensa*, 'Hampa se apodera de Managua', 7 May 1993; *La Prensa*, 'No habrá control de ola delictiva en 1994', 2 Nov. 1994.
51 *La Prensa*, 'El crimen: acontecer diario', 15 July 1995; *Barricada*, 'Una violación cada 24 horas', 10 Apr. 1995.
52 D. Rodgers, 'Youth gangs and violence in Latin America and the Caribbean: a literature survey', 19; J.L. Rocha, *Violencia juvenil y orden social en el Reparto Schick: Juventud marginada y relación con el estado*, 9–10; J. Hernández Pico, 'Juventudes en territorios de violencias', *Envío*, no. 398, May 2015.

In its upsurge of post-war violence, Nicaragua was far from unique. During these same years, a parallel increase in criminal gangs was underway in El Salvador and Guatemala as their lengthy Cold War-era armed conflicts also came to an end. Gangs like the Mara Salvatrucha-13 (MS-13) and the Mara-18 quickly emerged and gave cause for significant social and security concern in Central America. This development was at least partially a result of patterns of transnational migration. Large numbers of poor and rural Guatemalan and Salvadoran refugees had fled their countries during the 1980s to Los Angeles, California, where many of their undocumented children became immersed in that city's violent youth gang culture. Upon deportation from the United States during the 1990s, these young men helped to bring new forms of criminal violence back to Central America.

While El Salvador, Guatemala, Honduras and Nicaragua had all experienced high homicide rates dating back decades, Nicaragua alone was able to reduce levels of criminality during the 1990s. Importantly, many of those who fled Nicaragua to the United States in the 1980s were members of the middle and upper classes who settled in Miami and were granted political asylum due to American opposition to the FSLN. Thus, large-scale deportations of alleged criminals from the United States were not among the challenges faced by the Nicaraguan security forces as they battled the expansion of crime in the 1990s.[53]

More important than migratory patterns, I argue, is the fact that the Nicaraguan police drew upon its revolutionary legacy and responded to the explosion of youth gangs using completely different strategies to those employed in the neighbouring republics. In those countries, where the police forces of the previous military dictatorships remained largely unreformed, the state used heavy-handed *Mano Dura* (iron fist) tactics which, at times, came close to targeting urban youth and the poor as a means of social cleansing. In addition to significant human rights violations against impoverished barrios, an unintended consequence of this state repression was the increasing militarisation of street gangs. Substantial sectors of the Northern Triangle police and security forces continued their complicity with the criminal activity and international drug trafficking which had begun under right-wing military regimes. In Nicaragua, on the other hand, the PN emphasised prevention and rehabilitation over outright police violence, even during Liberal President Arnoldo Alemán's declared 'war against gangs' in 1999.[54] These Nicaraguan gangs, known as *pandillas*, were neighbourhood-based groups that had never evolved into the feared transnational *maras* operating elsewhere in the isthmus. The founders of the Nicaraguan police force still 'didn't want to be like Somoza's Guardia',

53 Rocha, 'Why no Maras in Nicaragua?'
54 *La Prensa*, 'Declaran la guerra a pandillas', 7 July 1999. According to José Luis Rocha, the PN was divided between Sandinista officers who aimed to continue the community-oriented model and 'economic elites' who pushed for more of a *Mano Dura* approach. J.L. Rocha, 'The political economy of Nicaragua's institutional and organisational framework for dealing with youth violence', 3.

and the PN maintained its opposition to harsh policies targeting the youth and working-class barrios.

Despite having the smallest security budget and the lowest police salaries in the region, criminality in Nicaragua quickly fell to levels more comparable with Costa Rica's than the countries of the Northern Triangle.[55] *Maras* from Honduras and El Salvador were unable to make inroads into Nicaragua. By 2007, the Nicaraguan government reported that only 20 gangs were operating in the country.[56] As they had done since the 1980s, the Nicaraguan police recognised the need to address youth criminality at the level of its social causes. The police worked with 'at-risk' youth via their schools, families, churches and non-governmental organisations (NGOs) like el Centro de Prevención (CEPREV).[57] 'Warring' groups of teenagers signed peace treaties, and youth sports leagues were established to provide a recreational outlet. In the process, the PN came to rely upon nearly 100,000 volunteers in its crime prevention efforts, including university students, psychologists and former gang members. Given its legacy of experimental 'open' and 'semi-open' prisons and cultural and literacy programmes for prisoners during the 1980s, Nicaragua also increasingly bucked 'the regional punitive trend', with notably lower sentences handed down to prisoners than in neighbouring countries.[58] With many prisons run by former revolutionaries, 'participation in reeducational programmes, which range[d] from schooling to cultural and church activities' was 'often rewarded with considerable sentence reduction'.[59] In their efforts to dismantle the street gangs, the PN could also draw upon intelligence provided by the dense organisational network of grassroots party activists at the community and neighbourhood levels forged during the revolutionary years. These one-time 'eyes and ears of the revolution' continued to serve as informants who provided detailed reconnaissance on gang activities to their Sandinista handlers in the PN.

Instead of the former Eastern Bloc countries, the PN now received training from Sweden, Spain and even the United States.[60] These years also witnessed a significant shift in the contributions of women to the police force. New attempts were made to provide services directly to women and children, beginning with the innovative Comisaría de la Mujer y la Niñez in 1993, which expanded over

---

55 *Barricada*, 'Policía nica es la peor pagada; entre los demás cuerpos de Centroamérica y Belice', 3 Aug. 1997.

56 Ministerio de Gobernación y Policía Nacional de Nicaragua, 'Atención y tratamiento a las pandillas' 6.

57 Policía Nacional de Nicaragua, *Sistematización del Modelo Policial Comunitario Proactivo de Nicaragua*; J.L. Rocha, 'From telescopic to microscopic: three youth gang members speak', *Envío*, no. 311, June 2007.

58 J. Weegels, 'Prisoner self-governance and survival in a Nicaraguan city jail', *Prison Service Journal*, 229 (Jan. 2017).

59 Ibid. As Weegels notes, this has not prevented the ever-present violence or overcrowding, but it has mitigated it to some extent.

60 R. Vivas Lugo, 'Todos los gobiernos han instrumentalizado a la policía para sus intereses', *Envío*, no. 351, June 2011.

time into a nationwide network of special female-run police stations that dealt exclusively with sexual, family and gender-based violence.[61] The PN went beyond merely integrating women, even establishing a Gender Council to assure all women on the force they would have the same opportunities for advancement as male officers.[62] Rather than serving solely as secretaries, receptionists and cooks, women participated at all levels in all branches and divisions. At the top level of the organisation's leadership, Eva Sacasa was appointed general commissioner and Aminta Granera, first commissioner.[63] A prominent female leader, First Commissioner Granera was one of the most popular public figures in the country for a long time. From a well-to-do family based in the city of León, she studied sociology, philosophy and theology at Georgetown University and, after briefly studying to become a nun, joined the Sandinista guerrillas. During the late 2000s and early 2010s, Granera received much of the credit for the PN's success.

With its efficacy in staving off the spread of organised crime, the PN was celebrated both domestically and internationally for its accomplishments and its model of community policing. Even conservative President Enrique Bolaños began to sing the praises of the erstwhile Sandinista Police in his bid for foreign investment. He proudly repeated that Nicaragua was 'without a doubt, the safest country in Central America and maybe in all of Latin America', if not 'the safest country in the hemisphere'.[64] While such claims certainly overreached, Nicaragua was now widely considered a Central American exception when it came to questions of policing, crime, violence and public safety.

Perverting the police: Daniel Ortega returns to office, 2007–18

In 2007 Sandinista leader and perennial presidential candidate Daniel Ortega returned to the presidency after 16 years out of office. The man who returned to office bore little resemblance to the radical militant of the 1980s. In 2000, he had entered into a power-sharing alliance with his right-wing foe, Liberal President Arnoldo Alemán. With the judiciary packed with party loyalists,[65] Alemán avoided jail time on corruption charges, and Ortega likewise was able to ensure that he would not face trial for sexual abuse allegations brought by his stepdaughter. While still using the language of 'socialism', the FSLN leader cut deals with the private sector and foreign investors, and was denounced for

---

61 *La Prensa*, 'Crean Comisaría de la Mujer', 9 Mar. 1993; *Barricada*, 'Inauguran comisaría de la mujer y la niñez', 26 Nov. 1993.
62 *La Prensa*, 'Mujeres policías crean su consejo', 9 Mar. 1996; Policía Nacional de Nicaragua, *Una historia que merece ser contada: Modernización institucional con equidad de género en la Policía Nacional de Nicaragua, 1996–2005*.
63 *La Prensa*, 'Policía tendrá dos nuevas comandantes el 5 de septiembre', 26 Aug. 1995.
64 *La Prensa*, 'Somos el país más seguro', 6 Sept. 2004; *El Nuevo Diario*, 'Bolaños ve 'avalancha de inversiones' en Nicaragua', 6 Dec. 2005.
65 E. Martínez Barahona, 'A politicized judiciary'.

the massive personal enrichment of his family and inner circle. Despite charges of creeping authoritarianism and corruption, the new Sandinista government soon earned widespread backing among the population due to the country's economic success and increased social spending in comparison to the neoliberal governments.

Despite corrupt high jinks at the highest levels of government, the PN continued to be lauded internationally for its role as a *muro de contención* (shield or wall) preventing the spread of drugs northwards and *maras* southwards. The levels of common crime and homicide rates continued to fall. During the 2006 presidential campaign, US Ambassador Paul Trivelli warned in secret that former president Ortega had provided protection to Colombian drug-traffickers in the 1980s and could do so again if re-elected.[66] Following his return to office, however, Ortega and the PN proved to be loyal partners of the US Drug Enforcement Agency (DEA) in its interdiction operations along the Atlantic Coast. Trivelli reported that, contrary to his predictions, during Ortega's first 12 months back in power, the Nicaraguan government had:

> achieved its highest level of annual narcotics seizures to date and proved to be an effective choke-point against traffickers of illegal narcotics, arms, and immigrants transiting through the region. Nicaragua also utilizes a community-policing model that has been successful in preventing the rise of national-level gang activities.[67]

Coming (in private) from an ambassador so vehemently opposed to the Sandinista government, this was high praise indeed.

Under Ortega's government, however, the PN's allegedly apolitical and nonpartisan nature was progressively destroyed. As we have seen, from its very foundation the police force had identified with a particular political project. This allegiance was maintained, despite 'professionalisation' and loyal service to administrations from different parties. With the return of the FSLN to power, however, the PN began to lose any institutional independence. As Ortega set about establishing an expansive network of patronage and corruption among party loyalists, the police were not immune to his perversion of the Sandinista legacy. Rumours abounded of police officers and other government supporters promised immunity for their illicit activities (such as drug trafficking), much as in Somoza's time. It became increasingly clear that to be a police officer required one to display allegiance to Daniel Ortega and his wife, Rosario Murillo. Ortega quickly placed loyal officials in top positions, forced those who wavered into retirement, and illegally allowed allies to remain in office beyond their constitutionally mandated limits. Reforms to the Constitution and to the new Police Law 872 in 2014 officially defined Nicaragua's policing

---

66 P. Trivelli, 'Nicaragua's most wanted Part I: the crimes of Daniel Ortega and his family', US Embassy Cable 1002, 5 May 2006, Wikileaks PlusD Database; P. Trivelli, 'Nicaragua's most wanted Part II: the crimes of the Sandinistas (FSLN)', US Embassy Cable 1003, 5 May 2006, Wikileaks PlusD Database.

67 P. Trivelli, 'Central American security requirements: Nicaragua', US Embassy Cable 2593, 14 Dec. 2007, Wikileaks PlusD Database.

as following 'a preventative, proactive and community-based model', thus codifying the approach developed over three decades of practice. However, the 2014 law, which declared him to be Supreme Chief of the PN, also greatly expanded Ortega's hold over the police force. Rather than reporting to the interior minister, the PN now took its orders directly from the President of the Republic. Sidelining broader civilian control, Ortega gained the personal ability, among many other new powers, to assign and retire police chiefs, extend officials in their roles for years without limit, and to assign members of the police force to serve in civil institutions.[68] The loyalty of the police was now to the head of the political faction to which its high command was universally aligned. Within the police, the worst aspects of its Sandinista legacy were accentuated in the form of a fanatical loyalty to 'el Comandante'. Campaign posters for the FSLN and pro-government iconography began appearing in police stations and the Sandinista hymn was sung alongside the national and police anthems.

A similar process of cooptation of government branches took place as Ortega loyalists dominated the military, the judiciary, the electoral system, the municipalities and the legislature. As Ortega was unconstitutionally re-elected twice in questionable elections (with First Lady Rosario Murillo becoming his vice-president in 2016), the repoliticisation of the PN under party control ran parallel to a generalised deterioration of its efficacy as an impartial force of law and order. While common crime rates continued to decline, a series of violent incidents led critics to challenge the effectiveness and autonomy of the police in its response to political conflicts. On repeated occasions, the PN stood idly by while armed government supporters – including paid gang members – attacked representatives of the political opposition during social and electoral protests. In 2014, during demonstrations against plans for an interoceanic canal on the Atlantic Coast, as well as mobilisations against the mining industry in Mina El Limón, the PN was called in to 'impose order'. Its excessive intervention was described by analyst and former police officer Elvira Cuadra Lira as constituting 'intimidation, illegal detentions, denunciations of torture, and the militarization of communities'.[69] In 2016, even the internationally celebrated police stations for women and children mentioned above were closed on the orders of a man who had been himself disturbingly accused of sexual abuse.[70]

Commissioner Aminta Granera's unconstitutional role at the head of the PN for more than a decade was further evidence of political distortions. As

---

68 E. Cuadra Lira, 'Reformas del sector seguridad en Nicaragua – cambios significativos en el paradigma de la seguridad'; R. Orozco, '¿El país más seguro de Centroamérica? La politización de las instituciones es el mayor riesgo a nuestra seguridad', *Envío*, 33, no. 390, Sept. 2014; R. Orozco, 'La Policía Nacional se ha desnaturalizado para garantizar la seguridad del régimen', *Envío*, no. 402, Sept. 2015.

69 E. Cuadra Lira, 'El nuevo protagonismo militar: Fuerzas armadas y poder'.

70 These branches later reopened in a far less-specialised form. *La Prensa*, 'Comisarías pasarían a Auxilio Judicial como parte de cambios en la Policía Nacional', 29 Jan. 2016; *La Prensa*, '¿Adiós a las Comisarías?', 31 Jan. 2016; *La Prensa*, 'Demandan al Gobierno a que reabra las Comisarías de la Mujer', 15 Sept. 2017.

noted above, Granera had become a much-loved public figure as a result of the police's renowned efficacy. Indeed, some even floated the idea of her as a potential presidential successor to Ortega. However, a secret US Embassy cable (released by WikiLeaks) of an interview between Granera and US Ambassador Robert Callahan provided a rare insight into the conflicts within the Ortega government. According to Callahan's report, Granera allegedly told the American Embassy that Ortega was 'completely crazy and a threat to the country', and that her popularity was the only thing that protected her from being purged for a more compliant loyalist.[71] Interestingly, for years after this conversation was made public, Ortega maintained Commissioner Granera in her position at the head of the PN, even after she had attempted to resign and much of her power had been transferred to Ortega confidant, Francisco Díaz. There were whispers that she had begun personally profiting from her role, in much the same way as other high-ranking Sandinistas had enriched themselves during FSLN's tenure. Others believed that she was being blackmailed or otherwise held hostage in her position. Indeed, she served in that job for well over a decade, far exceeding the five-year tenure followed by all previous police chiefs.[72] She would only depart – in disgrace – after the 2018 wave of political violence.

In fact, the political opposition increasingly targeted the figure of Granera for criticism. In July 2015, police carrying out anti-drug trafficking operations in the neighbourhood of Las Jagüitas in Managua opened fire on a vehicle they mistakenly believed to be transporting cocaine. In the process, they killed an innocent young woman and two children.[73] The incident shocked the Nicaraguan public and raised serious questions as to the tactics the PN was using in its successful 'War on Drugs'. The tragedy was quickly politicised. As a weeping Granera begged for forgiveness and promised to punish the officers for their use of deadly force (while following orders), protesters called for her resignation. In November 2017, another tragic event took place in La Cruz de Rio on the Atlantic Coast, in which the army killed a family of five, including two children, during what police described as an anti-narcotics operation. *La Prensa*, claimed that the targets of the operation had been armed government opponents.[74] Seen together, such militarised actions suggest that excessive force and repression by the army in the country's rural borderlands had become a clandestine counterpoint to the internationally recognised 'preventative, proactive and community-based' policing in the cities. In response to accusations that civilian deaths at the hands of the government amounted to extrajudicial

---

71 R. Callahan, 'Merida initiative: Nicaragua formally joins, but Police Chief Granera in dire straits', US Embassy Cable 433, 27 Apr. 2009, Wikileaks PlusD Database.
72 *La Prensa*, 'Orteguismo va por toma total de Policia', 7 Apr. 2011; Cuadra Lira, 'Reformas del sector seguridad en Nicaragua'.
73 *La Prensa*, 'Policías masacran a familia inocente', 13 July 2015.
74 *La Prensa*, 'Padre e hijos, víctimas del Ejército en La Cruz de Río Grande', 17 Nov. 2017; *La Prensa*, 'Policía Nacional justifica la masacre del Ejército en la Cruz de Río Grande', 15 Dec. 2017.

killings, the Nicaraguan government submitted a January 2018 report acknowledging a series of deadly operations, while lauding the achievements of the past decade. 'In Nicaragua', they reminded readers,

> there are no cartels, no organized crime structures, no maras, no clandestine runways that facilitate the land[ing] of planes carrying drugs, we are not a country that serves a storage-point for drugs, and we do not have the levels of criminality found in our neighbouring countries.[75]

Despite wariness about the emerging details of deadly police and military operations against alleged criminals, few Nicaraguans understood how deep the rot within the PN went.

The extent to which the Ortega government had perverted the police into a personal, praetorian force was definitively revealed in April 2018 when it was confronted with its first major political crisis. Although it is still unclear precisely who gave the order to do so, the PN's anti-riot forces began firing live rounds against opposition protesters. A force launched with the simple goal that it 'didn't want to be like Somoza's Guardia', now flooded into the streets alongside illegal paramilitaries to unleash deadly force against the protesting students, who were described by the government as 'demonic', 'terrorists' and 'vandals'. With no apparent sense of irony, the government referred to the deadly assaults against the demonstrators' roadblocks as 'clean-up operations', the same term used by the GN for its own actions when recapturing cities from the young rebels in 1978 and 1979. In Nicaragua, it had once again become 'a crime to be young'. The web of Sandinista informants that had been used so effectively in community policing was now utilised to identify and target those students who had participated in marches or built barricades in each neighbourhood. Unlike the Somoza period, the government did not declare a state of siege and the army remained in their barracks (although there were rumours that well-trained soldiers were among the paramilitary forces). However, the PN's long-time commitment to human rights, civil liberties and due process, which had been significantly eroded during the decade of Ortega rule, was now jettisoned outright in its struggle to defend 'El Comandante'.

Conclusion

By the end of 2018, an ostensible calm had returned to Nicaragua, with the disgraced Ortega holding on to power and hundreds of protesters, branded 'terrorists', behind bars and facing the prospect of long prison sentences. Hundreds of parents remained without justice for their murdered children, with not a single police officer or paramilitary facing charges for the crimes committed. The Nicaraguan government blamed all of the events that took place after the outbreak of the protests on a US-backed conspiracy, and dismissed human rights reports compiled by the Organization of American States and the

---

75 Gobierno de Nicaragua, 'Libro Blanco: incidencias de elementos delincuenciales de Nicaragua en el período 2007–2017' Report presented to Diplomatic Corps, 16 Jan. 2018.

United Nations. With Aminta Granera finally removed from the leadership of the PN (following a second resignation attempt in April) and whisked out-of-sight in the wake of the bloodbath, Francisco 'Paco' Díaz – related to Ortega through the marriage of their children and accused of human rights violations – was officially promoted to head the institution. Masaya police chief Ramón Avellán, widely criticised for brutal repression in that tense city, was promoted to the post of PN sub-director. Many police officers who bloodied their hands in the crackdown now felt that their futures were bound up in the survival of the Ortega government. In contrast, the hundreds of police officers who refused to join in the repression and remained loyal to the founding values of 'love and good relations with the people', now faced harassment, arrest and – allegedly – worse at the hands of their former comrades.

Sooner or later, the Ortega government will fall from power, but it is unclear whether Nicaragua's once-exceptional record of public safety and low crime rates will return. Indeed, the very government that opened 2018 with the boast that 'we do not have the levels of criminality found in our neighbouring countries', spent the rest of the year obliterating that positive legacy through its actions. It is entirely possible that police actions have so damaged the rule of law that Nicaragua will emerge from the crisis accompanied by a dramatic rise in social violence. Those government supporters given complete impunity to commit human rights violations on behalf of Ortega are unlikely to hand over the heavy weaponry provided by the government. Evidence exists to show that some of these groups are already making the transition from political violence to other forms of profitable criminal activity.

Unquestionably, a cycle in the history of law enforcement in Nicaragua has ended. For all its vaunted success, particularly during the 1990s and early 2000s, the PN ultimately failed in its most fundamental aim: to never 'be like Somoza's Guardia'. Many PN achievements trace their origins to the Sandinista Revolution, with its *mística* and its vision of its officers being the 'guardians of the people's happiness'. However, its deep commitment to a particular political party meant that, just as Ortega perverted the Sandinista legacy to suit his aims, the worst aspects of police culture were dramatically enhanced. The Nicaraguan police officers were exceptional for many years thanks to their revolutionary roots, standing head and shoulders above their Central American neighbours when it came to crime, human rights and community relations. However, with the return of the FSLN to political power, this exceptional historical origin proved a liability. It is doubtful whether any other police force in Central America today would be willing to commit such extreme violence against protesters on behalf of an individual political figure or party. The PN has irretrievably destroyed its reputation through its role in political repression and, just as a wholesale reform was necessary after the fall of the Somoza regime, the Nicaraguan police force will need to be wholly transformed again following a political transition.

Bibliography

(1981) *La justicia en la revolución: memoria del seminario jurídico Silvio Mayorga, Corte Suprema de Justicia, Nicaragua, Mayo de 1981* (Managua).

Bautista Lara, F.J. (2004) *Policía, seguridad ciudadana y violencia en Nicaragua: breves ensayos y un testimonio* (Managua).

Beretta, G. (1986) 'Nicaragua: una mujer en un puesto de decisión. Entrevista a Doris Tijerino', *Pensamiento Propio*, 32 (Apr.): 22–5.

Black, G. (1981) *Triumph of the People: The Sandinista Revolution in Nicaragua* (London).

Booth, J.A. (1985) *The End and the Beginning: The Nicaraguan Revolution* (Boulder, CO).

Borge, T. (1988) 'Intervención ante los CDS de Managua, 26 de febrero de 1981', in *Los primeros pasos: la Revolución Popular Sandinista* (Managua): 116–40.

Cajina, R. (2009) 'Reforma del sector seguridad ciudadana, transición política y construcción democrática. Ley 290 y Ley 228', *Mirador de Seguridad: Revista del Instituto de Estudios Estratégicos y Políticas Públicas* (Feb): 35–57.

— (2013) 'Security in Nicaragua: Central America's exception', Inter-American Dialogue (Jan.).

Chuchryk, P.M. (1991), 'Women in the revolution', in T.W. Walker (ed.), *Revolution and Counterrevolution in Nicaragua* (Boulder, CO): 143–65.

Cruz, J.M. (2011), 'Criminal violence and democratization in Central America: the survival of the violent state', *Latin American Politics and Society* 53 (4): 1–33.

Demokratizatsiya (2004) 'Tropical Chekists: the secret police legacy in Nicaragua', 12 (3): 427.

The Economist (2012) 'A surprising safe haven: crime in Nicaragua', 28 Jan. 2012.

— (2014) 'A broken system: crime in Latin America', 12 July 2014.

Gambone, M.D. (2001), *Capturing the Revolution: The United States, Central America, and Nicaragua, 1961–1972* (Westport, CT).

Granera Sacasa, A. and S. Cuarezma Terán (1997) *Evolución del delito en Nicaragua, 1980–1995* (Managua).

Grigsby, W. (2006) '¿Tenemos la Policía que nos merecemos?', *Envío*, 290.

Grove, L. (1986) 'Rebels without a cause in Managua', *Washington Post*, 10 Aug.

Hernández Pico, J. (2015) 'Juventudes en territorios de violencias', *Envío*, 398 (May).

Intelligence Digest (1979), 'Nicaragua: hostile US media', (Apr.) 6.

Inter-American Commission on Human Rights (1978) *Report on the Situation of Human Rights in Nicaragua: Findings of the 'On-Site' Observation in the Republic of Nicaragua, October 3–12, 1978*. General Secretariat, Organization of American States.

Kruijt, D. (2008) *Guerrillas: War and Peace in Central America* (London).

Malone, M.F.T. (2015) 'Why do the children flee? Public security and policing practices in Central America', Carsey Research National Issue Brief. University of New Hampshire, Carsey School of Public Policy.

Mansilla, L.A. (1980) 'Nicaragua: la insurrección y la guerra victoriosa. Entrevista a Octavio Cortés', *Araucaria de Chile*, 9: 17–41.

Martínez Barahona, E. (2012) 'A politicized judiciary', in D. Close, S. Martí i Puig and S.A. McConnell (eds.), *The Sandinistas and Nicaragua Since 1979* (Boulder, CO).

Millett, R. (1977) *Guardians of the Dynasty* (Maryknoll, NY).

Núñez de Escorcia, V. (1985) 'Justice and the control of crime in the Sandinista Popular Revolution', *Crime and Social Justice*, 23: 5–28.

Orozco, R. (2014) '¿El país más seguro de Centroamérica? La politización de las instituciones es el mayor riesgo a nuestra seguridad', *Envío*, 390 (Sept.).

— (2015) 'La Policía Nacional se ha desnaturalizado para garantizar la seguridad del régimen', *Envío*, 402 (Sept.).

Palmer, S.H. (1972) *The Violent Society* (Lanham, MD).

Pérez, J. (2004) *Semper fidelis: el secuestro de la Guardia Nacional de Nicaragua*, (Managua).

Pérez, O.J. (2015), *Civil-Military Relations in Post-Conflict Societies: Transforming the Role of the Military in Central America* (New York).

Policía Nacional de Nicaragua (2011) *Sistematización del Modelo Policial Comunitario Proactivo de Nicaragua* (Managua).

— (2005) *Una historia que merece ser contada: Modernización institucional con equidad de género en la Policía Nacional de Nicaragua, 1996–2005* (Managua).

Powell, D.R. and K.B. Youngs (1970) 'Report of the Public Safety Program and the Nicaragua National Guard', Office of Public Safety, Agency for International Development, US State Department, June.

Rocha, J.L. (2007) 'From telescopic to microscopic: three youth gang members speak', *Envío*, 311 (June).

— (2005) *The Political Economy of Nicaragua's Institutional and Organisational Framework for Dealing with Youth Violence*, Crisis States Research Centre Working Papers Series (London).

— (2013) *Violencia juvenil y orden social en el Reparto Schick: Juventud marginada y relación con el estado* (Washington, D.C.).

— (2006) 'Why no Maras in Nicaragua?' *Envío*, 301 (Aug.).

Rodgers, D. (1999) 'Youth gangs and violence in Latin America and the Caribbean: a literature survey', Latin American and Caribbean Region Sustainable Development (Washington, D.C.).

United Nations and Statistical Office (1960) *Demographic Yearbook 1960* (New York).

— (1967) *Demographic Yearbook 1966* (New York).

— (1968) *Demographic Yearbook 1967* (New York).

van de Velde, B. (2011) 'Revolutionary policing: a case study about the role of La Mística and El Espíritu in the Nicaraguan Police institution and in the lives of its fundadores', Utrecht University master's thesis.

Vivas Lugo, R. (2011) 'Todos los gobiernos han instrumentalizado a la Policía para sus intereses', *Envío*, 351 (June).

West, W.G. (1987) 'Vigilancia revolucionaria: a Nicaraguan resolution to public and private policing', in C.D. Shearing and P.C. Stenning (eds.), *Private Policing* (Beverly Hills, CA), 147–71.

Wilson, R.J. (1991) 'Criminal justice in revolutionary Nicaragua: intimations of the adversarial in socialist and civil law traditions', *The University of Miami Inter-American Law Review* 23 (2): 269–387.

World Bank (2011) *Crime and Violence in Central America: A Development Challenge* (Washington, D.C.).

2. 'The revolution was so many things'

Fernanda Soto

That day we woke up with electricity. In 2006, in Mulukukú, such luxuries could not be regarded as good news – it meant a wake was taking place.[1] In the early morning, all the members of the household gathered in the kitchen.[2] We all wanted to know who had died the previous night. Guillermo, while serving himself a cup of coffee, announced the news: 'Somebody killed Don Julio Hernández.' Don Chinto, a neighbour who had just arrived from downtown Mulukukú, added: 'I heard a *mozo* killed him. Well, that old man was arrogant.'[3] Guillermo, taking his place at the kitchen table, said: '*Mozos* are not like they used to be, when people would yell at them and they would keep silent.'

Julio Hernández was one of the richest men in town. Some said he had made a lot of money by not paying back loans he received during the 1980s and by taking his poor neighbours' land. His death seemed an act of poetic justice: as punishment for all the harm he had done, one of his workers had finally killed him. According to Don Chinto 'He shot him three times and then fled to Paiwas … the police are after him but I doubt they will get him.' After hearing the story, I wondered: was it because of the revolution that '*mozos* are not like they were before'?

That question stayed with me during most of 2006, when intense discussions about the Sandinista Revolution dominated public debate. Memories were particularly relevant at that time, an electoral year when it seemed the Sandinista National Liberation Front (FSLN) might return to power (as it eventually did). As Nicaraguans debated whether or not they should vote for the FSLN, their choices were guided by their memories of the revolutionary years, memories that were highly contested. Sandinistas, particularly those linked to the FSLN, described the revolution as a moment of profound positive change, while opponents described those years as the dark night of Nicaragua's

---

1 In 2006, Mulukukú was not yet connected to the national power grid, and the town had electricity from 9 am to 9 pm.
2 I was living with a group of nuns and we shared our meals with the people who worked with them in a local educational programme they ran.
3 All the names used in the article have been modified. In Nicaragua a *mozo* refers to a rural labourer.

F. Soto, 'The revolution was so many things', in H. Francis (ed.), *A Nicaraguan Exceptionalism? Debating the Legacy of the Sandinista Revolution* (London: University of London Press, 2019), pp. 45–59. License: CC-BY-NC-ND.

history. For those who saw its legacy as positive, the revolution had led to the construction of new political subjects characterised by solidarity, strong organisation and a politicised analysis of the world. Those on the opposite side referred to another legacy, one of economic backwardness and authoritarian rule.[4] For both Nicaragua was exceptional, that is, exceptionally better or worse than other Central American nations.[5]

Having myself been raised in a Sandinista family, I grew up with positive and romantic renditions of that past. Those memories were problematised later on, while working in the countryside. There I heard about the 'many other things' the revolution was, which are part of the 'forgotten' episodes of the hegemonic Sandinista memory. They are kept outside of the Sandinista narrative because some preceive them as a possible threat to the party and, thus, to the revolution itself. This does not mean that they are absent from public debate. On the contrary, in 2006 reports of these episodes were ubiquitous in Nicaragua, repeatedly reiterated by the FSLN's opposition.[6] As you will see in this chapter, a few Sandinista supporters also gave voice to more critical memories, but they tended to do so only in private.

For Beatriz Sarlo, the forgotten episodes that are remembered 'establish a hierarchy of value: what matters and what doesn't matter'.[7] For her, giving a significant place to politics entails discussing such hierarchies.[8] The forgotten episodes buried in the memories of the Sandinistas draw attention to the hierarchies that were at play in the past and, thus, to the politics of memory in Nicaragua. I agree with her that to give a significant place to politics when analysing Sandinista memories entails discussing its hierarchy of value. To reflect about what is remembered, who remembers and how they ought to remember in public can guide us in that endeavour. First and foremost, those questions invite us to discuss who gets to define such arrangements and the issues that move them.

Alongside the forgotten, we find the 'silent lessons' of the revolution: they are what we – individually and collectively – make of that moment. These lessons

---

4 E.g., since 2006 government campaigns have referred to the post-2006 period as Nicaragua's second Sandinista Revolution. They emphasise words like 'solidarity', 'unity' and socialism as well as Christianity (as religious values are equated with revolutionary ones). The FSLN's political opponents, in contrast, highlight government corruption and repression. Roberto Orozco, an independent researcher, analysed the assassination of peasant leaders in the Ayapal region; he says: 'Remember that the population is denouncing arbitrary detentions, assassinations, disappearances. All this is sending a message about the serious situation lived in Ayapal; this is a surge of activities, and they [the FSLN] are applying the same prophylaxis (as they say in their jargon) used in the eighties.' I. López and E. Romero, 'Asesinan a productor de Ayapal que denunció en La Prensa maltrato del Ejército', *La Prensa*, 18 Apr. 2016.

5 Carlos Vilas offers a 'balanced' political analysis of that decade in *El legado de una década*.

6 Among the opposition parties was la Resistencia, known as the Contras (counterrevolutionary forces) in the 1980s, and the Conservative party – the Movimiento Renovador Sandinista (MRS) – formed by Sandinistas who had broken with FSLN.

7 B. Sarlo, 'Los intelectuales, la tierra fértil del kirchnerismo'; 21.

8 Ibid.

are sometimes maps, but they can also be thought as binoculars that we use to gaze at the landscape and choose the safest route to take. We can get a glimpse of these lessons by paying attention to what people say – or do not say – about the past, but, mostly, by taking a close look at *how* they choose to voice these memories.[9] These lessons speak about our relationship with the past and today's dominant hierarchy of value.

I understand the forgotten and the silent lessons not as providing evidence of the failures or achievements of the revolution, but as part of the fabric of social change. Together they tell us a story, one about plans that unfolded in unforeseen ways and the red flags that appeared along the way. They reveal the untouchable creeds of the revolution: a belief in the primacy of the vanguard, in the responsibility to uplift the 'poor', the conviction that all opposition from below was the result of 'a lack of revolutionary consciousness', and the overconfidence of revolutionaries who assumed they knew it all. They also speak about people touched by solidarity and generosity, by dreams, faith, hope and the committed attempt of thousands to change Nicaragua's society.

This chapter is about the 'many other things' the revolution brought. It relates the stories of three peasants (a woman and two men) who supported the revolution. These accounts of the harshness of revolution in the midst of a war and its aftermath are permeated by the expectations awakened by revolutionary discourse and memories tarnished by the revolution's inability to live up to those expectations. They are also stories of social change, which offer a more nuanced and complex perspective on the past. This introduction is followed by a historical contextualisation of the region in which I collected the narratives, the three testimonies and the conclusion.

The revolution in the countryside

November 2006 marked what Sandinistas in Nicaragua have called the beginning of its second revolution. In 2006, after 16 years of what were known as neoliberal governments, the FSLN (popularly known as El Frente) was elected to rule the country. Seven months before the elections I moved to Siuna and then to Mulukukú.[10] The first is an ex-mining town in the Northern Caribbean Autonomous Region of Nicaragua, 318 km to the north-east of Managua. The second is a mid-size peasant town, 70 km southwest of Siuna. Mulukukú was famous during the 1980s because it was the base for the largest military training school of the Sandinista People's Army (EPS by its Spanish acronym). People from this region, like most rural habitants in Nicaragua, did not overwhelmingly

---

9   Michel-Rolph Trouillot writes a valuable and intellectually remarkable analysis of the making of silences in and about Haiti's history, and their impacts on the present for both Haitians and those of us and born on this side of the Atlantic: *Silencing the Past: Power and the Production of History*.

10 Both towns are now capitals of municipalities that hold the same name.

support the revolution. On the contrary, most joined or were sympathisers of the Contras (the counterrevolutionary forces).[11]

During the 1980s, for many Nicaraguan peasants the revolution meant a substantial increase in state interference in their lives. While programmes such as the literacy campaign were welcomed, agrarian reform was a source of conflict. The Sandinista government wanted to transform peasant practices – deemed 'backward' – and modernise the countryside through the formation of state-owned agricultural enterprises and rural cooperatives.[12] State policies pushed peasants into rapidly changing their organisational strategies.[13] However, the logic of collective work promoted by the state was in direct opposition to local conceptions of prosperity based on the idea of intense individual work, especially among small farmers and peasants.[14]

The Siuna-Mulukukú region was no exception. At the time, it was part of the agrarian frontier, a region of recent colonisation where peasants deforested the area in order to have access to land for agriculture and ranching. As Larson stresses, historically the agrarian frontier has been characterised by a lack of infrastructure and minimal state presence.[15] In Siuna-Mulukukú, the spatial organisation of communities (in some places it can take an hour to reach your closest neighbour) reflected a preference for less collective forms of life, shaped by 'conquest narratives' that emphasised the domestication of nature by men's hard labour.[16]

In the 1980s, rural inhabitants of the agrarian frontier felt that cooperatives not only threatened their well-being but also disrespected their way of life. Not surprisingly, peasants in those regions were reluctant to participate in cooperatives. Only Sandinista sympathisers (many of whom had collaborated with the guerrillas) and landless rural workers willingly joined the first cooperatives.

By 1982, as a result of pressure from the Sandinista state, cooperatives had been organised in most rural communities of Siuna-Mulukukú. They were small, made up only of community members, and they followed the Credit

11 Alejandro Bendaña has compiled testimonies of the peasants who joined the Resistencia and the reasons that moved them to do so in *Una tragedia campesina: testimonios de la Resistencia*.
12 See: INRA, 'Marco estratégico de la Reforma Agraria'. Paper presented at the Latin American Sociology Congress, Departamento de Propaganda y Educación Política del FSLN, Managua, 1981; V. Rueda Estrada, *Recompas, recontras, revueltos y armados: posguerra y conflictos por la tierra en Nicaragua 1990–2008*; M.J. Saldaña-Portillo, *The Revolutionary Imagination in the Americas and the Age of Development*, 109; E. Baumeister, *Estructura y reforma agraria en Nicaragua (1979–1989)*. See also the chapter by Jose Luis Rocha in this book.
13 CIERA, *La mosquitia en la revolución*.
14 See L. Horton, *Peasants in Arms: War and Peace in the Mountains of Nicaragua, 1979–1994*, for a similar analysis about people from another rural community in the agrarian frontier of Nicaragua.
15 A. Larson, *Tendencias actuales de la frontera agrícola: las contradicciones entre conservación y desarrollo*, 7. See also ibid. for a description of the agrarian frontier in the northern region of Nicaragua.
16 F. Soto, *Ventanas en la memoria: recuerdos de la revolución en la frontera agrícola*.

and Saving Cooperatives model (CCS by its Spanish acronym): their members shared a government loan but worked their land individually. In 1983, with the increase of Contra armed groups in the countryside, the government decided to move people to larger cooperatives that were closer to roads or towns. The goal was to offer protection, facilitate access to basic services like healthcare and education, and to exert better control over the population. At that time, cooperatives in Siuna were no longer centred on productive activities – they became Cooperativas de Auto-Defensa (Self-Defence Cooperatives).[17]

If the government had faced difficulties in convincing people to work collectively, it was even harder to persuade them to leave their land and move to Self-Defence Cooperatives. Most had to be forced to do so. The Sandinista army led the displacement, exacerbating frictions between peasants and the army. The first to move were those peasants who had already been threatened by the Contras, followed by those who feared the army. Many others believed the process was a plot to take their land away and either decided to stay put on their ranches or to join the Contras.

Lupe, a peasant who stayed in his community until mid 1984, said:

> We decided to stay because nobody likes to leave their things. Initially the community had 44 families. I know because I was a teacher at the time and I did the local census. But by 1984 only four families were still there. But, how could we [his family] leave if my father and I had put all our lives in that land?[18]

Even though compulsory military service was not officially introduced until September 1983, male cooperative members in rural areas like Siuna were drafted as early as 1980, in order to create the Sandinista Peoples' Militia. They formed the first battalions sent to the Coco River and the Puerto Cabezas region in 1981 (where the 'Red Christmas' Operation took place) and many of them remained in the Sandinista army until 1990.[19] The military draft only increased tension in the region and accelerated rejection of the revolution. Many peasants preferred to join the Contras voluntarily, rather than be forced to join the Sandinista army. By 1984 most men were fighting and only women, children and elderly people lived in the Self-Defence Cooperatives. Unable to produce their own staples and dependent on state aid for food, medicines and tools, they were also the main target of Contra attacks.

The region's rural areas became a war zone and most people migrated to towns, cooperatives or Honduran refugee camps. At great personal risk, some families decided to stay on their ranches to defend their property. They had no access to education or healthcare (as teachers and nurses were targeted by the Contras), they could not move freely around their property, and they lived in

17 See the chapter by David Cooper in this book.
18 Interview, 26 May 2007.
19 This is the popular name for the Sandinista operation that forced the displacement of 39 Miskitu communities from the Río Coco, in the wake of counterrevolutionary attacks along the border with Honduras.

constant fear of being taken by either army. To survive, they had to navigate between the two armies, the Sandinistas and the Contras.

By the mid 1980s it had become clear that those in the region who supported the Sandinista government were a minority. Many of these Sandinistas had been guerrilla collaborators who were satisfied with the social programmes offered by the government. And while most resisted leaving their ranches for as long as they could, in the end they agreed to join the cooperatives in the hope that when the war was over, the revolution would fulfil its main promise of a better life for all. In 2006 Don Chepe, a guerrilla collaborator, summarised their experiences in the 1980s and 1990s:

> During the war both sides suffered and we could not work in peace. In the '90s we worked but we lacked direction, we lacked support, although there were fewer armed people bothering us. We hope now [with the FSLN victory] that they fulfil what they promise. We hope that little by little we can see changes.[20]

As in the past, hopes were placed in the FSLN – but people like Don Chepe were the exceptions and they were the ones whom I was interested in understanding. I wanted to know why some peasants supported the revolutionary process and the FSLN in a region where most either joined the Contras or fled to Honduras. Their stories differ from the idealised, hegemonic Sandinista memory which cast solidarity as an ever-present aspect of processes promoted by the revolution. Nevertheless, the more negative parts of their accounts do not invalidate their positive memories of that time, nor have they precluded their continuing support for the revolution.

'Many things'

Concha

Concha, the daughter of a guerrilla collaborator, was 12 years old when her family migrated to Siuna. They were originally from Boaco, but had to leave their land because 'there the poor could not live in peace'. In the 1970s all her family supported the Sandinista guerrillas. She proudly recalls: 'My two sons were very small and they also supported the Frente.' In 2006, Concha was a 65-year-old widow, her husband having died during the war. When recalling her life in a Sandinista cooperative she said:

> People from the cooperative lied to us. When the Frente lost the election they told us that the Contra would come to kill everybody and a lot of people left in fear. I was one. I left my chickens, my cows, my corn. Eight days later I went back and didn't find anything. The cooperative leaders had taken all our things ... Yes, it is true we had to share but not in that way ...
>
> ... and let me tell you, we did not live a peaceful life in the cooperative because we were a lot of people and we did not have food. Yes, the Frente gave us some

20 Interview, 6 Dec. 2006.

supplies but it is not the same as when you grow your own food. We lived in frail houses, we got all wet during winter [rainy season]. We decided to stay there to try to survive [the war]. The ones who were smart, the bosses in the cooperatives, they sold our corn, they stole our cows and did so many other things, I know what they did and I don't forget who they are.[21]

For Concha the years in the cooperative were hard. The leadership was corrupt and took advantage of its power to make money from collective resources. She later added: 'I don't blame the Frente for what happened in the cooperative, I blame the cooperative leaders. They were the ones who took away all we had, they were the ones who lied to us.' Her story was quite different from official stories, narrated by men, about the Sandinistas cooperatives. These referred to solidarity, companionship, communal support and protection. In contrast, women like Concha recalled the difficulties they had faced during that time. In the end, it was they who had spent the most time in the cooperatives.

Jacinta, a nun with whom I lived in Mulukukú and who had worked in Concha's cooperative during the 1980s, partially agreed with her. She knew about the difficulties people experienced in the cooperative, and she considered the FSLN to carry most of the responsibility for them. Jacinta thought the FSLN should have trained and assisted people in better ways. She said:

People in the cooperative were not prepared to live and work like that. People took what the Frente gave them as a gift. I remember once getting there and people telling me that a tiger had eaten 400 cows.[22] They were telling me that and did not do anything! When have you heard of a peasant who lets a tiger eat all his animals?[23]

According to Jacinta, the cows were not eaten by a tiger but sold by the cooperative leaders. For her, the FSLN's political project was not wrong in itself, but making it a reality was the challenge. Her story underlines the difficulty of calling for solidarity at a time when war requires rapid and aggressive action. It also speaks to the complexities of managing collective projects on Nicaragua's agrarian frontier, especially projects that were designed by state functionaries who did not always understand or value people's knowledge and ways of life. Today 'rural change' continues to be an important leitmotif in the FSLN's narrative. 'Solidarity' remains part of this political discourse, but the emphasis is on employment and access to individual loans, rather than on attempts to create cooperatives in the countryside.[24]

---

21 Interview, 9 Dec. 2006.
22 In Nicaragua jaguars are known as tigers.
23 Interview, 25 May 2006.
24 Discussions concerning the FSLN's current relations with cooperatives and initiatives are linked to what is called '*economía social*'. See S. Cáceres, 'Somos protagonistas del desarrollo rural, *Envío*, no. 385, Apr. 2014.

Guillermo

At the time I met Guillermo he was in his late fifties. Originally from a small community close to Siuna, he spent most of the 1980s in the Sandinista army. In the 1990s he started working with a group of nuns in Mulukukú in various educational projects. He lived close to the nuns' house and we shared most of our meals together. He almost never talked about politics. What he really liked to do was recall stories of his youth – at such moments he would sometimes touch on the war in the 1980s. He described the places he was sent to fight, the rivers he had to cross and one could see through his stories that he still felt the weight of the dead bodies he had carried then.

His community became a cooperative in the early 1980s, but by 1984 most of its members had been relocated to a larger one because of the war. When I asked him about his experience of working collectively he told me: 'In the cooperative we had a good harvest and a bad harvest and after that I don't know because I was drafted.' I asked him once: 'Guillermo did you ever think of joining the Contra?' He told me what nobody else had dared to say:

> 'Yes, once, when they [the Sandinista police] put me in jail, I was in Puerto Cabezas, I wasn't carrying my ID and wasn't wearing my military uniform. I was coming back from my community to the military base. The Sandinista Police were on the road, checking men's ID. Those who didn't have them were sent to jail. I was one of them. As we got to the Police Station they put us in line and, one by one, each of us were sent inside a room. As I waited for my turn, I could hear a thumping sound coming from the room. I got goose bumps just thinking about what they were doing there and said to myself: 'No, I'm not going to let them do that'. I didn't even wait for them to put me inside the room; as the policeman approached me I knocked him down. He fell to the floor. I was prepared to receive a beating from all the other cops but they didn't do anything. They picked up the guy on the floor and went back to the room. After a while they came out, told all the other men in line to go home and left me in prison for a week, as a punishment. Only after a week was I able to go back to my battalion.[25]

Unfortunately, I'm unable to translate this violent episode with all the comic undertones he gave it in the telling. Guillermo's narration made us both laugh at times, especially when he described the astonished faces of the policemen. He was not carrying his ID or wearing his uniform because he feared being intercepted by the Contras on his way to Puerto Cabezas. If they had found him with a military ID, it would have meant a death sentence.

Guillermo never publicly said that he was a Sandinista or supported the Frente. He did not like to participate in political activities nor to offer his political opinions: 'because people get upset when talking about politics'. However, when people asked him for his thoughts, he was open and sincere. When recalling the revolution, he spoke with great passion at times, while at others making light of the sad moments he had endured. And often preferred

25 Interview, 15 Nov. 2006.

not to say much at all about certain matters. Without fear, he also recounted the things he thought were wrong. An example of this was his experience of police aggression, one that made him think about joining the Contras. However, in his stories it always seemed that, despite the mistakes, something made up for them which led him to continue supporting the revolution, such as the one about the return to his ranch.

When Guillermo told his superior that he wanted to leave the army and return to his community, he was sent to jail again. He spent a couple of weeks there until his superiors completed an internal investigation which confirmed that he was not leaving the army to join the Contras. They authorised his return, but when Guillermo got to his ranch, he found another family in residence there. A man told him that the government had given them that land and he had a piece of 'paper' (a title) to prove it. Guillermo, who also had a title, went to the Agrarian Development Ministry in Siuna.[26] He made an appointment with the director and told him:

> 'Look, in my ranch I found a man who says that you gave him that land. What about the title I have' – he pointed to the title he was showing to the director – 'does it have any value?' 'Yes, it does', the director replied and then turned to his left and told his assistant: 'We messed things up here', to which she replied: 'You are the one who messed this up because I only write what you dictate.'[27]

Laughing at the story, Guillermo said, 'That young woman was very smart.' Although he got his ranch back, his wife had not waited for him during the war. He later started working for the Church and decided to finish high school. His stories never showed resentment towards the police, the Sandinista army or the Sandinista government. He did not overlook the unfair treatment he had experienced at the hands of the police and the army's or the government's mistakes. But in his stories one could see that he still believed the revolution was a better option. He could defend himself, he entered state offices and was heard by those in authority.

The abuse of power by the Sandinista police and army in the 1980s forms part of the forgotten episodes of the FSLN narrative, in much the same way that the Contras' abuse of power comprises part of their forgotten episodes.[28] Unlike Guatemala and El Salvador, in the 1990s Nicaragua's government did not create a truth commission to investigate human rights abuses committed by both armies. The peace agreement concluded at the time involved legally condoning these occurrences. It was argued that if peace was to be achieved, then forgiveness was needed from both sides.[29]

---

26 Ministry of Agrarian Development and Institute of Agrarian Reform (MIDINRA).
27 Interview, 20 Nov. 2006.
28 See Vilas, *El legado de una década*, 43.
29 Rueda Estrada, *Recompas, recontras, revueltos y armados*, 404.

Raul

Raul's views regarding the Sandinista government were different from Guillermo's. He was born in Matagalpa and he migrated to Siuna with his family in the late 1970s, fleeing Somoza's Guardia. In Matagalpa he became involved with the Socialist party and supported the guerrillas. He liked to recall: 'I was not from the 19 of July generation, I'm from the Pancasán generation', underlining that his relationship with the FSLN dated from the 1960s and not from 1979, like most peasants in the region.[30] When he recalled the late 1960s he said: 'We [peasants] ignored our rights, we lived in the *montaña* and spent perhaps ten years there, working. Nobody would visit us to teach us anything.'[31]

Most of his stories revolved around the war and the defeat of the revolution in the 1990s. In his recollections, one could see a strong critique, frustration and even resentment towards the FSLN. He said he was dissatisfied with the way the party had treated them – the peasants – after the Sandinistas' electoral defeat in 1990. He mentioned once that he thought some of the FSLN members had lost their Sandinista values, that many 'thought they were "too important" and forgot about the rest'.

The root of Raul's complaints was what the opposition called the '*piñata*': the distribution of state goods among FSLN members after its 1990 electoral defeat.[32] The FSLN argued that these appropriations were necessary to ensure that the party had economic resources in the future. However, the decision exacerbated the economic gap between Sandinistas and led to ethical contradictions. Raul's comment that 'after giving my youth to the FSLN, I was left broken', while other Sandinistas acquired properties and became rich, made this all too evident. His words were bittersweet. Contrary to what he had been told and believed – that the peasants would always come first – when I interviewed him in early 2007, he felt that they had been left with the 'dregs'. He told me: 'You can see it, there are no peasants in the FSLN directive, nor in other governmental positions. During the time the FSLN ruled [in the 1980s], only one, Benigna Mendiola, got to be a deputy.'

He recalled how he had left his land in the 1980s to join the cooperatives and how, later, he left the cooperative to work with the party. In 1990, when the FSLN lost the election, he tried to return to the cooperative to claim a piece

---

30   Pancasán is a mountainous region located in the municipality of San Ramón, Matagalpa. In 1967, the National Guard uncovered a guerrilla column in the area and assassinated almost all of its members. The guerrillas had built a strong alliance with a local peasant union and an intense repression of peasants in the region followed, leading either to their assassination or their forced migration to regions such as Siuna. Soto, *Ventanas en la memoria*, and M. Baltodano, *Memorias de la lucha Sandinista* (Managua, 2010).

31   In Nicaragua, '*montaña*' is a synonym for 'the bush', that is, a space not yet 'conquered by agriculture'. The *montaña* was the place where the Sandinista guerrillas hid from Somoza's National Guard in the years before 1979 and it was also the place where the Contra War was fought in the 1980s.

32   A *piñata* is a clay pot filled with sweets. At children's parties, the *piñata* is broken and the sweets shared out.

of land but its leadership did not accept him back. He then visited an FSLN political leader in Siuna and, with his support, was able to get a house with a title in his name. Raul said: 'If they had not given me that little house I would have been left without anything.' Afterwards, he was able to recover part of the land he had abandoned before joining the cooperative. He told me:

> After the defeat [1990], people were trying to live on ... I travelled to Managua searching for Jaime. When we met I told him 'I need your support to legalise my land', Jaime responded: 'For God's sake, how could you have waited so long to legalise your land.' I got really mad at him and replied: 'Don't fuck with me, aren't you also responsible for what happened? You came to my house and told me to join the cooperative and leave my land, and now I've lost almost all of it. You told me that we were going to have time to "fix things" in the future. Now I want to recover some of it.'[33]

Raul was referring to Jaime, an ex-guerrilla member, with whom he had worked before 1979 and during the 1980s. In the 1990s many cooperative members returned to their ranches to find that new owners had taken over their land. Many others did not dare to return, fearing retaliation from the Contras. The economic conditions of the 1990s were, for many, more complex than those that pertained in the 1980s, made worse by the fears raised by the uncertainty of the post-war period. Raul concluded:

> I don't regret having supported the FSLN and the revolution, but I don't like the attitude of some people there [in the party] and I feel we, peasants, have lost political spaces. Sometimes I feel they used us, because before they used to tell us a *chagüite* and now they say: 'Wait, we will talk later.'[34]

Raul was upset – he was not poorer than other Sandinista peasants in Siuna, but he felt he deserved more political and economic recognition from the FSLN. He was not unhappy with the enrichment of party members, but because he had been left out of the division of spoils. I asked him once, 'Would you do it again? Would you participate again in the *guerrilla* and the revolution?' His answer was categorical:

> No, now what I see is ambition ... Once Oscar [another ex-*guerrillero*] came to visit me. I told him: 'Oscar, look, if I had known that things were going to be like this, I swear to God I wouldn't have done it. I would have worked to support my children.'[35]

During the early 1990s, the distribution of goods among FSLN members and the unequal privileges some of them enjoyed were controversial issues, which continue to be controversial today. Questions are constantly raised about how government resources are used, how they are distributed, and how decisions are taken at the national and local levels.[36] In this book, Cooper and Francis's

---

33 Interview, 11 June 2007.
34 To tell a *chagüite* is to give a speech full of empty promises. Interview, 11 June 2007.
35 Ibid.
36 S. Martí i Puig, 'Nicaragua: la consolidación de un régimen híbrido'; also Vilas, *El legado de una década*.

chapters analyse how different communities participate in decision-making processes at the communal and local levels. Their work is extremely important for gaining an understanding of issues such as participation, local conceptions of social and economic rights, communal agency and government responsibilities in present-day Nicaragua.

Remember Julio Hernández?

Returning to the story with which this chapter began, ultimately we heard the news that the person who killed Julio Hernández was not a *mozo* but a *mandador*.[37] The police never caught him.

But the question remains: did the revolution ensure that *mozos* were not as passive as they had been before? The answer is both yes and no. Certainly, before the revolution there were courageous *mozos* who confronted their arrogant bosses, but there is no doubt that the revolution upset Nicaragua's 'social balance' for Sandinistas and anti-Sandinistas alike. In 1991, Dora María Téllez, a revolutionary *comandante*, said: 'The Nicaraguan peasantry's struggle has gone beyond my expectations; although it was counterrevolutionary, it took the FSLN's political programme. The Contras ... are out there, demanding their rights as peasants.'[38] Lynn Horton makes a similar argument when she asserts that: 'Among peasants who fought with the contras in defence of pre-revolutionary values and relationships, the struggle itself and the example of the FSLN transformed their attitudes and expectations. Anti-Sandinista Quilalí peasants of the postwar period were no longer the quiescent peasantry of a decade earlier.'[39]

Indeed, the Sandinista Revolution made many Nicaraguans feel like 'architects of their liberation', as the lyrics of the FSLN's hymn reminded the population. Peasants were not excluded, whether they were Sandinistas or anti-Sandinista. Many felt they were constructing their own history, one where they were not subjects any more, but rather active participants in a project. The challenge was to make that project a reality, to change an unequal society in the midst of a war and an economic embargo, to navigate internal disagreements about how change might be achieved and to overcome entrenched structures of hierarchy and privilege.[40]

In that context, it is no surprise that the revolution's attempt to overturn Nicaragua's social balance was filled with contradictions, both personal and collective. As Concha's testimony shows, some peasants were given leadership roles in state projects defined by people who had preconceived ideas about who the peasants were, what they 'needed' and how to 'support' them. While some

---

37 Also known as *capataz*, or the boss of farm workers. He worked for the ranch owner.
38 *Envío*, 'Los recontras: campesinos armados con amplia base social', no. 119, Sept. 1991.
39 Horton, *Peasants in Arms*, 17.
40 A nuanced analysis of Cold War geopolitics is necessary here to understand Nicaragua's situation at that time.

local leaders ended up doing the best they could, others took advantage of those opportunities to reproduce traditional conceptions of leadership. As the case of Guillermo shows, peasants were able to enter official spaces where many had not been welcomed before; at the same time, many were repressed by the Sandinista police and army. Finally, as Raul recalled, few peasants had political leadership roles as the FSLN reproduced inequalities within its own party structure, and those few leaders did not participate as equals in decision-making nor in the redistribution of wealth. In the end, inequalities coexisted alongside social changes – these are the 'many other things' the revolution represented.

As mentioned above, the memories recorded in this chapter are forgotten episodes and within them we find the silent lessons of the revolution. These are visible in political initiatives, personal understandings and collective actions. One does not always find a causal relationship between the forgotten and the silent lessons, and examples of the latter often lack moral 'grandiosity'. However, both speak about ways in which some people make sense of the past, as well as the complexities of social change.

For some, the main silent lesson is that one must work within the dominant economic structure in the hope that, eventually, part of the revolutionary dream can be made a reality – a tactic made more complex by the fact that everyone interprets the revolutionary dream in their own way. For others, the silent lesson is to constantly recall those years, or to choose to keep their revolutionary memories to themselves. One colleague, noting the lack of discussion about the Sandinista Revolution in university classrooms in Nicaragua, recounted how surprised one of her students was to learn about the Sandinista patriotic military service of the 1980s. The student later found out her father had been drafted and spent two years of his youth fighting in 'the *montaña*' without ever mentioning that experience to his children.

For yet others, the silent lesson entails a profound scepticism about any attempt to remake Nicaraguan society, sometimes accompanied by considerable anger about the revolution itself. Perhaps, as Rancière states, 'The current scepticism is the result of a surfeit of faith.'[41] In some cases, that faith endured and was passed on to the next generation. I saw that faith in my parents' eyes but also in Concha's, Guillermo's and Raul's. I could see the gleam in their eyes when they remembered the revolution. To me, it was the gleam of remembering not just dreams, but a collective attempt to make those dreams come true. As Sofia Montenegro says when recalling those years:

> Despite all the FSLN's deficiencies, it is the political force that has triggered something historically unique in the country: the taking of power by the popular classes, the general consensus for the insurrection, as well as the thousands of vital experiences, big and small, individual and collective, which allowed us to know the unforgettable experience of touching the sky with our hands.[42]

41 J. Ranciere, 'La imagen intolerable', 103.
42 S. Montenegro, '¿Es revolucionario el FSLN?', *El Nuevo Diario*, 14 May 1994, 9.

The Sandinista Revolution, despite its successes and failures, despite its pains and glories, opened up a space for Nicaraguans to imagine themselves and their society in new ways. In the end, the revolution is about forgotten episodes and silent lessons, but also about collective attempts to make dreams a reality. It is the vibrancy of that collective endeavour that, for many, made the revolution exceptional.

Bibliography

Baltodano, M. (2010) *Memorias de la lucha Sandinista* (Managua).

Baumeister, E. (1998) *Estructura y reforma agraria en Nicaragua (1979–1989)* (Managua).

Bendaña, A. (ed.) (1991) *Una tragedia campesina: testimonios de la Resistencia* (Managua).

Cáceres, S. (2014) 'Somos protagonistas del desarrollo rural. No queremos el tripartismos del gobierno, exigimos guatripartismo', *Envío*, 385 (Apr.), www.envio.org.ni/articulo/4820 (accessed 20 Apr. 2019).

CIERA (1981) *La mosquitia en la revolución* (Managua).

Envío (1991) 'Los recontras: campesinos armados con amplia base social', 119 (Sept.), www.envio.org.ni/articulo/684 (accessed 20 Apr. 2019).

Horton, L. (1998) *Peasants in Arms: War and Peace in the Mountains of Nicaragua, 1979–1994* (Ohio).

INRA (1981) 'Marco estratégico de la Reforma Agraria'. Paper presented at the Latin American Sociology Congress, Departamento de Propaganda y Educación Política del FSLN (Managua).

Larson, A. (2002) *Tendencias actuales de la frontera agrícola: las contradicciones entre conservación y desarrollo* (Managua).

López, I. and E. Romero (2016) 'Asesinan a productor de Ayapal que denunció en LA PRENSA maltrato del Ejército', *La Prensa*, 18 Apr., www.laprensa.com.ni/2016/04/18/politica/2020505-asesinan-productor-ayapal-denuncio-la-prensa-maltrato-del-ejercito (accessed 20 Apr. 2019).

Martí I Puig, S. (2013) 'Nicaragua: la consolidación de un régimen híbrido', *Revista de Ciencia Política*, 33 (1): 269–86.

Montenegro, S. (1994) '¿Es revolucionario el FSLN?', *El Nuevo Diario*, 14 May.

Ranciere, J. (2010) *El Espectador Emancipado* (Buenos Aires).

Rueda Estrada, V. (2015) *Recompas, recontras, revueltos y armados: posguerra y conflictos por la tierra en Nicaragua 1990–2008* (México).

Saldaña-Portillo, M.J. (2003) *The Revolutionary Imagination in the Americas and the Age of Development* (Durham, NC).

Sarlo, B. (2013) 'Los intelectuales, la tierra fertile del Kirchnerismo', *Cuadernos de Literatura*, XVII: 18–33.

Soto, F. (2011) *Ventanas en la memoria: recuerdos de la revolución en la frontera agrícola* (Managua).

Trouillot, M. (1995) *Silencing the Past: Power and the Production of History* (Boston, MA).

Vilas, C. (2005) *El legado de una década* (Managua).

3. Nicaraguan food policy: between self-sufficiency and dependency

Christiane Berth

During the celebrations for World Food Day 2015 in Nicaragua, the Food and Agriculture Organization (FAO) representative, Verónica Guerrero Rodríguez, highlighted the fact that by significantly reducing malnutrition, Nicaragua was among the few countries to have achieved the first UN Millennium Goal.[1] In fact, the percentage of undernourished people in the country had decreased from 54.4 per cent in 1990 to 16.6 per cent in 2015.[2] After Daniel Ortega returned to power in 2006, the government launched a number of programmes to improve the country's nutritional situation, such as the Zero Hunger Program and the Healthy Patios Project. Some of these projects revived concepts from the early 1980s, when the Sandinistas had adopted a highly ambitious food policy that attracted the attention of the international nutrition community. The Sandinista government's apparent success since 2006 contrasts sharply with the deterioration of the Sandinista food policy in the late 1980s. By 1990, when the Sandinistas lost the elections, the nutritional situation in the country was disastrous.

In this chapter, I argue that the Sandinistas' continuous struggle with economic dependency impeded the revolutionaries' attempts to make Nicaragua more self-sufficient. Despite the reforms of the early 1980s, including a new food distribution system, agrarian reform and price regulation, food production did not advance as quickly as the revolutionaries had hoped. Consequently, Nicaragua continued to depend on food imports and, when foreign exchange became scarce, relied increasingly on food aid. With the looming economic crisis in the mid 1980s, the gap between political propaganda and social realities increased. The Contra War and the US economic blockade, as well as the Sandinistas' political strategies in the countryside, contributed to shortages that undermined the self-sufficiency project. In the end, the Sandinista government opted for a strategy of 'economic adjustment' which reversed some of the

---

1 The aim of this Millennium Goal was to halve the proportion of people suffering from hunger between 1990 and 2015.
2 H. Montez Rugama, 'FAO elogia lucha contra el hambre', *El Nuevo Diario*, 8 Oct. 2015.

C. Berth, 'Nicaraguan food policy: between self-sufficiency and dependency', in H. Francis (ed.), *A Nicaraguan Exceptionalism? Debating the Legacy of the Sandinista Revolution* (London: University of London Press, 2019), pp. 61–86. License: CC-BY-NC-ND.

important social reforms of the early 1980s. By 1988, hunger was back in Nicaragua, when average caloric intakes fell below the levels documented by nutritional surveys in 1953–54.[3]

Some researchers have argued that the disastrous nutritional situation was the result of neoliberal economic policies in the early 1990s.[4] This chapter, however, proposes a somewhat different interpretation. The failure to guarantee Nicaraguans a stable food supply in the second half of the 1980s contributed to the demise of the Sandinista Revolution. The disastrous nutritional situation then worsened further with the elimination of free healthcare, the introduction of neoliberal economic policies, and the neglect of small landholders by the post-1990 Unión Nacional Opositora (UNO) government. Despite a slight reduction in the late 1990s, poverty rates remained extremely high until 2005, when they were 48.3 per cent, and then began to decrease from 2006 onwards.[5]

Despite the setbacks of the 1980s, the revolutionary experience laid the foundations for an approach to food policy that is, in some ways, distinctive. The Sandinista Revolution left a legacy of peasant networks that reorganised in the 1990s and mobilised for improvements in the Nicaraguan countryside. The Nicaraguan section of La Vía Campesina (LVC) evolved out of these networks and campaigned for a food sovereignty law in Nicaragua.

Although the food sovereignty approach reprised some important elements of the Sandinistas' 1980s food policy, the new setting is different. The Ortega government is unwilling to challenge the private sector and has therefore subordinated demands for the restriction of food imports to the regulations of trade agreements. While several of the new programmes resemble the 1980s projects in name, they are conducted in a different political context: the new *caudillismo* or 'populist left regime with hybrid economic features'[6] that Ortega has established in Nicaragua since 2007. In this chapter, I evaluate Sandinista food policy across three periods: the expansive, ambitious food policy of the

3   M. Flores et al., 'Estudios dietéticos en Nicaragua: I. Municipio de San Isidro, Departamento de Matagalpa'; M. Flores, 'Estudios dietéticos en Nicaragua: II. Barrio de San Luis, Ciudad de Managua'.

4   S. Linkogle, 'Soya, culture and international food aid: the case of a Nicaraguan communal kitchen', 97; W. Godek, 'The institutionalization of food sovereignty, PhD diss., Rutgers University, 2014, 164–5.

5   Poverty decreased from 50.3 per cent of the population in 1993 to 47.9 per cent in 1998 to 45.8 per cent in 2001. R. Spalding, 'Poverty politics', 221–2; A. Acevedo Vogl, 'Estamos en un punto de inflexión y deberíamos preocuparnos', *Envío*, no. 404, Nov. 2015. The last survey on living standards conducted by INIDE (Instituto Nacional de Información de Desarrollo) claimed that poverty had decreased from 42.5 per cent in 2009 to 29.6 per cent in 2014. However, economist Adolfo Acevedo Vogl criticised the definition of poverty used by the survey (i.e. daily expenditure of less than US$1.81), suggesting it was too low. The World Bank has amended its definition of poverty for Latin America to include all those with a daily expenditure of less than US$4. In addition, INIDE has not published the database for the survey. A FIDEG (Fundación Internacional para el Desafío Económico Global) survey concluded that in 2013 the poverty level was still 40.5 per cent of the population. FIDEG, 'Dinámicas de la pobreza en Nicaragua 2009–2013', 2014, 4.

6   R.J. Spalding, *Contesting Trade in Central America: Market Reform and Resistance*, 208.

first years after the revolution (1979–82), the period of crisis and adjustment (1984–8) and the period of erosion (1988–90). In the last section, I discuss continuities and discontinuities in the neo-Sandinista food policy after 2007. Research on food sovereignty in Nicaragua has provided important insights into the politics around food during the last decade. Nevertheless, I propose that there is a need for a broader analysis which incorporates agrarian change, consumption and food distribution to explain both the reduction of malnutrition and its continuing prevalence in rural Nicaragua today.

Initial euphoria, 1979–82

The slogan 'Let's all sow the land', which appeared on a Nicaraguan Food Program poster, called on people to participate in food production. The illustration shows a peasant couple with the man holding his machete triumphantly aloft, while the woman holds a basket of vegetables on her arm. This poster formed part of early Sandinista campaigns to increase food production in Nicaragua.[7] Projects in the early 1980s set ambitious goals: the aim was to reach self-sufficiency by 1982 – and this in a country where food imports had increased significantly in the decades prior to revolution.

'It may be concluded that the theme of FOOD and especially that of National Food Self-Sufficiency and Food Security is considered to have a very high political priority in contemporary Nicaragua' was how Otto van Teutem, FAO representative in Nicaragua, ended his report on World Food Day in 1982.[8] His statement demonstrates that the international organisations working in Nicaragua also saw the new energy with which the Sandinistas were pursuing their revolutionary food policy. It aimed at guaranteeing a basic food supply to all Nicaraguans and was based on four pillars: 1) the increase of basic grain production; 2) the promotion of local food consumption; 3) the democratisation of the supply system; and 4) the regulation of prices. Up to 1982, the revolutionaries created new institutions, invested more resources, developed ambitious production schemes and launched broad-based education campaigns. In general, the Sandinistas promoted a 'mixed economy', with three sectors: private enterprise, mixed firms and a state sector. In contrast with other revolutionary regimes, they refrained from a complete nationalisation of production.[9]

During the period of initial euphoria, the Sandinistas introduced credits for basic grain producers, democratised the supply system, and mobilised people to consume locally produced food. The new distribution network, managed by the Empresa Nacional de Alimentos Básicos (ENABAS), included popular stores, rural distribution points and popular supermarkets. External aggression

7   The poster is reprinted in O. Núñez Soto, 'Unser Land: unsere Revolution', 104.
8   O. van Teutem, 'Report on World Food Day 1982 – Nicaragua, 2 Nov. 1982'. ESH WFD IN 4/9 NIC, FAO Archives.
9   R. Sola Montserrat, *Un siglo y medio de economía nicaragüense: las raíces del presente*, 54–55; J. Austin, et al., 'The role of the revolutionary state in the Nicaraguan food system'.

played a key role in expanding these ambitious reforms. Shortly after taking over the US presidency in January 1981, Ronald Reagan announced that his government would cancel credits for wheat imports from Nicaragua. Soon afterwards, in May 1981, the Sandinistas launched the Nicaraguan Food Program (PAN) to coordinate Nicaragua's new food policy.[10] The cancellation of the wheat credits also sparked the first campaign to promote corn as an anti-imperialist, revolutionary food. The campaigns included visual references, Mesoamerican legends, cooking competitions and songs. The first corn festivals mobilised thousands of Nicaraguans around local food security.[11] More than 30 years later my interviewees remembered the campaigns with enthusiasm.[12] At the same time, government propaganda increasingly promoted the aim of self-sufficiency. In late 1981, PAN director Pedro Antonio Blandón announced that Nicaragua planned to reach self-sufficiency in basic grains by 1982.[13] To stimulate food production in the cities, the Sandinistas also launched an urban gardening campaign.

The global nutrition community observed Nicaraguan efforts with interest. After the world food crisis in the early 1970s, there was intense debate about the correct approach to global nutritional problems. The Sandinista revolutionaries attracted attention because they prioritised basic grain production and seemed willing to change land distribution structures as well as invest resources in improving the nutrition of the poor. Consequently, the FAO, WHO and UNICEF financed a large number of nutritional projects during the 1980s. Their work, as well as the general interest shown in Nicaragua's policy, attracted many people from the nutritional community to the country. They combined work at Sandinista institutions with research on the food system. For example, Solon Barraclough the US economist and UN Research Institute for Social Development (UNRISD) director, initiated a collaboration that shaped the work of the Nicaraguan research centre, Centro de Investigaciones y Estudios de la Reforma Agraria (CIERA).[14] Conceived of as a research institution to support agrarian reform and food policy, the centre applied UNRISD's food system methodology in many of its surveys.

As the Sandinista government began to cooperate closely with the FAO in the early 1980s, food security was incorporated in Nicaraguan policy. Moreover, the FAO supported several projects under its Food Security Assistance Program.[15]

10 Although the programme's symbol was the corncob, the organisation's acronym is the Spanish word for bread.
11 *Barricada*, 'Xilonem, respuesta y compromiso', 12 May 1981, 3.
12 Interview, María Josefina Gurdián Mántica (Doña Piñita), Managua, Aug. 2012. Interview, Rosario Montes Orozco, León, Sept. 2012.
13 P. Candia, 'El proyecto PAN trascendencia y obstáculos', *Barricada*, 20 June 1981, 3; *Barricada*, 'Consigna del PAN, producir', 22 June 1981, 1, 7; *Barricada*, 'Blandón evalúa 5 meses del PAN', 28 Sept. 1981, 1, 5; *Barricada*, 'PAN, unificar políticas en 1982', 16 Dec. 1981, 5.
14 S. Barraclough, *A Preliminary Analysis of the Nicaraguan Food System* (Genf, 1982).
15 E. Saouma to J. Wheelock, 1 Sept. 1981. FA 13/1 FSAS ODG Old, FAO Archives.

At international conferences, Nicaragua suggested the establishment of a regional Food Security Council built on Latin American solidarity and intra-regional trade.[16] In internal political debates, however, the concept of self-sufficiency remained more significant. In 1987, the Nicaraguan Constitution addressed the issue of food security, asserting the right of Nicaraguans to be protected against hunger, backed up by state guarantees for adequate availability and equitable distribution.[17] In the political discourse of Nicaragua in the 1980s, the term 'food sovereignty' did not appear. However, some elements of Sandinista food policy anticipated demands subsequently raised by the food sovereignty movement. These were the emphasis on local consumption and production, agrarian reform, and the right to define the local food system autonomously.[18]

The first publications by international experts reflected contemporary enthusiasm and presented Nicaragua as a model for other countries of the Global South. For example, Joseph Collins, founder of the US initiative Food First, held up Nicaragua as a model for countries that lacked large budget resources for their food policy.[19] James Austin et al. concluded that 'in spite of extremely adverse circumstances ... the Sandinista Revolution has made significant achievements in the areas of food policy and agricultural development'.[20] However, the experts were also aware that these ambitious projects faced enormous challenges.

The new food policy faced two main obstacles: first, the structure of the Nicaraguan economy was highly dependent on agro exports, and, second, the policies of the Somoza dictatorship had reinforced this dependency. In particular, cotton cultivation had expanded in Pacific Nicaragua, taking up the best soils from the 1950s on. By contrast, basic grain production had moved to the inferior soils of the Nicaraguan interior.[21] When the Sandinistas came to power in July

16 FAO, *Report of the Seventeenth FAO Regional Conference for Latin America: Managua, 30 August to 10 September 1982*.

17 Article 63: 'Es derecho de los nicaragüenses estar protegidos contra el hambre. El Estado promoverá programas que aseguren una adecuada disponibilidad de alimentos y una distribución equitativa de los mismos', Constitución política de 1987, http://legislacion.asamblea.gob.ni/normaweb.nsf/bbe90a5bb646d50906257265005d21f8/8339762d0f427a1c062573080055fa46?OpenDocument

18 See, e.g., the 2016 definition on La Vía Campesina's homepage: 'Food sovereignty prioritises local food production and consumption. It gives a country the right to protect its local producers from cheap imports and to control production. It ensures that the rights to use and manage lands, territories, water, seeds, livestock and biodiversity are in the hands of those who produce food and not of the corporate sector. Therefore, the implementation of genuine agrarian reform is one of the top priorities of the farmer's movement': https://web.archive.org/web/20160305031659/http://viacampesina.org/en/index.php/organisation-mainmenu-44.

19 Solon Barraclough argued similarly that 'the Nicaraguan experience in dealing with its food problems will probably be highly relevant for some other Central American countries'. *A Preliminary Analysis*, 11.

20 Austin et al., 'The role of the revolutionary state'; 35.

21 Between 1960 and 1979, cotton exports increased by 381 per cent, beef exports by 335 per cent and sugar exports by 349 per cent. B.N. Biondi-Morra, *Revolución y política alimentaria: Un análisis crítico de Nicaragua*, 49, 57–9; Sola Montserrat, *Un siglo y medio*, 29, 35–9; J.A. Booth, *The End and the Beginning: The Nicaraguan Revolution*, 60–6.

1979, the initial situation they faced was unfavourable. The civil war of the late 1970s had brought food production to a standstill, making food supply during the insurrectional period difficult. Consequently, the revolutionary government's first priority was to resume food production.

In the countryside, many peasants hoped that agrarian reform would follow immediately after the revolution, allowing them to produce on their own land. However, the first wave of Sandinista expropriation favoured large state farms instead of individual peasant production. In 1979, the Sandinistas transformed the enterprise and landholdings of the Somoza family and National Guard officers into state enterprises that would continue export production to earn foreign currency but would also increase basic grain production to ensure local supply. By contrast, after the enactment of the first agrarian reform law in 1981, land distributions proceeded slowly. During the first period up to 1984, cooperatives benefited most, receiving more than 80 per cent of all distributed land. Many peasants who had dreamt for a long time of possessing their own land felt betrayed.[22] At the same time, relations between peasants and ENABAS suffered from problems concerning the new system of guaranteed prices the latter had introduced. For example, peasants considered prices offered for basic grains to be too low as inflation was on the rise. Next, trading with ENABAS had its disadvantages because the enterprise paid by cheque instead of cash. Since local banks could not always cash cheques, this often meant that peasants had to travel further afield.[23]

Although theoretically basic grain production took absolute priority, the need for foreign exchange undermined the food policy agenda. The Nicaraguan economy depended strongly on the export of cotton, coffee and sugar, the result of which was that the government had to support their production in order to secure foreign currency. The resources assigned to agro-export enterprises meant that basic grain production received insufficient assistance, because of the general scarcity of agricultural inputs. In addition, export agriculture and basic grain production also competed for labour.[24]

The first evaluations by the Sandinistas of the new food policy showed mixed results: agricultural production still faced difficulties, as Figure 1 below demonstrates. In particular, corn production had declined after 1978. Although it recovered with the 1980/81 harvest, corn production did not reach pre-war levels again until the late 1980s. The production of beans and rice also recovered in the early 1980s, but not sufficiently to keep up with the increasing demands of a growing population. This gap is reflected in the first surveys on post-revolutionary consumption.

---

22 E. Dore, 'The great grain dilemma. Peasants and state policy in revolutionary Nicaragua', 102–4, 115–17; E. Baumeister, *Estructura y reforma agraria en Nicaragua (1979–1989)*, 123.

23 A.H. Saulniers, 'State trading organizations in expansion: a case study of ENABAS', 119; S. Martí i Puig, 'The origins of the peasant-Contra rebellion in Nicaragua, 1979–87', 12.

24 L.J. Enríquez, *Harvesting Change: Labor and Agrarian Reform in Nicaragua 1979–1990*, 84–5.

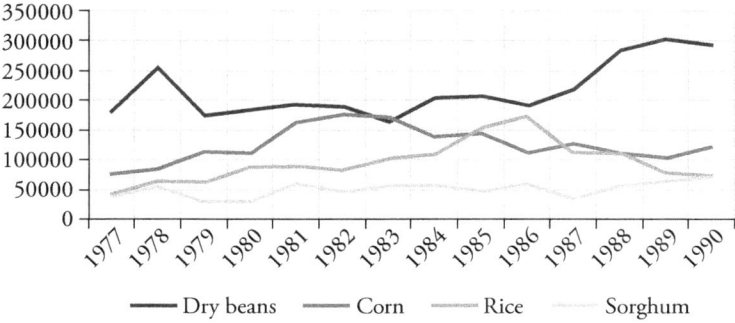

Figure 3.1. Basic grain production, 1977–90 (in t).

Surveys conducted in the early 1980s reveal the mixed results of the Sandinista food policy: despite increasing per capita consumption of basic foodstuffs, people judged their nutritional situation to be worse after the revolution. It must be noted that the surveys encountered many difficulties, such as the limited availability of updated statistical data on the population, basic grain production and income. CIERA's first investigation in 1982 into popular consumption in ten Managuan districts revealed discontent among the inhabitants. Taking meat as the main indicator of good nutrition, more than 40 per cent of the interviewees contended that their nutrition had worsened in the previous two years and only 8 per cent believed that their diets were better.[25] While this was certainly true in terms of meat consumption, the supply of rice, wheat flour and eggs had improved.[26] The supply of basic foods also increased as the government subsidised the cost of basic grains, sugar, milk and vegetable oil until 1984. It was the first time in Nicaraguan history that a government had distributed subsidised food on such a large scale.[27]

Throughout the 1980s, revolutionary propaganda revalorised traditional Nicaraguan food against imported ingredients and processed food. Contemporary surveys on consumption indicate limited success, however. In the early 1980s, people in the poor districts of Managua still spent considerable

25 Centro de Investigación y Estudios de la Reforma Agraria (CIERA), *Distribución y consumo popular de alimentos en Managua*, 78.
26 *Barricada* published data on per capita consumption between 1977 and 1982, based on MIDINRA (Ministerio de Desarrollo Agropecuario y Reforma Agraria) and MICOIN (Ministerio de Comercio Interior) data. These statistics show a decline in per capita milk consumption while other data indicate an improvement. In general, statistical information from the revolutionary years is sometimes contradictory. Especially in the years of economic crisis, the scope of surveys remained limited. See C.M. Vilas, 'Nicaragua. I. Scientific research in a revolutionary setting. The case of Nicaragua', 11–13, 54–55.
27 Data on rural consumption are scarce, but the few existing surveys indicate that peasants could supply themselves with meat and basic grains. However, the lack of tools and the other means necessary to undertake daily work affected their living conditions and prompted discontent.

sums of money on processed food such as Maggi soup or biscuits. Similarly, the demand for milk powder remained high throughout the 1980s.[28] The government promoted fish as a healthy alternative to meat, frescos beverages instead of soft drinks, and corn instead of wheat. In the early 1980s people attended corn festivals in large numbers, started urban gardening projects and developed creative substitutes for scarce products. Nevertheless, it proved difficult to make comprehensive changes to Nicaraguans' consumption habits. Some advances were made with the introduction of new staples such as soy and potatoes, production of which was stimulated by development projects, and to an extent their consumption improved local diets during the crisis of the late 1980s.[29]

By the time CIERA published the results of the consumer survey in 1983, the situation in Nicaragua had worsened: from 1981, the US began supporting armed opponents of the revolution – the Contras – who attacked Nicaragua from their bases on its borders. The Contra War demanded resources that could otherwise have been spent on social projects. It also affected basic grain production: in the war zones storage and infrastructure were destroyed and peasants displaced.[30] Worse still, prices of Nicaragua's most important export products on the world markets fell, which led to a deep financial crisis.

Ongoing dependency and the turn to economic adjustment, 1984–8

With the Contra War and the looming financial crisis, dependency and scarcity became ever more visible in Nicaraguan society. By 1985, military expenditure made up 50 per cent of the national budget. Due to US pressure, many international financial institutions had blocked funding for Nicaragua. At the same time, prices for agrarian export products remained low, which exacerbated the scarcity of foreign currency. There had been shortages of basic grains since the early 1980s, reinforced by natural disaster, but in 1984 the situation worsened. The Nicaraguan economy became a 'shortage economy'[31] and this had many negative consequences for Nicaraguan consumers, who had to bear the time-consuming search for food and the erosion of real wages. Long lines formed outside shops and frequently consumers were unable to acquire basic products

---

28 Centro de Investigación y Estudios de la Reforma Agraria, *Distribución y consumo popular*, 12–13.

29 On potatoes, see Evaluación externa. Retrospectiva y prospectiva del proyecto agropecuario MAG-COSUDE. Estelí, Nicaragua, 10–22 June 1991. E2025A#2002/145#2340, Bundesarchiv Bern; on soy, see H. Simon, 'Probleme und Perspektiven von Frauenförderung vor dem sozio-ökonomischen Hintergrund Nicaraguas, 128–48.

30 T.W. Walker, *Nicaragua: Living in the Shadow of the Eagle*, 92–5.

31 The term was coined by the economist János Kornai, who analysed the historical development of economies in central, eastern and south-eastern Europe from the 1950s. It refers to chronic shortage of important goods as a result of the economy's structure. B. Tomka, *A Social History of Twentieth Century Europe*, 242. Even if the Nicaraguan economy was not entirely planned, structural problems caused the lack of products available to consumers.

such as sugar, wheat, toilet paper or soap. In 1984, Managuan supermarkets reported the first violent protests by consumers, who smashed windows to gain access to food.[32] Simultaneously, black markets witnessed rapid growth. In Managua, informal trade was concentrated at the largest Managuan market, the Oriental, where speculators offered scarce goods at exorbitant prices. By 1984, the Sandinistas had intensified control measures, for example, by introducing a consumer card system for the distribution of rice, beans, salt, sugar, corn, oil, soap and matches.

As outlined above, agricultural production had not advanced sufficiently to guarantee a basic grain supply to all Nicaraguans. By 1983, the lack of foreign currency further undermined production as the government was facing serious difficulties in importing necessary agricultural inputs, such as tools and fertilisers. This shortage was particularly acute for technology-based crops, such as rice, whose production fell significantly between 1983 and 1986. The growing dependency on imports and food aid went, paradoxically, hand in hand with a radicalisation of the discourse on self-sufficiency. For instance, the FSLN newspaper *Barricada* characterised urban gardens as 'trenches against hunger'.[33] In illustrations, peasants' tools were portrayed as weapons, which is indicative of the militarisation of political propaganda in the mid 1980s.[34]

A closer look at rural communities reveals, however, that the countryside did not fight unconditionally at the Sandinistas' side, either in the military conflict or in agricultural production.[35] This was the result of the contradictory Sandinista agrarian policy during the early revolutionary years. The Agrarian Reform Law resulted in very little land being distributed to small peasants, because Sandinista elites at the agriculture ministry favoured large-scale agriculture. They designed huge, spectacular projects that failed to address Nicaraguan realities.[36] By contrast, advocates of a small peasants strategy formed the majority at CIERA, but their arguments were not heard until it became apparent that more peasants were supporting the Contras. By the mid 1980s, the Sandinistas had accelerated land distribution, were paying higher prices for basic grains, and had implemented a new rural supply network.[37]

To alleviate the general supply situation, the government relied increasingly on external food aid, a trend set in 1981, when more than 77.3 million tons of food were received. Throughout the decade, wheat, corn and rice were the most

32 *Barricada*, 'Abastecimiento irregular en barrio Bello Horizonte', 17 Aug. 1984, 10.
33 Translation from Spanish original. *Barricada*, 'Huertos: lucha contra el hambre y el bloqueo', 3 June 1985, 3.
34 See, e.g., *Barricada*, 'Trabajo y defensa ... un solo frente de combate', 10 June 1985, 8.
35 I.A. Luciak, *The Sandinista Legacy: Lessons from a Political Economy in Transition*, 123–4; L. Horton, *Peasants in Arms: War and Peace in the Mountains of Nicaragua*, 1979–1994, 158–60.
36 S. Ramírez, *Adiós Muchachos: A Memoir of the Sandinista Revolution*, 168. Joseph Collins had expressed similar fears in the mid 1980s in *Nicaragua: Was hat sich durch die Revolution verändert? Agrarreform und Ernährung im neuen Nicaragua*, with the assistance of F. Moore Lappé et al, 148–51.
37 Luciak, *The Sandinista Legacy*, 124–31; E. Baumeister, 'Agrarian reform', 239–40.

important donated products. This made it possible to guarantee supply quotas at times of difficulty, but it also silently undermined Nicaragua's policy of becoming more independent from external aid. Between 1982 and 1984, western European governments, Canada and the European Economic Community (EEC) provided large amounts of aid, while food donations from socialist countries increased significantly after 1983, and had become the most important source of aid by 1984.[38] This reflects a general shift in external aid for the revolutionary project. On the one hand, the United States exercised diplomatic pressure that made even strong allies cave in to their demands. On the other, early enthusiasm was fading. Some European governments criticised Sandinista policy as undemocratic and thus reduced their economic aid considerably.[39] Although, owing to Socialist support, the total amount of aid remained more or less stable, Sandinista leaders were continuously seeking to acquire new sources, which also meant adapting to donors' agendas.[40] For example, the Sandinistas never publicly criticised the FAO and incorporated the international organisation's self-image into Sandinista political propaganda. In the end, food aid strengthened the demand for wheat products and powdered milk, which further weakened the self-sufficiency project. In spite of some voices expressing concern about external dependency, in most cases the Sandinistas glorified the aid in public ceremonies as a way of demonstrating their strong international reputation. For example, while they idealised East German food aid as an expression of proletarian internationalism, archival documentation reveals a clear struggle for influence in Cold War terrain.[41] Moreover, the German Democratic Republic (GDR) hoped to acquire Nicaraguan export products, such as coffee, that could help to alleviate its supply problems.[42] As the economic crisis became ever more visible, GDR consultants commented critically on the lack of adequate economic strategies.[43]

In fact, by 1983, conflicts on the future of Nicaragua's economic policy had emerged. Faced with a lack of access to foreign currency, Sandinista politicians began to question whether an expansive social policy was still possible. This contentious discussion among political leaders and experts lasted for several

38 R. Garst, *La ayuda alimentaria al istmo centroamericano*, Colección Temas de Seguridad Alimentaria 13 (Panamá, 1992), cuadro 15. The data are based on the statistics from the Nicaraguan Ministry of Exterior Cooperation.
39 K. Christiaens, 'Between diplomacy and solidarity: western European support networks for Sandinista Nicaragua', 21 (4) (2014).
40 S. Barraclough et al., *Aid that Counts: The Western Contribution to Development and Survival in Nicaragua*, 73.
41 *Barricada*, 'RDA entrega el trigo donado', 9 June 1981, 1, 5. Documentation from German state archives reveals that the GDR competed eagerly with Federal Germany to provide food aid, as diplomats from both German states saw this as a means of portraying a positive image of their political system. Each carefully observed every step their rivals made.
42 This expectation was not entirely fulfilled as Nicaragua could not deliver all the promised products during the mid 1980s.
43 Müller, Bericht über die Beratertätigkeit Monat Jan./Feb. 1985, 11.2.1985; Müller, Bericht über die Beratertätigkeit im Zeitraum November/Dezember 1984, 10.12.1984. BArch DE 1/58123.

years. Alejandro Martínez-Cuenca, foreign trade minister, favoured an adjustment solution, while others still dwelt on structuralist approaches. With elections in 1984, they postponed making a decision until 1985, when the first signs of hyperinflation were already becoming visible. In February 1985, the Sandinistas launched the first economic adjustment package, including budget cuts, the elimination of most food subsidies, increased taxes and a devaluation of the Nicaraguan currency. With the new economic strategy, food policy became less important.[44]

While external advisers' early publications about Nicaragua's food policy had been overwhelmingly positive, by the mid 1980s their evaluations had become more critical. Joseph Collins' third, extended version of his book, published in 1986, openly expressed his disillusionment. First, he argued, food policy was no longer a political priority. Next, he strongly criticised the reliance on technology and large-scale production which meant that small producers received only limited technological support. Finally, he said, PAN suffered from bureaucratic chaos, inadequately educated staff and a lack of resources.[45] By that point, researchers' interest in publishing on Sandinista food policy had also faded away. Although basic elements of the policy, such as the distribution system, still existed, the economic crisis weakened the system's capacities. The Sandinistas launched increasingly militant campaigns blaming external enemies, such as the speculators, for the scarcity of goods.

The erosion of Sandinista food policy, 1988–90

The situation steadily worsened in the second half of the 1980s. Between 1985 and 1987, Nicaraguans faced an 85 per cent erosion of real wages. The government was incapable of halting inflation, which reached 747 per cent in 1986; 1,347 per cent in 1987 and 33,000 in 1988.[46] The crisis eroded the country's food policy and the capacity to store and manage food donations.

Many products were not available through official supply channels, obliging people either to search for substitutes or pay exorbitant prices on the black market. In spite of all the Sandinistas' efforts to bring the Managuan Oriental market under control, informal trade continued to grow, as official wages did not keep up with inflation. Many state employees reduced their working hours so as to engage in other survival activities. Criticism grew hand-in-hand with eroding living standards, eventually even by the FSLN newspaper in 1987. Several writers, such as the Nicaraguan poet Gioconda Belli, rejected the official interpretation that speculation was the main enemy of the revolution and suggested the reintroduction of food subsidies.[47]

44 A. Martínez Cuenca, *Sandinista Economies in Practice*, 65–6; Ramírez, *Adiós Muchachos*, 166; Sola Montserrat, *Un siglo y medio*, 100–1; J. Ricciardi, 'Economic policy', 247–73.
45 Collins, *Nicaragua*, 154–64.
46 Ricciardi, 'Economic policy', 261; D. Close, *Nicaragua: The Chamorro Years*, 128–9.
47 G. Belli: ¿Quienes son los especuladores?', *Barricada*, 25 Feb. 1987. Similar doubts about the line between commerce, illegal speculation and poor people's activities were raised by D.

After the first adjustment measures, the government's economic policy continued to divide leading Sandinista politicians. The government consulted external advisers, among them the US economist Lance Taylor from the Massachusetts Institute of Technology (MIT) and Daniel Ibarra Muñoz, the former treasury secretary for Mexico, who worked as a consultant for the Comisión Económica para América Latina y el Caribe (CEPAL). By 1988, the Central American peace negotiations had advanced to the stage where the Sandinistas believed that the conflict could be settled and the time for economic reforms had come. Finally, the market and structural adjustment advocates won out.[48]

In February 1988, the government introduced a first adjustment package that included a 10 per cent budget cut, the dismissal of 8,000 public employees and the introduction of a new currency. It soon became apparent that the measures were not enough to stop inflation. As people continued to suffer from poor supply lines and unaffordable prices, they lost confidence in the government's economic policy. In June 1988, a second adjustment package was implemented that devalued the new currency and introduced higher prices for public services, wage liberalisation and the elimination of the last food subsidy for milk.[49] Still the economic situation did not improve. Furthermore, measures to alleviate the social crisis had only limited effects.[50] In October 1988, Hurricane Joan hit the country, an additional blow to the Nicaraguan economy. The hurricane shattered the Caribbean coast, causing a total of more than US$839 million worth of damage.[51]

The 1988 adjustment was a radical turning point, as the influence of market mechanisms in the mixed economy increased. Simultaneously, the Sandinistas reduced the scope of their expansive social policy. A closer look at PAN shows that Nicaragua's food policy was eroded during the transition that began in 1988. While PAN's shrinking number of employees still drew up ambitious plans to attract foreign funding, the institutional capacity for their implementation was limited. As Harald Juch, a German development cooperation employee remembers, the staff lacked nutritional knowledge and showed no interest in engaging in public education campaigns any more. At the same time, a large corruption scandal affected the programme.[52] Similarly, ENABAS adapted to

Martínez, 'Reintegrar al trabajo a los especuladores', *Barricada*, 26 Feb. 1987, 3.

48 Martínez Cuenca, *Sandinista Economies*, 69–73.

49 Close, *Nicaragua: The Chamorro Years*, 124–5; G. Dijkstra, *Industrialization in Sandinista Nicaragua: Policy and Practice in a Mixed Economy*, 136–9; Anlage 3: Übersicht über die Maßnahmen zur weiteren Durchführung der Wirtschaftsreformen, Stand vom 10.10.1988. BArch DE 1/58121.

50 To alleviate the social effects of the crisis, the government introduced a wage increase of 500 per cent, on the face of it a high amount. However, the real wage increase was estimated at just 200 per cent as the new wage system eliminated other incentives. Dr Bothe, ZK-Berater, Nicaragua an Dr Schürer, Vorsitzender der Staatlichen Planungskommission, 25.2.1988. BArch DE 1/58122; Dijkstra, *Industrialization in Sandinista Nicaragua*, 136–9.

51 CEPAL, 'Damage caused by Hurricane Joan in Nicaragua', 3.

52 H. Juch, 'Unser revolutionärer Alltag: Teil 2', Tagebuch Comics Zeichnungen Fotos, unpublished manuscript, 1989, 7–13.

market mechanisms and abandoned the goal of equal access to distribution points and storage facilities.

The economic crisis reversed the social advances of the early revolutionary years. Average caloric intakes for Nicaraguans fell continuously until 1989. Between 1976 and 1986, the average per capita caloric intake in Nicaragua had ranged between 2,000 and nearly 2,400 kilocalories (kcal). In 1986, it started to fall: first to 1,932 kcal in 1987, then to 1,610 kcal in 1988 and finally to 1,591 kcal in 1989 – a 22.5 per cent decline.[53] By 1988, average caloric intakes had fallen below 1,800 kcal, which is below the current FAO's definition of hunger.[54] Health surveys also indicated that malnutrition among children had once again increased.[55] Nevertheless, Sandinista leaders refrained from mentioning hunger in internal political propaganda, as this would have been a public acknowledgement of failure. The economic crisis and the hurricane also strongly affected food production.

The devastation caused by Hurricane Joan led to the erosion of 10,000 hectares of arable land, and destroyed seeds, food processing facilities, warehouses and storage units. In total, 15,700 head of cattle, 15,000 pigs and 460,000 head of poultry were killed, further adding to the country's grave meat shortages. The CEPAL diagnosed 'a serious food shortage' and estimated that agricultural production would decline by 17 per cent.[56] Moreover, the lack of fertilisers and other agricultural inputs mainly affected the large-scale production of rice, milk and meat. For example, milk production declined by 64.9 per cent and beef production by 38.1 per cent between 1978 and 1989. Rice production had increased by 1982, but then fell by 40.8 per cent between 1982 and 1989.[57] Despite increasing the production of corn and beans after 1987 – a marker of the success of the new peasant strategy – the overall situation remained disastrous. Food aid reached a new peak of more than 185 million tons in 1988. These donations temporarily alleviated the situation but could not resolve the supply crisis.[58] As the Sandinistas realised that wages at state institutions did not allow people to make ends meet, they introduced a special aid package guaranteeing low-cost basic food to around 190,000 state employees.[59] This measure was

---

53 Program Briefing Paper for Potential CARE Food Assistance Activities in Nicaragua, 4 Apr. 1990, Box 1218, CARE Archives. Protein consumption levels ranged from 50.7 to 56.3 grams (g) between 1976–85, fell to 49.8 g in 1986 and then to 37.6 g in 1989. CARE obtained these data from PAN.

54 FAO defines hunger as the inability of a person to acquire sufficient food for more than a year, taking a minimum level of kilocalories as an indicator. The organisation establishes the average need at 2,100 kilocalories per person.

55 As the economic crisis also undermined the state's capacity to generate reliable data, surveys sometimes only cover limited samples, which makes comparisons difficult.

56 CEPAL, 'Damage caused by Hurricane Joan in Nicaragua', 10.

57 Data from FAOSTAT, http://faostat3.fao.org/home/E (accessed 23 Apr. 2019).

58 Garst, *La ayuda alimentaria al istmo centroamericano*, cuadro 15.

59 The AFA (*arroz, frijoles, azúcar*) package included ten pounds of rice, ten pounds of beans and five pounds of sugar per month.

meant to ensure that government institutions could keep working, but it left vulnerable groups unprotected.

Far from Managua, global political changes indicated that aid from the Eastern bloc would decline, a fact that local Soviet advisers communicated to Sandinista politicians.[60] Owing to the crisis Hurricane Joan had left in its wake, the government introduced a third adjustment programme in early 1989, which drastically slashed state expenditure by 44 per cent. As a consequence, the government dismissed a further 35,000 state employees and reduced its responsibility for state enterprises.[61] During the peace process negotiations in February 1989, the Sandinistas agreed to bring the national elections forward to February 1990, meaning that 1989 became a pre-electoral period. In their election campaign the opposition argued that the United States would revive economic aid if they were to win, thereby improving the prospects for the Nicaraguan economy.[62] To counter this, Sandinista political propaganda claimed that Soviet support would definitely continue, even though the leadership knew this was not the case. Sandinista politicians continued to honour Soviet diplomats with reception ceremonies for donations, even as the political transformation of the Eastern bloc began.[63]

Contemporary surveys on adjustment policies indicate Nicaraguans' growing disillusionment and discontent. For example, the ITZANI research institute interviewed more than a thousand people in five Managuan districts in spring 1989. Two-thirds perceived their personal economic situation to be worse than the year before. Only 20 per cent viewed the economic policy as good, with more than 70 per cent expressing a critical opinion: 24 per cent judged the situation as bad, 14 per cent as terrible and 36 per cent as indifferent. Finally, 25 per cent believed that the government was unwilling to find a solution for the country's economic problems.[64] The poor economic situation, combined with people's desire for peace, contributed to the Sandinista electoral defeat.

Overall, Sandinista food policy embarked on a course to becoming more self-sufficient, but faced a dependency dilemma. Given the scarcity of resources, the promotion of basic grain production would have weakened the agro-export sector which generated foreign exchange. Hence, the Sandinistas followed an alternative course which also reflected the existence of different factions within government institutions. Visions of giant state enterprises producing food proved unsuccessful, while peasants' expectations that they would receive individual landholdings were fulfilled too late. After the shift to peasant production and the liberalisation of basic grain prices in the mid 1980s, the production of corn and

60 D.M. Ferrero Blanco, 'Daniel Ortega y Mijail Gorbachov: Nicaragua y la URSS en los últimos anos de la Guerra Fría (1985–1990)'.
61 Ricciardi, 'Economic policy', 266–7.
62 Close, *Nicaragua: The Chamorro Years*, 126.
63 *Barricada*, 'Llega embarque de arroz URSS a San Juan del Sur', 24 Jan. 1990, 6.
64 J.W. Soule, 'The economic austerity packages of 1988 and their impact on public opinion', *International Journal of Political Economy*, Fall (1990).

beans did increase. However, this success came too late and was too limited to guarantee the growing Nicaraguan population access to basic food. This failure undermined the government's campaigns to strengthen the consumption of local food.

After the 1990 elections, the deepening social crisis and occasional price shocks continued to affect the Nicaraguan people. By 1992 some 50 per cent of the population was suffering from malnutrition. The UNO (National Opposition Union) government led by President Violeta Chamorro (1990–7) followed a neoliberal economic policy that was supported by a new influx of US economic aid and the cooperation of international financial organisations. Although the nutritional situation was severe, the food policy of the Chamorro government was left at the margins. International organisations, such as the FAO, criticised the strong external dependency of the Nicaraguan food system.[65] A limited number of Sandinista projects were continued by NGOs in the 1990s, while agricultural organisations fought to improve the situation in the countryside. During the late 1990s and early 2000s, food policy focused on fighting the consequences of Hurricane Mitch, which hit the country in 1998 and caused another food crisis. Corruption scandals discredited ENABAS and President Arnoldo Alemán (1997–2002) exploited food aid for electoral purposes.[66]

Although initially the FSLN deeply opposed the UNO government, after a year it had taken a more conciliatory stance. By the late 1990s, the FSLN had already abandoned its aim of revolutionary change and entered into an alliance with the governing Partido Liberal Constitucionalista (PLC), which can only be explained by the profound transformation of the party throughout the 1990s. Some of the FSLN leadership joined the country's economic elite by taking control of state property during the political transition, a process commonly known as the piñata.[67]

In 2006, thanks to electoral reforms established during the pact period, Daniel Ortega won the elections with 38 per cent of the vote and once again became president. Researchers have characterised his second presidency as a new *caudillismo* or a 'populist left regime with hybrid economic features'.[68] Contrary to other left-wing Latin American governments, Ortega has maintained more institutional continuity and refrained from a strong redistributive policy, eschewing nationalisation, land reform or price controls.[69] Nevertheless,

65 FAO, Representación en Nicaragua, 'Informe Anual: Julio 92 a Junio 93', 1–2; FAO, Representación en Nicaragua, 'Informe Anual: Julio/94 a Junio/95', 10–11.
66 Nitlápan–*Envío* Team, 'Time for a pact or time for a reflection?', *Envío*, no. 204, July 1998; J.L. Rocha and I. Cristoplos, 'Las ONGs ante los desastres naturales: vacíos y oportunidades', *Envío*, no. 212, Nov. 1999.
67 A. Pérez Baltodano, 'Political culture'; Ramírez, *Adiós Muchachos*, 32; A. Zamora, 'Some reflections on the piñata', *Envío*, no. 180, July 1996.
68 Spalding, *Contesting Trade*, 208.
69 Ibid., 208–10.

his government initiated an anti-poverty policy that was much broader than previous governments' efforts. The new government's package included programs such as Zero Usury and Zero Hunger. The basis for this policy was Nicaragua's new alliance with ALBA-TCP (Alianza Bolivariana para los Pueblos de Nuestra América – Tratado de Comercio de los Pueblos),[70] whose funding permitted the expansive social policy. Ortega's new allies put fewer restrictions on economic aid than European donors, who limited their support after Ortega's 2011 unconstitutional re-election.[71]

Continuity and change in Sandinista food policy

The new Ortega government's food programmes display some similarities with those of the 1980s – rhetorically at least. The government included an urban gardening project in its national development plan, reactivated ENABAS and continued the corn festivals. Some continuities with the 1980s food projects do exist, for example, ENABAS launched a 'Food for the People' project with the aim of establishing a just market system.[72] However, I argue that the heart of 1980s Sandinista food policy has not been restored: food subsidies, price regulations and land distribution are absent from the new programmes. More importantly, the neo-Sandinistas have made no attempt to break with the capitalist economy. Thus far, public debates and research have focused on the Zero Hunger Program and the food sovereignty law, because these initiatives are embedded within broader regional or global political initiatives. No systematic evaluation of Nicaraguan food politics has been made since 2006, so what follows is a broad summary of the most important trends until 2016.

The 1980s Sandinista food policy laid the groundwork for the food sovereignty debate by prioritising locally produced food and demanding the right to shape the local food system. Furthermore, the Sandinista Revolution left a legacy of active peasant organisations mobilising for change and debating agrarian issues. During the 1980s, these peasant organisations and conferences on agrarian reforms established a process of exchange that favoured the rise of the LVC (the transnational peasant movement), with the Asociación de Trabajadores en el Campo (ATC) and the Union Nacional de Agricultores y Ganaderos (UNAG) as founding members.[73] In 1997, Sandinista deputy Dora Zeledón launched the first initiative for a food security law. The proposal rejected the

---

70 The alliance was founded in 2004 by Venezuela and Cuba as an alternative to the Free Trade Area of the Americas (FTAA). The two nations agreed on terms for the petroleum trade and intensified exchanges in the areas of health and education. Later, Bolivia in 2006, Nicaragua in 2007, Ecuador in 2009 and several Caribbean nations joined ALBA.
71 S. Martí i Puig and D. Close, 'The Nicaraguan exception?', 299–300. E.g., Denmark ended bilateral development cooperation with Nicaragua in 2012, while other countries, such as Germany and Finland, announced their intention to evaluate and reduce their programmes.
72 Alianza de los pequeños productores organizados, con ENABAS y los CPC, 'Creación de Red de Mercado Justo', 2007.
73 W. Godek, 'Challenges for food sovereignty policy making: the case of Nicaragua's law 693'.

perception of food as merchandise and suggested that 50 per cent of Nicaragua's food supply should be provided by national production. Food aid distribution, which the law considered to be 'unfair competition' for local production, would be limited to exceptional supply crises resulting from natural disasters and other unforeseen events.[74] In the years after 1997, although the initial proposal was modified several times, the government of President Enrique Bolaños (2002–7) remained unwilling to pass the legislation.

In Nicaragua, the concept of food sovereignty gained traction after the 2001 World Forum on Food Sovereignty. From then on, LVC member organisations began to discuss a new initiative for a food sovereignty law. In 2004, 40 organisations from Nicaraguan civil society founded the Grupo de Interés Soberanía y Seguridad Alimentaria y Nutricional (GISSAN) to promote the law. As that name indicates, the debate over concepts continued among the initiative's supporters, because the term 'food security' seemed more familiar and concrete to many of them. In 2005, GISSAN member organisations worked on a new draft for a law that Deputy Wálmaro Gutiérrez (FSLN) introduced to the National Assembly in 2006.[75] When the National Assembly discussed the law in June 2007, the new Ortega government was already in power.

With Ortega's electoral victory, it seemed more likely that the law would be approved. However, the legislation prompted contentious discussions and National Assembly deputies rejected the law during its second reading. The private sector was particularly opposed to Article 5, which prohibited imports of genetically modified food. The business community feared that the law would also affect the implementation of the Central America Free Trade Agreement (CAFTA) and convinced PLC members to oppose the project. After the first initiative failed in 2007, the FAO joined the effort and the law project was deradicalised. Those articles which permitted the creation of grain reserves and price regulations were eliminated from the draft legislation. In addition, Article 9 of the law clearly established that state policies should not touch free enterprise and commerce, which meant a surrender to market mechanisms.[76] The deradicalisation of the law reflected the government's interest in avoiding further conflicts with the private sector and the IMF. While discussions about the legislation continued, the government launched the Zero Hunger Program as a core element of its anti-poverty policy.

The Zero Hunger Program has generated a contentious debate as critics accused the Sandinistas of political favouritism. Its name was inspired by the Brazilian 'Fome Zero' programme. Launched in 2003 by President Luiz Inácio Lula da Silva, the programme included cash transfers for poor families, favourable interest rates for family farmers and a school meals programme. The

74 Asamblea Nacional de la República de Nicaragua, 'Iniciativa de ley "Ley de Seguridad Alimentaria"', unpublished manuscript, 1998.
75 Godek, 'The institutionalization of food sovereignty', 175–81.
76 B. Müller, 'The loss of harmony: FAO guidance for food security in Nicaragua'; Godek, 'Challenges for food sovereignty policy making'.

Nicaraguan project, however, had a narrower focus, mainly providing peasants with the necessary basic inputs for food production. It distributed a package of animals, seeds and construction materials worth US$2,000 to 75,000 peasant families. Critics bemoaned the programme's lack of transparency with regard to the selection of beneficiaries, as well as the fact that it was not incorporated into a broader strategy against malnutrition. A 2007/2008 evaluation suggests that the selection criteria for the programme were too vague, allowing political considerations to play a role, which in turn led to regions in Central Nicaragua such as Masaya being favoured.[77] The question of whether the focus on peasant farmers was the result of lessons learned in the 1980s, or simply an attempt to jump on the bandwagon of the Brazilian initiative, remains the subject of further research.[78]

Efforts to revive 1980s projects are also visible in food distribution and urban gardening. The state distribution agency ENABAS resisted privatisation during the 1990s, but its capacities were significantly reduced. The neo-Sandinista government revived the enterprise and started reconstructing food storage facilities with ALBA funding. In addition, ENABAS launched the Programa Nacional de Distribución de Alimentos para el pueblo, which aimed to create a new network of state distribution points. According to the enterprise's homepage, it has founded more than 3,800 distribution points in about a hundred Nicaraguan municipalities.[79] However, no systematic research has been conducted on the programme's effects.

Three years after taking over government, the Sandinistas also relaunched urban gardening projects. Starting in 2010, with two projects in Los Laureles district in Managua and Ciudad Sandino, the so-called Healthy Backyard Program was incorporated into the national development plan for 2012 to 2016.[80] During that period, the idea was that 250,000 gardens would be involved throughout the country. The gardening projects also aimed at increasing fruit and vegetable consumption. Evaluations by geographer Laura Shillington demonstrate that local inhabitants sometimes disagreed with international project staff about which plants would be most beneficial for their gardens.[81]

The idea of strengthening local food consumption is also visible at the corn festivals. After the Sandinista defeat these festivals had continued at the regional level and became more touristy. In Jalapa and Matagalpa, especially, the tradition remained strong. Between 2005 and 2015 their mottoes have emphasised

---

77 P. Kester, *Informe evaluativo (2007–2008): Programa Productivo Alimentario (PPA) 'Hambre Cero'*, 17; Spalding, 'Poverty politics'.

78 Rose Spalding argues that the government launched the Zero Hunger Program having possibly learned from its experiences in the 1980s. Ibid., 233.

79 https://web.archive.org/web/20170426210719/http://www.enabas.gob.ni/enabas (accessed on 2 July 2019).

80 FAO, 'Urban and peri-urban agriculture in Latin America and the Caribbean: Managua'.

81 L.J. Shillington, 'Right to food, right to the city: household urban agriculture, and socionatural metabolism in Managua'.

Nicaragua's role as a significant corn producer, for example '*La gran milpa de Nicaragua*' (2008) or '*Jalapa con su maíz ... orgullo de mi país!*' (2009).[82] At the 2011 corn festival in Matagalpa, the local FSLN mayor clearly favoured the food sovereignty movement. He argued staunchly that it was necessary to rescue Nicaraguan culinary traditions for future generations, and that its food was a patrimonial value of Nicaraguan culture and formed part of the country's food sovereignty.[83] After 1999, corn production increased significantly, peaking in 2003, and fluctuating between 443,700 and 545,938 tons in the following years.[84]

In the last two decades, basic grain production has increased, reducing the dependency of the Nicaraguan food system on external sources. In 2011/2012, Nicaragua was among the least dependent Central American countries in terms of basic grain trade.[85] However, per capita food availability decreased after 2004 owing to low yields, which could create further supply problems in the future.[86]

Compared to the early 1990s, the nutritional situation in Nicaragua has improved considerably in the last two decades. Rates of malnutrition fell from 50 per cent (1990–2) to 38 per cent (1995–7) to 25 per cent (2000–2). According to recent FAO data, the situation has improved further with a reduction in malnutrition from 22.3 per cent in 2007 to 16.6 per cent in 2015.[87] However, undernourishment is still a major problem. Between 2009 and 2013, an average of 23 per cent of Nicaraguan children suffered from chronic malnutrition.[88] In rural areas, the situation remains depressing, with poverty rates exceeding 50 per cent.[89]

Conclusion

The Sandinista Revolution established ambitious aims: to break with export dependency, democratise access to food and guarantee all Nicaraguans a basic supply of food. In the early revolutionary years, the government and mass organisations designed creative campaigns, which mobilised thousands of people, with the goal of ensuring local food security. The Sandinista policy also gained the support of international organisations, such as the FAO, WHO

82 *El Nuevo Diario*, 'Preparan feria del maíz en Jalapa', 28 Aug. 2008; *El Nuevo Diario*, 'Jalapa con su maíz... orgulllo de Nicaragua', 17 Sept. 2009.

83 Transcription from my sound recording at the event, Apr. 2011.

84 Statistics from FAOSTAT, http://faostat3.fao.org/home/E (accessed 23 Apr. 2019). The peak production in 2003 was 588,599 tons, followed by 443,730 tons in 2004 and 545,938 tons in 2013.

85 FAO, 'Panorama de la seguridad alimentaria y nutricional en América Latina y el Caribe 2011: altos precios de los alimentos: oportunidades y riesgos', 2011, 63–6.

86 G. Bornemann et al., 'Desafíos desde la seguridad alimentaria y nutricional en Nicaragua', 34.

87 Statistics from FAOSTAT, http://faostat3.fao.org/browse/D/FS/E (accessed 23 Apr. 2019).

88 Unicef, 'At a glance: Nicaragua', www.unicef.org/infobycountry/nicaragua_statistics.html (accessed 23 Apr. 2019).

89 INIDE, 'Results of the National Households Survey on Measurement of Level of Life, 2014', 2015, http://www.inide.gob.ni/Emnv/Emnv14/Poverty%20Results%202014.pdf (accessed 23 Apr. 2019).

and UNICEF. In addition, bilateral development cooperation fostered many revolutionary projects to increase food production. However, these ambitious plans faced enormous challenges because of the dependency of the Nicaraguan economy on agro exports, war and the economic blockade. Moreover, Sandinista agrarian policy remained contradictory. Until the mid 1980s, it promoted large-scale, modern agriculture, while giving peasants less support. This was one of the reasons why basic grain production did not expand as rapidly as it should have done.

Within the Central American context of the early 1980s, Nicaragua's food policy, with its strong focus on self-sufficiency, was exceptional. Looking at other Global South countries, however, it is possible to identify similarities with the Nicaraguan approach. After attaining political independence in the 1950s and 1960s, many Asian and African countries developed self-sufficiency projects. Political independence was linked to economic independence and control of food resources. As in Nicaragua, these countries struggled to find a balance between self-sufficiency, food aid and Green Revolution strategies. Research on these self-sufficiency projects has not yet been completed, and it is not clear whether experts from the international nutrition community were involved in these efforts. The evidence for Nicaragua indicates that, starting from the early 1980s, international organisations and bilateral support from individual countries influenced strategic decision-making about food policy.

Nicaragua is a prime example of the many small countries with dependent economies in the Global South that experienced regime changes and became Cold War hotspots in the 20th century. After 1979, experts from both Cold War blocs struggled for influence over Sandinista politics in different areas. Products from both fronts of the Cold War entered Nicaraguan territory in the form of food aid, a phenomenon that was extensive in Central America but also happened in other Global South countries.

During a short honeymoon period, international organisations and NGOs promoted Nicaragua as a model for food policy in the Global South, and Nicaragua disseminated proposals for self-sufficiency and regional food security alliances at international conferences. These ambitious projects, however, faced serious economic limitations: the nation's dependency on agro exports generated conflicts around resources, basic grain production did not expand sufficiently, and tensions weakened the relationship between Sandinistas and the peasants.

By 1985, the Nicaraguan economy had entered a severe crisis and the supply situation became steadily worse. Because of this, the Sandinista government had to rely increasingly on food imports and aid, which undermined the self-sufficiency project. The reliance on donations also implied a growing surrender to the donors' political agendas, visible in the numerous reception ceremonies for food aid. With the 1988 adjustment programmes, the ambitious food policy was completely eroded. The financial crisis reversed state institutions' capacity to store food, manage the incoming donations, and implement the projects financed by external donors. Simultaneously, the strengthening of market mechanisms reversed the democratisation of the food distribution network. Finally, the failure of the Sandinistas to guarantee a stable basic food supply during the crisis years contributed significantly to its electoral defeat in 1990. In the early 1990s, the UNO government neglected food policy, despite widespread malnutrition. At the same time, the food system remained highly dependent on imports whose lower prices harmed local food producers who were unable to compete.

However, the Sandinistas Revolution left an active network of peasant organisations that continued to mobilise for social change. They contributed to the campaign for a food sovereignty law in the early 2000s. The close collaboration between the Sandinistas and FAO in the 1980s had introduced the principle of food security into Nicaraguan politics. Later on, important elements of the Sandinista food policy were taken up by the food sovereignty movement, such as the priority for locally produced food, agrarian reform and the autonomous definition of the local food system. After the 2001 World Forum on Food Sovereignty, the issues of food security and food sovereignty were debated intensely in Nicaragua. With the FSLN electoral victory, favourable conditions for the proposed legislation seemed to have arrived, but in the event, the law was passed in a watered-down form.

Although names and rhetoric are similar, the framework for neo-Sandinista food policy differs from that of the 1980s. While the Sandinistas based their policy on the idea of a mixed economy, the Ortega government and the new Sandinista economic elites have accepted capitalism and adapted their policies accordingly, taking care not to endanger agreements with the IMF or violate CAFTA rules. Unlike other Latin American left-wing governments, the Ortega government has not embarked on profound changes in economic structures or land distribution. Nevertheless, social policy is a higher priority than it was for previous Nicaraguan governments. In fact, poverty and malnutrition from 2005 to 2015 decreased significantly. Moreover, Nicaragua has become less dependent on grain imports than other Central American countries. However, reliance on external sources is still a problem: the Ortega government changed the country's foreign alliances, which created a dependency on ALBA funding. The deep economic crisis in Venezuela has made ALBA support more uncertain, which might also endanger the neo-Sandinistas' social policy. Because of this, malnutrition could rise again, given Nicaragua's vulnerability to natural disasters, dependency on volatile external resources and low basic grains productivity.

Bibliography

Acevedo Vogl, A. (2015) 'Estamos en un punto de inflexión y deberíamos preocuparnos', *Envío*, 404 (Nov.), www.envio.org.ni/articulo/5106 (accessed 29 Apr. 2019).

Asamblea Nacional de la República de Nicaragua (1998) 'Iniciativa de ley "Ley de Seguridad Alimentaria"'.

Austin, J., J. Fox and W. Kruger (1985) 'The role of the revolutionary state in the Nicaraguan food system', *World Development*, 13 (1): 15–40.

Barraclough, S. (1982) *A Preliminary Analysis of the Nicaraguan Food System* (Geneva).

Barraclough, S., A. van Buren, A. Garriazzo, A. Sunderam and P. Utting (1988) *Aid that Counts: The Western Contribution to Development and Survival in Nicaragua* (Amsterdam).

Baumeister, E. (1991) 'Agrarian reform', in T.W. Walker (ed.), *Revolution and Counterrevolution in Nicaragua* (Boulder, CO), pp. 229–45.

— (1998) *Estructura y reforma agraria en Nicaragua (1979–1989)* (Managua).

Biondi-Morra, B.N. (1990) *Revolución y política alimentaria: un análisis crítico de Nicaragua* (México, DF).

Booth, J.A. (1985) *The End and the Beginning: The Nicaraguan Revolution*, 2nd edn. (Boulder, CO).

Bornemann, G., O.N. Cuadra, C. Narváez Silva and J.L. Solorzano (2012) 'Desafíos desde la seguridad alimentaria y nutricional en Nicaragua' (Managua), www.oxfamblogs.org/lac/wp-content/uploads/2013/05/Desaf%C3%ADos-desde-la-seguridad-alimentaria-y-nutricional-en-Nicaragua.pdf (accessed 23 Apr. 2019).

CEPAL (1988) 'Damage caused by Hurricane Joan in Nicaragua: its effect on economic development and living conditions, and requirements for rehabilitation and reconstruction', www.cepal.org/publicaciones/xml/3/40893/Hurricane_Joan_Nicaragua_1988.pdf (accessed 29 Apr. 2019).

Centro de Investigación y Estudios de la Reforma Agraria (CIERA) (1983) *Distribución y consumo popular de alimentos en Managua*, Colección Cmdte. Germán Pomares Ordóñez (Managua).

Christiaens, K. (2014) 'Between diplomacy and solidarity: Western European support networks for Sandinista Nicaragua', *European Review of History*, 21 (4): 617–34.

Close, D. (1998) *Nicaragua: The Chamorro Years* (Boulder, CO).

Close, D., S. Martí i Puig and S.A. McConnell (eds.) (2012) *The Sandinistas and Nicaragua since 1979* (Boulder, CO).

Collins, J., with F. Moore Lappé, N. Allen and P. Rice (1986) *Nicaragua: Was hat sich durch die Revolution verändert? Agrarreform und Ernährung im neuen Nicaragua* (2nd edn., Wuppertal).

Dijkstra, G. (1992) *Industrialization in Sandinista Nicaragua: Policy and Practice in a Mixed Economy* (San Francisco, CA).

Dore, E. (1990) 'The great grain dilemma. Peasants and state policy in revolutionary Nicaragua', *Peasant Studies*, 17 (2): 96–120.

Enríquez, L.J. (1991), *Harvesting Change: Labor and Agrarian Reform in Nicaragua 1979–1990* (Chapel Hill, NC).

FAO (1983) '*Report of the Seventeenth FAO Regional Conference for Latin America: Managua, 30 August to 10 September 1982* (Rome).

— (1993) Representación en Nicaragua, 'Informe Anual: Julio 92 a Junio 93'.

— (1995) Representación en Nicaragua, 'Informe Anual: Julio/94 a Junio/95'.

— (2011) Panorama de la seguridad alimentaria y nutricional en América Latina y el Caribe 2011: altos precios de los alimentos: oportunidades y riesgos'.

Ferrero Blanco, D.M. (2015), 'Daniel Ortega y Mijail Gorbachov: Nicaragua y la URSS en los últimos anos de la Guerra Fría (1985–1990)', *HISPANIA NOVA, Revista de Historia Contemporánea*, 13: 26–53.

FIDEG (2014) 'Dinámicas de la pobreza en Nicaragua 2009–2013', http://liportal.giz.de/fileadmin/user_upload/oeffentlich/Nicaragua/30_wirtschaft-entw/FIDEG_POBREZA_2009-2013.pdf (accessed 24 Sept. 2019).

Flores, M. (1956) 'Estudios dietéticos en Nicaragua: II. Barrio de San Luis, Ciudad de Managua', *Boletín Sanitario: Edición especial dedicada a labores de INCAP en Nicaragua*, 31–51.

Flores, M., T.H. Caputti and Z. Leytón (1956) 'Estudios dietéticos en Nicaragua: I. Municipio de San Isidro, Departamento de Matagalpa', *Boletín Sanitario: Edición especial dedicada a labores de INCAP en Nicaragua*, 2–21.

Garst, R. (1992) *La ayuda alimentaria al istmo centroamericano*, Colección Temas de Seguridad Alimentaria 13 (Panamá).

Godek, W. (2014) 'The institutionalization of food sovereignty: the case of Nicaragua's law of food and nutritional sovereignty and security' (Rutgers University PhD thesis).

— (2015) 'Challenges for food sovereignty policy making: the case of Nicaragua's law 693', *Third World Quarterly*, 36 (3): 526–43.

Horton, L. (1998) *Peasants in Arms: War and Peace in the Mountains of Nicaragua, 1979–1994* (Athens, OH).

Juch, H. (1989) 'Unser revolutionärer Alltag: Teil 2', *Tagebuch Comics Zeichnungen Fotos*.

Kester, P. (2009) *Informe evaluativo (2007–2008): Programa Productivo Alimentario (PPA) 'Hambre Cero'* (Managua).

Linkogle, S. (1998) 'Soya, culture and international food aid: the case of a Nicaraguan communal kitchen', *Bulletin of Latin American Research*, 17 (1): 93–103.

Luciak, I.A. (1995) *The Sandinista Legacy: Lessons from a Political Economy in Transition* (Gainesville, FL).

Martí i Puig, S. (2001) *The Origins of the Peasant-Contra Rebellion in Nicaragua, 1979–87*, Institute of Latin American Studies Research Paper 54 (London).

Martí i Puig, S. and D. Close. (2012) 'The Nicaraguan exception?', in D. Close, S. Martí i Puig and S. McConnell (eds.), *The Sandinistas and Nicaragua since 1979* (Boulder, CO), pp. 287–307.

Martínez Cuenca, A. (1992) *Sandinista Economies in Practice – an Insider's Critical Reflections* (Cambridge, MA).

Müller, B. (2013) 'The loss of harmony: FAO guidance for food security in Nicaragua', in B. Müller (ed.), *The Gloss of Harmony: The Politics of Policy Making in Multilateral Organisations* (London), pp. 202–26.

Núñez Soto, O. (2007) 'Unser Land: unsere Revolution', in O. Bujard and U. Wirper (eds.), *Die Revolution ist ein Buch und ein freier Mensch: Die politischen Plakate des befreiten Nicaragua 1979–1990 und der internationalen Solidaritätsbewegung* (Cologne), pp. 92–107.

Pérez Baltodano, A. (2012) 'Political culture', in D. Close, S. Martí i Puig and S. McConnell (eds.), *The Sandinistas and Nicaragua since 1979* (Boulder, CO), pp. 65–90.

Ramírez, S. (2012) *Adiós Muchachos: A Memoir of the Sandinista Revolution* (Durham, NC).

Ricciardi, J. (1991) 'Economic policy', in T. Walker (ed.), *Revolution and Counterrevolution in Nicaragua* (Boulder, CO), pp. 247–73.

Rocha, J.L. and I. Cristoplos (1999) 'Las ONGs ante los desastres naturales: vacíos y oportunidades', *Envío*, 212 (Nov.), www.envio.org.ni/articulo/974 (accessed 23 Apr. 2019).

Saulniers, A.H. (1987) 'State trading organizations in expansion: a case study of ENABAS', in M.E. Conroy (ed.), *Nicaragua: Profiles of the Revolutionary Public Sector* (Boulder, CO), pp. 95–126.

Shillington, L.J. (2013) 'Right to food, right to the city: household urban agriculture, and socionatural metabolism in Managua', *Geoforum*, 44: 103–11.

Simon, H. (1991) 'Probleme und Perspektiven von Frauenförderung vor dem sozio-ökonomischen Hintergrund Nicaraguas: Das Fallbeispiel der "nutricionistas populares" von Ciudad Sandino' (Freie Universität Berlin Diplomarbeit, Soziologie).

Solá Montserrat, R. (2007) *Un siglo y medio de economía nicaragüense: las raíces del presente* (Managua).

Soule, J.W. (1990) 'The economic austerity packages of 1988 and their impact on public opinion', *International Journal of Political Economy* (Fall): 34–45.

Spalding, R. (2012) 'Poverty politics', in D. Close, S. Martí i Puig and S. McConnell (2012) *The Sandinistas and Nicaragua since 1979* (Boulder, CO), pp. 215–43.

— (2014) *Contesting Trade in Central America: Market Reform and Resistance* (Austin, TX).

Tomka, B. (2013) *A Social History of Twentieth Century Europe* (Hoboken, NJ).

Vilas, C.M. (1988) 'Nicaragua. I. Scientific research in a revolutionary setting. The case of Nicaragua', SAREC Documentation, Research Surveys, Stockholm.

Walker, T.W. (ed.) (1991), *Revolution and Counterrevolution in Nicaragua* (Boulder, CO).

— (2003) *Nicaragua: Living in the Shadow of the Eagle*, (4th edn., Boulder, CO).

Zamora, A. (1996) 'Some reflections on the piñata', *Envío*, 180 (July), www.envio.org.ni/articulo/3019 (accessed 23 Apr. 2019).

4. On Sandinista ideas of past connections to the Soviet Union and Nicaraguan exceptionalism*

Johannes Wilm

Nicaraguan views on relations between Nicaragua and Eastern Europe/ the former Soviet Union in the 1980s, is the focus of this chapter. Much has been written about the nature of these relations,[1] but little about Nicaraguan and Sandinista perceptions of that situation and how these have informed Nicaraguan actions. The hypothesis presented here is that the seemingly contradictory behaviour and relations between Nicaragua and the Soviet Union during that period in the 1980s can be explained by the tendency of many key Nicaraguan Sandinistas to place historical agency for events that happen in country in their Nicaraguan hands. While Sandinistas are quick to point to Nicaragua's relationship of economic dependence with the United States during Somoza's time and liberal opposition rule between 1990 and 2007, they do not view the country's relationship with the Soviet Union as having had the same dependence. Nicaragua is thought of as acting independently of its economic circumstances, acting on the world stage as if it were a major power, which makes it an exception when compared to its neighbours. It is likely that Sandinistas' support for this view has permitted the most powerful Nicaraguan leaders, including President Daniel Ortega, to act as they do and to gain support throughout the country for their actions.

---

* My thanks to Mark Jamieson and Dennis Rodgers, who initially pointed out that the collected material on Nicaraguan students in Eastern Europe was significant; to Stephen Nugent and Casey High for their many comments on a chapter on a similar theme in my PhD thesis, which influenced the final outcome of this chapter; to Michael Böhner who spent much time explaining the structures of solidarity with Nicaragua as viewed by GDR-solidarity activists; to the many Sandinista informants of all ages who gave up their time to be interviewed and, in many cases, also hosted me; to the participants of the Central America research conference at the Institute of Latin American Studies (ILAS) in London in spring 2015, whose feedback was of great importance; to Sarah Zurhellen who helped with the final wording of this contribution; and to Hilary Francis for her work editing this collection.

1 P. Shearman, 'The Soviet challenge in Central America'; E. Dominguez Reyes, 'Soviet relations with Central America, the Caribbean, and members of the Contadora group'; J. Suchlicki, 'Soviet policy in Latin America: implications for the United States'; R. Berrios, 'Relations between Nicaragua and the socialist countries'.

J. Wilm, 'On Sandinista ideas of past connections to the Soviet Union and Nicaraguan exceptionalism', in H. Francis (ed.), *A Nicaraguan Exceptionalism? Debating the Legacy of the Sandinista Revolution* (London: University of London Press, 2019), pp. 87–102. License: CC-BY-NC-ND.

The Nicaraguan concept of 'agency', or *protagonismo*, differs sharply from the understanding of the term that is prevalent among some academics. Historians in particular tend to think of agency as the effort expended by people who have dreams and try to achieve things, but are ultimately limited by structures. For example, Tanya Harmer argues that Chilean agency in the run-up to the 1973 coup has been underestimated – but she makes it clear that for it 'does not equal power'. An emphasis on Latin Americans' agency does not, she believes, imply a belief that Latin Americans had the power then to 'radically remake the world and their place in it'.[2]

The term 'agency', as it is used here, is much more expansive and closer to anthropologist David Graeber's understanding of 'historical agency': the capacity of a subject to make history or to change the course of history.[3] In other words, having historical agency does not simply mean acting or being able to pressure others to act: it requires having the power to change things. Historical agency. Understood this way, it is the ability to diverge from the 'normal' path of events conditioned by external circumstances. Graeber's approach has much in common with the idea of *protagonismo* used in Nicaraguan popular discourse. Declarations about the existence of *protagonismo* are found throughout Nicaraguan society. It is not uncommon to hear younger Sandinista leaders discuss the '*protagonismo*' of young people in the revolutionary process, because – so the argument goes – young people are less bound by existing rules and customs, and are therefore more willing to try something new. In this chapter, the Nicaraguan understanding of the concept is favoured because it offers an overview of Nicaraguan perceptions about where historical agency lies, rather than an analysis of where agency can objectively said to be found.

This emphasis on agency in Sandinista discourse might seem surprising. Sandinista political thought is fully grounded in dependency theory and the idea that Nicaragua's poverty was the result of an exploitative, unequal relationship with the United States. In a sense, it is precisely this consciousness of structural constraints that drove Nicaraguans' expansive understanding of agency. This connection is clear in Stephen Henighan's discussion of the work of Sergio Ramírez, the Sandinista politician and author. Henighan shows how Ramírez' belief, grounded in dependency theory (Nicaragua is a 'backward, dominated nation'), leads directly to his conviction that '"it is necessary to consolidate national identity" in a project of national liberation'.[4]

---

2 T. Harmer, 'Tanya Harmer, *Allende's Chile and the Inter-American Cold War*', H-Diplo Roundtable Review, 14 (1) (n.d.), D. Walcher and D. Labrosse (eds.), https://issforum.org/roundtables/PDF/Roundtable-XIV-2.pdf. (accessed 27 Apr. 2019).

3 D. Graeber, 'Epilogue to the disastrous ordeal of 1987', 1996.

4 S. Henighan, *Sandino's Nation: Ernesto Cardenal and Sergio Ramírez Writing Nicaragua, 1940–2012*, 450.

Nicaragua's relationship with the Eastern bloc

The Frente Sandinista de Liberación Nacional (FSLN), the radical element in the opposition to the US-sponsored Somoza dictatorship in Nicaragua since the early 1960s, succeeded in taking power on 19 July 1979, after a final revolutionary insurrection that had started in 1978 and led to about 30,000 deaths.[5] During the 1980s and until the FSLN lost power in 1990, Nicaragua was an ally of Eastern Europe and the Soviet Union. However, the origins of the connection between Nicaragua and Eastern Europe, as well as Cuba, in the 1980s are not entirely clear. On the one hand, some early FSLN leaders had previously been part of the Moscow-allied Partido Socialista Nicaragüense (PSN). The most well-known among these was Carlos Fonseca Amador, who wrote a book about his 1957 experience in Moscow.[6] On the other, according to currently available evidence, the Nicaraguan revolutionaries did not have connections with Moscow during the 1970s. Even after taking power, the future President Daniel Ortega's initial conversations were with US President Jimmy Carter in September 1979. The talks led to a loan of US$2 million. Furthermore, relations between the US embassy and the Sandinistas were friendly in the first months after the takeover.[7] Some US political commentators even argued that this was an opportunity for the United States to take on the role of supporting a revolutionary government, which, until then, had been one occupied exclusively by the Soviet Union and Cuba.[8]

At the same time as the connection to the Soviet Union expanded gradually during the first year of Sandinista government, the United States was replaced as Nicaragua's main trading partner. It is not entirely clear which of these was the cause and which the effect. By October 1979, US analysts claimed they had seen evidence that Cuba had 50 advisers in Nicaragua.[9] In February 1980, after several months of delay, a narrow majority in the US House of Representatives approved a meagre US$75 million in aid to Nicaragua. This had been promised earlier, but 60 per cent of it was earmarked to go to private businesses, and any expenditure on education projects involving Cuban teachers was prohibited.[10] The amount was much less than the Sandinistas had hoped for and tiny when compared with US$1.5 billion debt that the Sandinistas had been asked to

---

5   L.H. Gelb, 'On arms for Nicaragua', *New York Times*, 29 Aug. 1979.

6   C. Fonseca Amador, *Un Nicaragüense en Moscú*.

7   A. Riding, 'Foreign policy set by Managua called realistic; U.S. seeks regime's confidence', *New York Times*, 9 Oct. 1979.

8   Gelb, 'On arms for Nicaragua'; A. Riding, 'Nicaragua after Somoza; after Somoza', *New York Times*, 3 Feb. 1980.

9   'U.S. analysts say Cuba is keeping forces abroad; Cubans poorly paid', *New York Times*, 21 Oct. 1979.

10   G. Hovey, 'House, by 5-vote margin, passes Bill on assistance for Nicaragua', *New York Times*, 28 Feb. 1980.

accept from the Somoza regime in 1979.[11] At this stage, it seemed clear that Nicaragua would have to find funding from an alternative source, and in March 1980, a Nicaraguan delegation led by Moisés Hassan, a member of the interim governing junta, signed a range of agreements with the Soviet Union.[12] This placed the country firmly in the camp of the Warsaw Pact countries, which also meant a freeze in their relations with the United States. Starting in the period 1981–3, Nicaragua received measurable military and economic aid from the Soviet Union, including tanks, wheat and credit for purchases.[13]

The change in Nicaragua's relationship with the United States during that first year can also be understood in terms of political differences and shifts in the later. Under President Jimmy Carter, the US had first tried to support a moderate opposition, without Sandinista participation, in the months prior to the taking of power in 1979. Once the Sandinistas were in power, however, the Carter administration did try to work with them. It was only when the promised aid package had to go through Congress, where it met the opposition of conservative Republicans, that restrictions were added to prevent the Sandinistas from aiding other armed groups. When they did so anyway, Carter suspended the aid (instead of cancelling it). It was only after President Reagan took office that the United States changed its strategy and began funding a war against the Sandinistas.[14]

Relations with the Soviet Union and its allies grew rapidly. Nicaragua's trade with the countries belonging to the Council for Mutual Economic Assistance (CMEA), the economic organisation that united the Soviet Union's closer allies, was only 1.1 per cent in 1980, but by 1987 this figure had risen to 48.6 per cent. By 1985, after Mexico stopped sending oil to Nicaragua due to its failure to pay, 90 per cent of petrol imports came from the Soviet Union.[15] In addition to such aid, advisers from these countries stayed in Nicaragua for extended periods, and in 1979–90, many Nicaraguan students pursued their education in allied socialist countries (although the total number of students who went abroad is not fully known). According to estimates, 20,000 students followed courses in Cuba,[16]

---

11 A. Riding, 'Nicaragua tries economic cure; concern among bankers', *New York Times*, 27 Nov. 1979.

12 'Nicaragua leaders sign pacts with Soviet Union', *New York Times*, 23 Mar. 1980.

13 Reyes, 'Soviet relations with Central America, the Caribbean, and members of the Contadora Group', 149–50.

14 W.M. Leogrande, 'Making the economy scream: US economic sanctions against Sandinista Nicaragua'.

15 F. Harto de Vera, 'La U.R.S.S. y la revolución sandinista: los estrechos límites de la solidaridad soviética', 89.

16 R. Zúñiga interview with Marlén Villavicencio: 'Ser internacionalista, para nosotros es un principio inalienable', 23 Nov. 2011.

4,500–5,500 in East Germany[17] and 8,200 in the Soviet Union (approximately 7,000 civilian[18] and 1,183 military).[19]

International and Nicaraguan perceptions of Nicaraguan-Soviet relations

The confrontation with the United States and the cooperation with Cuba and Eastern Europe ended up as a major part of the Sandinista reality of the 1980s, so it is not strange that many Nicaraguans who lived during that time have developed an opinion about it. Additionally, events in Nicaragua became world news during much of the 1980s. Nicaraguan understandings of cooperation between Sandinista Nicaragua and the communist bloc differed substantially from the views that prevailed elsewhere. For US President Ronald Reagan, the Soviet Union had obtained 'a beachhead in North America'. Reagan feared that '[u]sing Nicaragua as a base, the Soviets and Cubans can become the dominant power in the crucial corridor between North and South America'.[20] While many outside Nicaragua disputed Reagan's assessment of the threat that Nicaragua posed, most people would probably accept the general idea that this was yet another manifestation of the Cold War between the Soviet Union and the United States.

Most scholarship on the relationship between Nicaragua and the Soviet Union dates from the 1980s. Unsurprisingly, given the immediate stakes, this work is extremely polarised. Some scholars argued that Nicaragua was heavily reliant on the Soviet Union, while others saw a much looser relationship. Jiri Valenta described the Sandinistas and the Soviet Union as long-time allies: '[F]rom the beginning the FSLN has been led by dedicated, Leninist-oriented revolutionaries with long-standing ties to the Cuban and (to a lesser degree) Soviet communist parties'.[21] Valenta also guessed that 'the KGB probably assisted in efforts to train, finance, and arm the FSLN through Cuban intermediaries',[22] though he failed to present any meaningful evidence to back up his claim. Among those who discerned less Soviet planning behind events, Peter Shearman argued that the revolution itself was regionally developed and financed through

17 M. Böhner to J. Wilm, 'Answer to the question "How many Nicaraguans studied in the GDR in the 1980s"', 24 Jan. 2016. Böhner is a former GDR-Nicaragua Solidarity activist and expert on GDR-Nicaragua relations. The question was posed by the author during personal correspondence with Böhner.
18 M. Espinoza to J. Leiva, 'Cantidad de estudiantes en la URSS, respuesta a la pregunta al Director del Centro Regional de Estudios Internacionales (CREI)', 23 Jan. 2016. Interview conducted in person.
19 Ejército de Nicaragua, 'Profesionalización del Ejército de Nicaragua', 91.
20 R. Reagan, 'Address to the nation on the situation in Nicaragua', 1986, mp3, Presidential Audio Recordings, 1/20/1981–1/20/1989, US National Archives, https://catalog.archives.gov/id/7450184 (accessed 26 Apr. 2019).
21 J. Valenta, 'Nicaragua: Soviet-Cuban pawn or non-aligned country?', 165.
22 Ibid., 167.

other local powers, such as Costa Rica and Mexico, and that it was only once the revolution had triumphed that 'the Soviet Union enter[ed] the picture as a major actor'. However, he went on to explain, Nicaragua was not likely to become part of the CMEA and, in that sense, was more distant from the central powers.[23] Similarly, Edmé Dominguez Reyes described the events of 1979 as having been a 'surprise' for the Soviet Union, and although it became a major source of aid for Nicaragua in subsequent years, he said the Soviet attitude toward Nicaragua was cautious and mindful of the possibility that the United States could become directly involved in a war with Nicaragua.[24] This diversity of views is partly a reflection of the academics' political differences, but it is also indicative of an ambiguity in the Sandinistas' position. Nicaragua's leaders seemed to be committed Marxists, possibly even Leninists, with views compatible with the Soviet Union's. They even abstained from voting against the Soviet occupation of Afghanistan at the United Nations.[25] At the same time, the country continued to have a mixed economy and maintained good relations with western European social democratic parties. In other words, the Sandinistas did not behave as if they were managed from Moscow.

This ambiguity was not present in the discourse about the relationship developed by Nicaraguan leaders in the 1980s, one that is still prevalent among Sandinistas today. Rather, Sandinista leaders asserted that Nicaragua was completely free of foreign influence. In 1981, Sergio Ramírez, at the time a member of the government junta and vice-president from 1985, said the following about the concerns of the United States:

> One of the things on which the government of the United States insisted recently was the supposed involvement of the Soviet Union with Nicaragua. It did this to convert the actual and real confrontation that there is between the United States and Nicaragua into a part of an East–West confrontation in Central America. We deny it once more because the only thing that is going on in Nicaragua is the confrontation between the United States and Nicaragua, because now we have the historical aspiration to be a free and independent country, not part of the orbit of influence of the United States and not part of the influence of any country in the world.[26]

This statement is in line with the Sandinista discourse of the time and the majority of views expressed by Sandinistas in the current period of Sandinismo. It was Nicaragua which had a conflict with the United States, it was Nicaraguans who contacted the Soviet Union; their relationship was one of equals, one in which their country was an independent actor; and it was not a relationship between colony and empire, as Reagan seemed to portray it.

---

23 Shearman, 'The Soviet challenge in Central America'.
24 Reyes, 'Soviet relations with Central America, the Caribbean, and members of the Contadora Group'.
25 Shearman, 'The Soviet challenge in Central America', 214.
26 *Envío*, 'Continuing tensions between Nicaragua and the United States', no. 7, Dec. 1981.

It must be noted that Ramírez spoke somewhat differently about the relationship with the Soviet Union after he left the FSLN. In 2007, writing about the 1987 peace negotiations, he commented that the Soviet Union had urged the Nicaraguan government at that time to agree to a negotiated solution because it could not see a military one. As Nicaragua depended on Soviet arms to continue the war, the Soviets' attitude was therefore a significant factor in the Sandinistas' decision to pursue the peace process.[27] Whether this represents a rare insight into the real, seldom-expressed thinking of a Sandinista elite, or whether Ramírez has reinterpreted past events, is hard to know. No matter what the case may be, such views are not in line with the arguments of rank-and-file Sandinistas or the public speeches of Sandinista leaders now or during the 1980s.

Treatment of former connections to the Soviet bloc after 2007

The extent to which Sandinista leaders had not forgotten their past connections to the Soviet bloc, and remembered the time when the Unites States was considered an enemy rather than an ally, became clear in the first years after their return to power in early 2007. At the annual celebration of the triumph of the Sandinista Revolution on 19 July 2008, President Daniel Ortega presented the Rubén Darío medal for cultural independence to Margot Honecker, the former education minister for East Germany and widow of Erich Honecker, the former general secretary of East Germany's old Socialist Unity Party.[28] Honecker had not appeared in public since going into exile in Chile in the early 1990s, and she was awarded the medal, given specifically for the help East Germany had given Nicaragua in the past. Discussing the former Soviet Union in 2007, Daniel Ortega repeated the position held in the 1980s – that it was Nicaraguans who made the decisions about Nicaragua and that the Soviet Union had respected these decisions.[29] Ortega views Russia as the continuation of the Soviet Union: in 2007 he said: '[W]hen we speak of cooperation with Russia, we are speaking of taking into account the relation that we had with the Soviet Union, when Russia was one of our supporters.'[30] In 2008, Ortega declared that Russia was 'illuminating the planet' with its 'struggle for peace and justice', while 'the Empire' (the United States) was threatening it militarily.[31] Further down the FSLN party hierarchy, one also found admiration for their former allies in the period after 2007. This section presents evidence from anthropological fieldwork undertaken in this context.

27 Sergio Ramírez, 'Lo que nos tocó de guerra fría', *El País*, 29 Aug. 2007.
28 AFP, 'Ortega condecora a viuda de Honecker con orden Rubén Darío', *El Universo*, 19 July 2008.
29 D. Ortega, 'No había tal conflicto Este-Oeste', 22 Aug. 2007.
30 US Embassy in Managua, 'Ortega administration at six months', Wikileaks Public Library of US Diplomacy (Nicaragua Managua, 2 July 2007), https://search.wikileaks.org/plusd/cables/07MANAGUA1622_a.html (accessed 27 Apr. 2019).
31 *La Prensa,* 'Ortega: "Rusia está iluminando el planeta"', 18 Sept. 2008.

At around the time that Honecker received the Rubén Dario medal, I had been interviewing spokespeople at the FSLN municipal headquarters in León over a period of several months about current political affairs. The secretary and several others who regularly passed through the office therefore recognised me as a regular visitor. When I announced I wished to ask about the circumstances leading to the decision to give the medal to Honecker, commenting that this was rather unusual as German media reports about her were generally unfavourable, the reaction was a combination of annoyance and surprise. I was told that the medal was something the 'entire German working class' should be proud of. Then, instead of finding an official to speak to me, I was asked to interview another person who was standing in line and had been to East Germany (that person had apparently experienced snow for the first time and had a wonderful stay all in all). Over the next year criticism of Eastern Europe regimes, in that first interview and most others I conducted with Nicaraguans who had studied in Eastern Europe, was almost non-existent. This was the case, I noticed, even among Sandinistas I met who had not been to Eastern Europe. Their descriptions of socialism in either region were similarly optimistic.

There were some exceptions to this rule. One former student described how everyone in East Germany had read *Das Kapital*: the bus driver, the person checking the ticket on the bus, the person sitting next to you. He ended his explanation by saying 'They had read the book while the other Germany had the money.' This could be interpreted as a criticism of the East German state, implying it had not been able to provide the same level of welfare for its citizens as had West Germany. Another informant, who presented himself as a supporter of the opposition party Movimiento Renovador Sandinista (MRS) and a critic of President Daniel Ortega, spoke about cases of rape, where Sandinista men had had sex with girls without their consent while studying in East Germany, and how he felt this had been brushed under the carpet. During the interview, it also became clear that the East Germans he had encountered were unaccustomed to what he saw as the Nicaraguan tradition of openly expressing different opinions during discussions. It is possible that some of my Nicaraguan informants chose not to tell me about less positive aspects of Eastern European socialism, as some may have assumed that I would identify with East Germany and not be too accepting of any criticism.

However, even if some Nicaraguans consciously filtered what they told me, this does not seem to counterbalance the number of positive stories. And while those who had been to East Germany were aware that living standards in Moscow and East Berlin were significantly higher than in Nicaragua at the time, they generally portrayed their relationship with the places they had visited as having been one of equality, not of an empire trying to influence Nicaraguan thinking. Also, the newfound relationship with Russia seemed to be generally understood as a revival of the connection with the Soviet Union, much as Ortega seems to have portrayed it. For example, Freddy, a gardener in León when I interviewed him in 2008, was trying to convince a younger Nicaraguan to 'go study in the Soviet Union' – a place he had been as a student and which he believed to be a great country and partner of the Nicaraguan Revolution.

Younger Sandinistas generally had a more distant relationship with the Soviet Union, although an awareness of that country still remained in Nicaragua. Jessica, a 23-year-old Sandinista who is part of the national directorate of communication workers of the Sandinista Youth (Sandinistas aged around 16–25 who work in TV and radio), explained that she first encountered the Soviet Union when talking with her Sandinista father during the opposition years: 'He told me there had been this country that had stood with the Nicaraguan Revolution during the 1980s.' On another occasion, one of the younger communicators said during a meeting: 'in a certain way we have been part of it', to which a more knowledgeable youth leader responded that Nicaragua had actually been a very distant ally of the Soviet Union, and that its connection to the Soviet Union had played out mainly in Nicaragua's political proximity and friendship with Cuba, an official ally of the Soviet Union. As in most such conversations, an emphasis was put on the egalitarian nature of the relationship.

Egalitarian connections and Nicaraguan exceptionalism

If Nicaraguans were on a par with their Eastern European and Cuban colleagues, in what sense did they define themselves as exceptional? This element was most apparent in discussions of the difference between Nicaragua and its Central American neighbours. Nicaragua was considered exceptional because it was the only Central American nation that had had a successful revolution. Although there were some revolutionary movements in El Salvador and Guatemala, the participants had not won state power. Interviewees also perceived that the other Central American nations were much more dependent on foreign powers. I asked Sandinista informants how they would describe relations between Costa Rica, Nicaragua's southern neighbour, and the United States. The answer was uniformly that Costa Rica was clearly a sort of colony of the United States. Comparisons between Nicaragua and the other Central American nations were particularly common in the summer of 2009, when a military coup against Honduran President Manuel Zelaya caused political confusion in the region. Manuel Zelaya had allied himself with the Sandinista government and Nicaragua just a year earlier. The country was set to implement some of the social programmes that Nicaragua had introduced shortly before, but the process was much slower. Prior to that, in the spring of 2009, I first heard the term 'the Sandinista countries', referring to the countries of Central America, and the idea seemed to be that Nicaragua would lead these other countries towards greater understanding. A professor at the UNAN-León portrayed the connection this way: 'It is only Nicaragua that is free to express itself. That does not mean that the other countries would not like to do so, but for various reasons it is Nicaragua that is the only country that can truly speak freely.'

When the coup happened, I went to Honduras and came back with a documentary about the Hondurans who were trying to combat what was happening. Members of the Sandinista Youth helped me show the documentary in the national theatre and they presented parts of it on national TV and radio. I was surprised that the main questions the various Sandinistas asked me when the microphones were off centred on the degree to which the Hondurans seemed less organised, and whether they had less understanding of international politics than Nicaraguans. These perceptions were repeated whenever Nicaragua's neighbours were brought up: even though Nicaragua had lower living standards, it was widely believed that their neighbours were the ones who lacked political development and were, therefore, forced to follow the plans of the 'empire'. In the generalised Sandinista view, historical agency was reserved for Nicaraguans.

Are Nicaraguan relations with Venezuela and Eastern Europe similar?

Through the portrayal of the former Soviet Union and Nicaragua as equal partners, the Sandinistas have built up a national discourse that somewhat obscures the fact that the Sandinistas, throughout most of their years in power, have had to rely on help from abroad. At the same time, along with the widespread belief in the country that Nicaraguan leaders act independently, Nicaragua has shown a certain level of divergence from the Soviet bloc's main political line.

When the Sandinistas returned to power in early 2007, the country again started to function somewhat independently, even though it was financed to a large degree by another country, this time Venezuela. Relations with Russia were re-established, but during the conflict between Georgia and Russia in 2008, it was Nicaragua who first – and rapidly – recognised the independence of the Georgian breakaway republics of South Ossetia and Abkhazia,[32] more than a year before Venezuela did so.[33]

In 2013, when former Central Intelligence Agency (CIA) employee Edward Snowden was asking a range of countries for asylum, Ortega made a conditional offer ('If circumstances permit it...') that was made public a few hours before Venezuela offered asylum, seemingly unconditionally.[34] It is likely that the offers from Venezuela, Nicaragua and, a day later, Bolivia were coordinated to some degree, but the fact that Nicaragua made the first offer did not go unnoticed by the Sandinistas. Among the young communication workers of the Juventud Sandinista, the exact order of who had offered asylum was mentioned frequently and it was taken as a sign that Nicaragua was playing a leading role.

Between 2007 and 2010 the United States changed its understanding of the relationship between the Sandinista government and Venezuela. In 2007, the US

---

32   DPA, 'Nicaragua reconoce independencia de Abjasia Y Osetia Del Sur', *Emol*, 3 Sept. 2008.
33   Red Voltaire, 'Venezuela reconoce a Abjasia y Osetia Del Sur', *Red Voltaire*, 20 Sept. 2009.
34   Clarín, 'Venezuela le otorgó asilo a Snowden, el topo de la CIA', *Clarin.com*, 5 July 2013.

embassy wrote in a confidential cable that '[a]lthough "national sovereignty" is a favorite leitmotif of Ortega's, he continues deferring to his Venezuelan counterpart'.[35] By 2009, after Nicaragua's recognition of South Ossetia and Abkhazia, the US embassy changed its wording, thereby acknowledging that Ortega had some level of historic agency, even though this role was restricted to recreating a situation in which Nicaragua would be a client state: 'We believe that Ortega wants to recreate the bipolar conflict and clientelism that once existed between Russia and the West in Central America.'[36] In 2010, a secret cable discussed why Ortega had made recent friendly overtures to the US ambassador. One of the possible reasons, it was speculated, could be that the efforts of the Nicaraguan government to establish relations with, and obtain funding from, countries other than Venezuela, such as Iran and Russia, had not yet produced the expected economic results.[37] While the tone regarding everything about Ortega and the Nicaraguan government was consistently negative, and at times accusatory, by 2010 it was tacitly accepted that the Sandinistas and/or Ortega were acting somewhat independently of the country that was financing their activities.

Older Sandinista informants who were politically active during the 1970s and 1980s tended to have a somewhat cautious view of Venezuela. They perceived Nicaragua as an independent actor, just as able as Venezuela, at times ideologically more educated, and with a greater experience of having government power. Those Sandinistas who were active during the 1980s almost seemed to think of Venezuela as a liability and that the concept of 21st-century socialism, which arrived in Nicaragua through Venezuela, was merely a less-thought-through alternative to the original principles of Sandinismo (without clearly defining what these were).

Conclusion

As we have seen, past and present understandings of Sandinismo are dominated by a sense of historical agency. The actions of Sandinistas and Nicaraguans are interpreted in this light, while the populations of neighbouring countries where revolutions were not successful are portrayed as being trapped in structures of dependency. The tendency to see local politics as the outcome of the actions of local actors is not unique to Nicaragua. For example, after the 1973 coup the Chilean dictatorial regime saw itself as taking a lead in fighting communism

---

35 US Embassy in Managua, 'Ortega administration at six months'.
36 US Embassy in Managua, 'Nicaragua and Abkhazia establish formal diplomatic ties', Wikileaks Public Library of US Diplomacy (Nicaragua Managua, 18 Sept. 2009), https://search.wikileaks.org/plusd/cables/09MANAGUA913_a.html (accessed 26 Apr. 2019).
37 US Embassy in Managua, '(U) Ortega and the U.S.: new-found true love or another still-born charm offensive?', Wikileaks Public Library of US Diplomacy (Nicaragua Managua, 25 Feb. 2010), https://search.wikileaks.org/plusd/cables/10MANAGUA115_a.html (accessed 26 Apr. 2019).

because the United States was not playing the role it ought to.[38] Until recently, international scholars have put too much emphasis on the United States when considering US–Latin American relations, leaving little-to-no room for Latin American agency.[39]

Nevertheless, the Sandinista emphasis on Nicaragua's historic agency continues to be emphasised. However, the view that Nicaragua, one of the poorest countries in the western hemisphere,[40] is somehow more able to exert historic agency than other larger Latin American countries which are less dependent on foreign aid, seems to lack a material basis. Nicaraguan poet Rubén Darío wrote, 'If the nation is small, one dreams it large.'[41] In a sense, the problems that Nicaragua face are so overwhelming that an exaggerated sense of the country's power is necessary to face these enormous challenges.

Yet somehow, Sandinista leaders and the Nicaraguan people have been able to put the country on the map and make Nicaragua one of the few Latin American countries capable of upsetting the president of the United States. Nicaragua has maintained international alliances and continued on its own very particular road to development. Even the World Bank emphasises that Nicaragua stands out in achieving 'shared growth' and notes that it is performing better than the Central American and the Caribbean averages.[42]

Parallels between the Soviet–Nicaraguan relationship in the 1980s and current links between Russia and Nicaragua are especially noteworthy. In one sense Ortega's efforts to renew Nicaragua's alliance with its former partner from the 1980s suggest a blinkered approach which ignores several changes that have taken place in world politics since then. Equally though, it points to the positive effects of Nicaraguan confidence. In 2010 US diplomats felt, according to US embassy cables released by Wikileaks, that Ortega's attempts to reconnect with former allies had failed, but these links have solidified in subsequent years. Nicaragua, simply by insisting on an alliance has obtained something that at first seemed impossible. Of course, these new links are being forged in a completely different world, and while the alliances of the 1980s were brokered on ideological terms, Nicaragua is now simply opting for capitalist Russia instead of the capitalist West. In this uncertain climate, the future of Nicaragua's international relations is precarious. But whatever the future holds, it is likely that Nicaraguans will continue to believe in their country's ability to defy structural constraints and act as a force to be reckoned with in the wider world.

---

38 T. Harmer, 'Fractious allies: Chile, the United States, and the Cold War, 1973–76'.
39 M.P. Friedman, 'Retiring the puppets, bringing Latin America back in: recent scholarship on United States–Latin American relations.', 621.
40 C. León, 'Nicaragua and IDA: an enduring partnership'.
41 R. Darío, *El viaje a Nicaragua e intermezzo tropical*.
42 León, 'Nicaragua and IDA'.

Bibliography

AFP (2008) 'Ortega condecora a viuda de Honecker con orden Rubén Darío', *El Universo*, 19 July, www.eluniverso.com/2008/07/19/0001/14/31E771E4D7D04929AE1254F90AF27B77.html (accessed 27 Apr. 2019).

Berrios, R. (1985) 'Relations between Nicaragua and the socialist countries', *Journal of Interamerican Studies and World Affairs*, 27 (3): 111–39.

Clarín (2013) 'Venezuela le otorgó asilo a Snowden, el topo de la CIA', *Clarin.com*, 5 July, www.clarin.com/mundo/Venezuela-otorgo-asilo-Snowden-CIA_0_950905013.html (accessed 26 Apr. 2019).

Darío, R. (2015) *El viaje a Nicaragua e intermezzo tropical* (Managua).

DPA (2008) 'Nicaragua reconoce independencia de Abjasia Y Osetia Del Sur', *Emol*, 3 Sept., www.emol.com/noticias/internacional/2008/09/03/320330/nicaragua-reconoce-independencia-de-abjasia-y-osetia-del-sur.html (accessed 26 Apr. 2019).

Ejército de Nicaragua (2009) 'Profesionalización del Ejército de Nicaragua', in *30 años de vida institucional 1979–2009* (Managua), https://ejercito.mil.ni/contenido/relaciones-publicas/publicaciones/docs/memoria-1979-2009.pdf (accessed 26 Apr. 2019).

Envío (1981) 'Continuing tensions between Nicaragua and the United States', (Dec.), www.envio.org.ni/articulo/3129 (accessed 26 Apr. 2019).

Fonseca Amador, C. (1981) *Un Nicaragüense en Moscú* (Managua).

Friedman, M.P. (2003) 'Retiring the puppets, bringing Latin America back in: recent scholarship on United States–Latin American relations', *Diplomatic History*, 27 (5).

Gelb, L.H. (1979) 'On arms for Nicaragua', *New York Times*, 29 Aug.

Graeber, D. (1996) 'Epilogue to the disastrous ordeal of 1987', http://www.hartford-hwp.com/archives/36/010.html (accessed 26 Apr. 2019)

Harmer, T. (2013) 'Fractious allies: Chile, the United States, and the Cold War, 1973–76', *Diplomatic History*, 37 (1): 109–43.

— (n.d.) 'Tanya Harmer, *Allende's Chile and the Inter-American Cold War*', H-Diplo Roundtable Review, 14 (1), D. Walcher and D. Labrosse (eds.), www.h-net.org/~diplo/roundtables/PDF/Roundtable-XIV-2.pdf (accessed 27 Apr. 2019).

Harto de Vera, F. (1991) 'La U.R.S.S. y la revolución sandinista: los estrechos límites de la solidaridad soviética', *Revista Africa América Latina*, 6: 87–93.

Henighan, S. (2014) *Sandino's Nation: Ernesto Cardenal and Sergio Ramírez Writing Nicaragua, 1940–2012* (Montréal).

Hovey, G. (1980) 'House, by 5-Vote margin, passes Bill on assistance for Nicaragua', *New York Times*, 28 Feb.

La Prensa (2008) 'Ortega: "Rusia está iluminando el planeta"', 18 Sept., www.laprensa.com.ni/2008/09/18/politica/1342230-ortega-rusia-esta-iluminando-el-planeta (accessed 26 Apr. 2019).

Leogrande, W.M. (1996) 'Making the economy scream: US economic sanctions against Sandinista Nicaragua', *Third World Quarterly* 17 (2): 329–48.

León, C. (n.d.) 'Nicaragua and IDA: an enduring partnership', *World Bank*, www.worldbank.org/en/country/nicaragua/publication/nicaragua-and-IDA (accessed 26 Apr. 2019).

New York Times (1979) 'U.S. analysts say Cuba is keeping forces abroad; Cubans poorly paid', *New York Times*, 21 Oct.

— (1980) 'Nicaragua leaders sign pacts with Soviet Union', *New York Times*, 23 Mar.

Ortega, D. (2007) 'No había tal conflicto Este-Oeste', 22 Aug., www.radiolaprimerisima.com/noticias/18655/daniel-ortega-presidente-de-nicaragua-no-habia-tal-conflicto-este-oeste (accessed 26 Apr. 2019).

Ramírez, S. (2007) 'Lo que nos tocó de guerra fría', *El País*, 29 Aug., https://elpais.com/diario/2007/08/29/opinion/1188338404_850215.html (accessed 24 Sept. 2019).

Reagan, R. (1986) 'Address to the nation on the situation in Nicaragua', mp3, Presidential Audio Recordings, 1/20/1981–1/20/1989, US National Archives, https://catalog.archives.gov/id/7450184 (accessed 26 Apr. 2019).

Red Voltaire (2009) 'Venezuela reconoce a Abjasia y Osetia Del Sur', 20 Sept., www.voltairenet.org/article162145.html (accessed 26 Apr. 2019).

Reyes, E.D. (1985) 'Soviet relations with Central America, the Caribbean, and members of the Contadora group', *The Annals of the American Academy of Political and Social Science*, 481: 147–58.

Riding, A. (1979) 'Foreign policy set by Managua called realistic; U.S. seeks regime's confidence', *New York Times*, 9 Oct.

— (1979) 'Nicaragua tries economic cure; concern among bankers', *New York Times*, 27 Nov.

— (1980) 'Nicaragua after Somoza; after Somoza', *New York Times*, 3 Feb.

Shearman, P. (1987) 'The Soviet challenge in Central America', *Proceedings of the Academy of Political Science*, 36 (4): 211–22.

Suchlicki, J. (1987) 'Soviet policy in Latin America: implications for the United States', *Journal of Interamerican Studies and World Affairs*, 29 (1): 25–46.

US Embassy in Managua (2009) 'Nicaragua and Abkhazia establish formal diplomatic ties', Wikileaks Public Library of US Diplomacy,

18 Sept. (Managua), https://search.wikileaks.org/plusd/cables/09MANAGUA913_a.html (accessed 26 Apr. 2019).

— (2007) 'Ortega administration at six months', Wikileaks Public Library of US Diplomacy, 2 July (Managua), https://search.wikileaks.org/plusd/cables/07MANAGUA1622_a.html (accessed 27 Apr. 2019).

— (2010) '(U) Ortega and the U.S.: new-found true love or another still-born charm offensive?', Wikileaks Public Library of US Diplomacy, 25 Feb. (Managua), https://search.wikileaks.org/plusd/cables/10MANAGUA115_a.html (accessed 26 Apr. 2019).

Valenta, J. (1985) 'Nicaragua: Soviet–Cuban pawn or non-aligned country?', *Journal of Interamerican Studies and World Affairs*, 27 (3): 163–75.

Zúñiga, R. (2011) Interview with Marlén Villavicencio: 'Ser internacionalista, para nosotros es un principio inalienable', 23 Nov., http://tortillaconsal.com/tortilla/es/node/10359.

5. Agrarian reform in Nicaragua in the 1980s: lights and shadows of its legacy

José Luis Rocha

Nicaragua embarked on an agrarian reform adventure in the 1980s, inspired by a revolutionary government that longed to make great transformations. Despite these grand dreams, however, initial reform was state-centric and progress was slow. The inadequacy of these early efforts led to the deterioration of relations between the state and the peasants in the countryside and the intensification of armed conflict. Agrarian reform measures were bitterly contested and their results were ambiguous – a conflict and ambiguity that has continued to mark the descendants of those affected by the original reforms. The 1980s was a time of bitterness for those whose land was confiscated and of jubilation for the beneficiaries of reform, but the 1990s brought compensation for those whose land had been confiscated, just as embargoes by banks transformed the original beneficiaries' joyous dream into a nightmare. Together, dubious and inadequate land titles, contested reallocations of land to former owners, and compensation awarded on the basis of fraudulent claims created a heavy burden of debt that Nicaraguan taxpayers are still servicing to this day. At the same time, ongoing uncertainty over land ownership continues to block access to loans, discourages long-term investment and undermines productivity.

From the beginning, agrarian reform was presented as an essential part of the exceptionalist ideal that the Sandinista Revolution expected to make flesh in Nicaragua: it was assumed that successful reform was the inevitable destination, and the path towards it was laid out with apparently clairvoyant clarity. In reality, though, an analysis of the actual trajectory of the reforms reveals constant oscillations between illusion and realism, principles and pragmatism, grandness and misery.[1] Agrarian reform was a stage on which different concepts, both reformist and anti-reformist, faced off against each other, leading the country to a point of no return – neither the restitution and compensation measures of the 1990s, nor the resurgence of extreme inequality in land ownership ever succeeded in restoring the status quo ante. The Sandinistas' agrarian reform did

1 J. Wheelock, *La reforma agraria sandinista*.

J. Luis Rocha, 'Agrarian reform in Nicaragua in the 1980s: lights and shadows of its legacy', in H. Francis (ed.), *A Nicaraguan Exceptionalism? Debating the Legacy of the Sandinista Revolution* (London: University of London Press, 2019), pp. 103–25. License: CC-BY-NC-ND.

not provide a blueprint that led ineluctably to exceptionalism; in practice, the collision between multiple initiatives, forces and circumstances ensured that property ownership was shaken up enough to introduce substantial changes in the way that land tenure was structured. For many, this shift was not as penetrating and widespread as it should have been, but its impact was significant enough so that 40 years later we can still discern its imprints, some of them etched in now-hard lava, while others are traced in sand. What were the reform's achievements and flaws? What legacy did it leave us, for better or worse? Did the agrarian reform make Nicaragua an exceptional country? If so, in what sense? The data in this section will provide tentative answers to these questions.

In 1979 the new Sandinista government inherited a system of land distribution that was dominated by a class known as the 'rural bourgeoisie'. Out of a total of 5.6 million hectares of land dedicated to agriculture, almost 2.1 million (36 per cent) were held in properties larger than 350 hectares. Small farms of less than 35 hectares only accounted for 17.5 per cent of the land in use.[2] Extreme inequality in the distribution of land was linked to inequality of access to credit: in the 1960s and '70s, 90 per cent of the loans destined for the agricultural sector went to the big agro-export landowners.[3] In agriculture the poor comprised 61.4 per cent of the economically active population. Of these, 36.5 per cent were smallholders who hired themselves out as workers at certain periods of the agricultural cycle, 17.4 per cent were farmhands who made up the permanent labour force on the big agro-export haciendas and 7.5 per cent were seasonal labourers who could only access full-time work during the coffee, cotton or sugar-cane harvests.[4]

After Somoza fled the country the question of land distribution was a primary concern of the Sandinista National Liberation Front (FSLN). The third decree issued by the new Government Junta of National Reconstruction ordered the confiscation of all properties owned by Somoza's family and his allies, including soldiers and officials of the defeated regime. Soon after, another decree expanded the scope of the confiscations to 'people connected with Somoza'. These two decrees affected 20 per cent of all farmland in Nicaragua. The confiscated land was known as the People's Property Area (APP). It was not distributed to individual farmers but instead organised into 1,500 state farms under the management of the newly created Nicaraguan Institute of Agrarian Reform (INRA).[5] Some 50,000 people, perhaps 13 per cent of all agricultural workers, were employed by the state in these enterprises. Despite these initial

---

2   Centro de Investigaciones y Estudios de la Reforma Agraria (CIERA), *La reforma agraria en Nicaragua 1979–1989*, vol. I, 292.
3   S. and J. Saravia-Matus, 'Agrarian reform: theory and practice. The Nicaraguan experience'.
4   C. Maldidier and P. Marchetti, *El Campesino-Finquero y el potencial económico del campesinado nicaragüense*, 15.
5   Saravia-Matus, 'Agrarian reform', 30.

measures most landless labourers and smallholders – a total of 322,549 people – remained in limbo.[6]

Initial reforms did not match the Sandinista government's revolutionary aims. In 1981, two years after the Sandinistas took power, the speech that announced the new Agrarian Reform Law noted that 1.2 per cent of the population still owned 47.1 per cent of the land, while 30 per cent of the rural population had no land at all.[7] Between 1979 and 1981 around 1.2 million hectares had been confiscated from Somocistas and senior National Guard officers, many of whom had mortgaged their land and escaped with the cash before the Sandinistas took power. Much of this land consisted of huge plantations with tens of thousands of agricultural workers, which the government did not consider suitable for distribution among peasants. In these early days of agrarian reform the government opted to expropriate huge farms such as La Fundadora and La Cumplida and convert them into state enterprises, and they also expropriated medium-sized properties that could be joined together and made into big state-run haciendas. One faction within the revolutionary government sincerely believed that breaking up large and medium-sized haciendas into small plots would reduce their productivity and jeopardise the generation of hard cash from exports. Beyond the problem of land distribution, the Sandinista state was also concerned with agricultural production and income generation, income which was essential if the revolutionary government was to secure the social transformation it promised. And all this in a context where the dark clouds of the US economic blockade and armed aggression, financed and managed by the Reagan government, could already be discerned. It was thus decided to add disused farmland to the properties subject to expropriation, and a year after the triumph of the revolution Sandinista officials began drafting the Agrarian Reform Law.[8]

The law streamlined the agrarian reform process and triggered a boom in different forms of property ownership. Fallow, underused or abandoned properties larger than 350 hectares in the Pacific region and 700 acres in the country's interior were subject to the new legislation. Even so, only 558 properties covering an area of 350,000 hectares were affected in the first phase of the programme (1981–4). Subsequently, Law 14, passed on 11 January 1986, legalised the confiscation of all disused or underused properties, regardless of their size.[9] This law accelerated agrarian reform and increased the bank of available land. At the risk of stating the obvious, it should be noted that these laws did not penalise large landowners as such, only those people who were letting their land lie fallow, something the country could ill afford. Nonetheless,

6   Ibid., 31.
7   Ley de Reforma Agraria, Decreto no. 782, Junta de Gobierno de Reconstrucción Nacional de la República de Nicaragua, 16 Oct. 1981; CIERA, *La reforma agraria*, vol. VIII, 58–89; *Envío*, 'The Agrarian Reform Law in Nicaragua', no. 3, Aug. 1981.
8   Wheelock, *La reforma agraria*, 52–3 and 56.
9   Ibid., 57–8 and 64.

there were substantial shifts in patterns of land distribution. In 1988, two years before the FSLN's electoral defeat, the private sector owned 2.6 million hectares of productive agricultural land, down from 5.6 million in 1979. Overall, the state had reallocated 48 per cent of productive agricultural land. In 1979 private properties larger than 350 hectares made up 36 per cent (2.1 million hectares) of the total available land. By 1988 this figure had dropped to 6.4 per cent or 350,000 hectares.[10]

Most of the reallocated land was absorbed by state farms – known as State Production Units (UPE) – and cooperatives. Of productive agricultural land, UPEs accounted for close to 12 per cent, while nearly 14 per cent ended up in the hands of cooperatives. Most (11.4 per cent) of this land was farmed by Sandinista Agricultural Cooperatives (CAS), whose members held a joint title to their property and carried out all work collectively. Credit and Service Cooperatives (CCS), where small farmers worked their own land but received credit via collective loans, were less common, comprising just 1.7 per cent of the total.[11] Overall, with almost a quarter of the land ultimately being farmed collectively in some form, the programme represented an unprecedented shift in patterns of agricultural land ownership. These shifts were clearly linked to the model of agrarian change promulgated by the Sandinista government. At the same time, other reformist pressures did not form part of the state's original plans and these forced the Sandinistas to take unforeseen decisions. These pressures, particularly the demands of the peasantry, also made their mark and, arguably, proved to be more durable than the state's efforts, because they came from below. The history of these collisions between state and non-state ideals gives the lie to any notion of exceptionalism forged directly and solely from the Sandinista programmes.

In 1984, the expropriation of farms was intended to increase the amount of land available for redistribution, but it was also a means of strengthening the government's hand in its fight against the Contras. Counterrevolutionaries were punished (the 1984 measures sanctioned the confiscation of lands belonging to anyone aiding the Contras) and allies were rewarded. Land awarded to Sandinistas and their allies helped to cement support, and state farms and cooperatives played an active part in the government's defence strategy by helping to repel Contra attacks. Above all, the state provided titles for those holding land following occupation or invasion, in effect legalising a de facto process of agrarian reform that had been unfolding since before the triumph of the revolution. These measures marked a change in FSLN policy, made possible by the impetus of the war and a shift in thinking among INRA leaders. The overall trend was simple – less state property and more peasant property – but the political and ideological battles that lay behind the changes were complex and contested. In the next section a discussion of the conflict between two trade unions that organised farmers and farmworkers – the Rural Workers Association (ATC) and the National Union of Farmers and Ranchers (UNAG) – sheds light

10 CIERA, *La reforma agraria*, vol. I, 292.
11 Ibid., vol. IX, 39.

on the wider ideological battle, revealing the stakes and positions held by the opposing camps.

ATC demands salaries, not land

The ATC was founded on 25 March 1978 as an organisation for agricultural and semi-proletarian workers. Within a year it had 47,851 members who acted as a logistical support network for the Sandinista guerrillas in the months leading up to the Sandinista Revolution. Its members cut communication lines, destroyed telephones and roads, joined the fighting and transmitted information, within a network that was organised geographically, dividing areas into units for each community and district.[12] After the revolution, the ATC organised the SACs (cooperatives which were initially called agricultural communes), made up of organised agricultural workers' collectives that seized Somocista farms and worked them collectively. In this way, the ATC as an organisation was aligned from the beginning with the Sandinista state's initial preference for maintaining large farm estates as single productive units, an approach that was meant to allow a greater concentration of capital, land and workers as well as facilitate their use of superior technology.

Originally peasants and farmers with small and medium holdings were also supposed to be included in the ATC. However, the difference between their perspectives and interests and those of salaried farmworkers made their coexistence within one organisation difficult. Peasants' demands for land were entirely different from workers' demands for higher wages, and the ATC's leadership was more interested in defending the farmworkers' interests.[13] When peasants founded UNAG, the ATC prioritised organising workers in state agrarian-reform enterprises. It replaced its district-by-district organisational structure with a network of local unions which had offices in the state farms. In 1983, despite the loss of peasant members who had moved to UNAG, the ATC had 44,413 members on its books.

Work in 'bureaucratic capitalism'

The ATC prioritised two lines of action: to raise productivity and to train workers so that they could take over management of the state farms in the future. In practice, however, the ATC's demands in the early years related chiefly to wages and the prices of consumer goods, because management of the haciendas was the preserve of state bureaucracy.[14] Farmworkers no longer answered to the farmer-boss but to the state-boss – the bureaucrat-boss characteristic of what Cornelius Castoriadis calls 'bureaucratic capitalism', based on the social division

---

12   CIERA, *La reforma agraria*, vol. VI, 60.
13   C. Vilas, *Perfiles de la revolución sandinista*, 271.
14   CIERA, *La reforma agraria*, vol. VI, 77, 83 and 85.

between the proletariat and a bureaucracy that excludes workers from managing the means of production.[15]

Although the ATC's intervention forced the enterprises to keep paying the wages of workers mobilised in the armed struggle against the Contras, there were many limitations to its achievements. For example, the unions were never able to get the bosses to make temporary workers permanent.[16] They were not even able to maintain the value of their wages: the nominal pay for piecework in the coffee harvest only went up by 0.15 córdobas between 1980 and 1983. In real terms, measured by purchasing power relative to inflation, this was a reduction of almost 40 per cent. Coffee pickers' wages were particularly vulnerable, even in times of good international prices. The price of some basic goods fell, but the drop in salaries was much more significant: the price of corn and beans dropped by at least 5 per cent while cotton pickers' wages fell by 28 per cent.[17]

The deterioration in wages went hand-in-hand with a declining work culture, made apparent in the wry joke which defined socialism as 'a system in which the state pretends to pay and the workers pretend to work'. A widespread belief was prevalent that the revolution should change the rules of the game and instigate a more relaxed work ethic, thus distinguishing itself from capitalist exploitation of the labour force. In fact, the working day dwindled to two or three hours, a phenomenon that was a key factor in the slowing of production during those years.[18] While farm workers waited for their historic vacation, those without land longed for more aggressive agrarian reform.

The UNAG is born, with a peasant seal

In April 1981, UNAG was born, supported by peasants who were poor but had experienced a rapid economic ascent during the coffee and cattle booms of the years immediately prior to the revolution's triumph. Many had collaborated with the guerrillas and were loyal to the FSLN, even when they did not necessarily share the Sandinistas' politics. At their initial 1981 gathering, in the Perla de Matagalpa theatre, 3,000 farmers with small and medium holdings, representing 100,000 peasants came together to break publicly with the Central Cooperative of Coffee Growers, a Somoza-era organisation whose middle-class anti-Sandinista members had hoped to create a broad front against the revolution. The peasants who met that day were to become the embryonic UNAG.[19]

Typical UNAG members owned a medium-sized portion of land and had been sidelined by the elite-dominated associations of agro exporters in the Somoza era. They were now targets of proselytizing work from those same

15 C. Castoriadis, *La sociedad burocrática*.
16 CIERA, *Las clases sociales en el campo de Jinotega*.
17 Vilas, *Perfiles*, 387.
18 CIERA, *La reforma agraria*, vol. VI, 95. M. Spoor, 'Rural employment and agrarian markets in transition: Nicaragua (1979–89)', 538.
19 CIERA, *La reforma agraria*, vol. VI, 80–1.

associations, but UNAG filled a gap and neutralised the agricultural elite's attempts to build opposition to the revolution. It sought to unite all farmers, regardless of their class status, to achieve hegemony among the rural sectors that had not been organised by the ATC. This interaction between classes helped to assuage the fears of many peasants, who already held land and employed a small workforce, and who felt threatened by the clamour for land from those who had no property of their own.[20] The farmers with small and medium holdings who had come together in UNAG were particularly anxious to secure long-term loans, agricultural supplies, technical assistance, new roads, participation in state institutions, and decision-making on prices and marketing. Farmers from this sector also pressured INRA to pass the Agrarian Reform Law in 1981.

Directed by the FSLN, UNAG initially worked with cooperatives and successfully urged many of its members to form CCSs. In the 1980s, 93 per cent of UNAG members belonged to cooperatives, largely the CCSs.[21] In 1984, as the Contra War heated up, UNAG sought to extend its social base to incorporate other farmers with similar portions of land who were not in cooperatives and even those portrayed – in Sandinista propaganda – as representatives of the 'patriotic bourgeoisie'. They were involved in the farming associations and commissions that promoted each crop and they energised the district committees of UNAG.

While the ATC dedicated itself exclusively to agricultural workers, UNAG recruited poor peasants through district outreach work as well as middle-income and well-off peasants, giving the organisation a particularily heterogeneous social base. This situation had disadvantages for some. The predominance of landowning peasants meant that UNAG's demands mirrored the concerns of the farmer with a medium-sized holding, who was worried about prices, access to markets, transport and the availability of agricultural inputs. It did not give the same voice to poor peasants clamouring for land.[22] In the early years of the revolution, the FSLN feared that demands for land by poor peasants, who had not been absorbed into state enterprises, might destroy the revolution's plans for national unity, which were predicated upon an alliance with the rural bourgeoisie. The FSLN was reluctant to give up this unity project and it did not want to distribute the land belonging to state enterprises, which were seen as the linchpin of national wealth. In other words, if the FSLN aspired to some form of exceptionalism, it expected to achieve it thanks to the productive capacity of the state and its vast supply of agricultural land, not by distributing land to small farmers.

As the economic crisis worsened, peasants grew increasingly frustrated with the FSLN's failure to respond to their demands. This eroded UNAG's power to

20 M. Merlet and C. Maldidier, 'El movimiento cooperativo, eje de la sobrevivencia de la revolución', 56.
21 CIERA, *La reforma agraria*, vol. VI, 133.
22 V. Fitzgerald and A. Chamorro, 'Las cooperativas en el proyecto de transición en Nicaragua', 30 (1987): 31.

unite farmers, although the organisation continued to attract new members. It became increasingly critical of the FSLN and its farming policy, especially after 1986, when it began to give voice to the peasants' demand for land. Projecting itself as the key mass organisation in the countryside, UNAG took the lead in peasant protests, changing both its discourse and its practice in the process. In 1986 UNAG's slogan was 'An organisation for struggle' – and the struggle was for land.[23] This shift ensured that UNAG recovered its previous strength.

Cooperatives = solidarity

The demands of UNAG's members collided with an ideological sacred cow: the veneration of collectivism. From the start, the Sandinista government had promoted cooperatives in order to forge 'a spirit of solidarity and cooperation' and overcome 'competitive and exploitative relationships among men'.[24] Competition was perceived as a capitalist evil that had to be suppressed. Solidarity was integral to the figure of the 'new man' and multiple devices were employed to promote it. In Nicaragua, this collectivist impetus sprang in part from an ideological debt to Sandino who, in the 1920s, said he was 'in favour of land belonging to the state' and inclined 'towards a cooperative regime' along the Río Coco.[25] Cooperatives were part of the FSLN's 1969 historic programme, which was committed to motivating and encouraging peasants to organise and take their destiny into their own hands and participate directly in the country's development.[26] These local precedents were reinforced by modes of thought common in revolutionary states, where a dichotomy between individualism (bourgeois and reactionary) and collectivism (revolutionary) prevailed. This opposition, and its role in the strengthening of the revolutionary state, are the subject of two books by Lynne Viola, whose work on the Soviet Union reveals divisions greatly similar to those that existed between the ATC and UNAG in Nicaragua.[27]

The emphasis on collectivism, therefore, was the result of a mix of local and transnational ideological currents. It was also driven by the perception that only large-scale units could deliver the material wealth so desperately needed by the fledgling Sandinista state. The economies of scale involved in working a large landholding made it possible to use irrigation and mechanisation, and to apply modern technology; operating as a group would also facilitate access to loans, technical assistance, the buying and storage of harvests, and the supply of agricultural inputs. The plan also included the provision of educational

---

23 Merlet and Maldidier, 'El movimiento cooperativo', 62.
24 CIERA, *La reforma agraria*, vol. VIII, 135.
25 Wheelock, *La reforma agraria*, 42.
26 Ibid., 44–5.
27 L. Viola, *The Best Sons of the Fatherland: Workers in the Vanguard of Soviet Collectivization* L. Viola, *Peasants Rebels under Stalin: Collectivization and the Culture of Peasant Resistance*.

programmes and health, housing and cultural services.²⁸ In 1988 the state even went so far as to exempt productive cooperatives from paying income tax.²⁹ The cooperativist project soon achieved wide coverage: by 1982, 2,849 cooperatives with 65,820 members had already been set up and controlled an area of some 700,000 hectares. By 1988, the project seemed to have gained even more ground, with 3,151 cooperatives and 76,715 members who controlled over a million hectares.³⁰ We must remember, though, that two kinds of cooperative existed: the CASs, which required a more complete form of collectivisation, and the CCSs, with a lighter touch, which collectivised administration but not cultivation. As the next section will show, these different types of cooperative evolved differently, in ways which again reflect the contested nature of agrarian reform.

UNAG v. MIDINRA, Bukharin v. Preobrazhenski

From its foundation, UNAG challenged Sandinista officials' view of the collectivisation process. In January 1980 INRA was merged with the agriculture ministry to form the Ministry of Agricultural Development and Agrarian Reform (MIDINRA), triggering what would become a long-running dispute between it and UNAG. Social scientist Peter Marchetti compared this controversy to the 1924 debate between Eugene Preobrazhenski and Nikolai Bukharin over the Soviet Union's New Economic Policy instituted between 1921 and 1929. Preobrazhenski favoured a rapid transition to socialism supported by the expansion of state enterprises and industrialisation, at the expense of the peasantry. Similarly, MIDINRA supported large-scale projects involving directly controlled state farms or fully collectivised CASs. This would allow the state to control the harvest and sale of crops, thereby securing a supply of cheap agricultural produce for the cities. Preobrazhenski and MIDINRA viewed the peasantry as 'backward', a seedbed of capitalism. Bukharin and UNAG held the opposing view. For them a more moderate approach to collectivisation was necessary in order to maintain an alliance with the peasantry. They also believed that a greater emphasis on individual production would help to limit the state's monopoly, make better use of the nation's productive potential, and ensure that the agricultural sector responded better to market forces.³¹

The Cooperatives Law expressed these conflicting visions by facilitating the creation of two types of cooperatives: credit and service cooperatives with individual land ownership (the CCS model) and production cooperatives with collective property (the CAS model). The CCS model was much more popular with farmers' groups because it was more flexible and did not involve

---

28 Wheelock, *La reforma agraria*, 136.
29 CIERA, *La reforma agraria*, vol. VIII, 148–9.
30 Ibid., vol. I, 304–6.
31 P. Marchetti, 'Semejanzas y diferencias en dos debates sobre el campesinado: la economía mixta y la vía al socialismo', 35–45.

collectivisation or a commitment to the state.[32] There were far fewer CAS cooperatives, partly because their foundation depended on the allocation of agrarian reform land. Initially the CSS cooperatives outnumbered the CAS by seven to one, in terms of both land and members. Landless peasants were the most willing to organise into a CAS, because establishing one involved the granting of new land. Middle-income peasant farmers who already had land and were interested in gaining access to loans were far more likely to form CCSs.[33] Cooperative status was a prerequisite for government loans, so many peasants registered as CCS members who did not comply with the minimal operational requirements. Many formally constituted CCSs never called a member's assembly and those who had joined never did anything together aside from filling in the paperwork needed to apply for a loan. The 1981 Cooperatives Law stipulated that 'the revolutionary state will grant farming cooperatives special financial support through programs that offer preferential interest rates'.[34] Actual practice went even further than this and cooperatives' debts were forgiven so frequently that non-repayment of loans became an implicit norm.

Despite the CCSs' early preponderance, it soon became clear that the CAS model would predominate. In 1982 the cooperative development strategy prioritised giving CASs access to land, loans and technical supplies, and CAS holdings grew substantially. At the start of the agrarian reform, cooperatives received an average of 11 to 12 hectares per member; by 1988 the CCSs were still within this range, but they now controlled an average of 20 hectares per member, chiefly because state farms had been converted into CAS cooperatives.[35] By 1986 the CASs had received 75 per cent of the land assigned by the agrarian reform to cooperatives and individual owners, with predictable consequences for the relative importance of the two models.[36] Between 1982 and 1988 the number of CAS cooperatives increased by 129 per cent, their membership grew by 217 per cent and the area of land they controlled expanded by 453 per cent. In contrast, the number of CCS cooperatives fell by 6 per cent, with a 14 per cent reduction in membership and a 38 per cent drop in landholdings.[37] Many of the CCSs which had existed in name only were disappearing, but the CCSs were also seriously affected by the war – the number of cooperatives fell by 17 per cent in the central region, the area of the country where most fighting took place, partly because CCS members were afraid of armed counter-revolutionaries accusing them of having links to the FSLN. In contrast, the war actually strengthened the CASs, as they owed a greater debt to the Frente. Significantly, the first bands of armed counter-revolutionaries – the MILPAS (Anti-Sandinista People's Militias) – appeared in 1980 in the northern part of the country, supported by owners of

32   CIERA, *La reforma agraria*, vol. V, 288–9.
33   Fitzgerald and Chamorro, 'Las cooperativas'; 31.
34   CIERA, *La reforma agraria*, vol. VIII, 145.
35   CIERA, *La reforma agraria*, vol. I, 305.
36   Fitzgerald and Chamorro, 'Las cooperativas', 37.
37   CIERA, *La reforma agraria*, vol. I, 304–5.

small and medium coffee farm and cattle ranches who feared that the growing nationalisation of the rural economy would lead to the confiscation of their property. The MILPAS leaders were former Sandinista guerrillas unhappy that confiscated land had been turned into state enterprises.[38]

The war forced the pace

The war meant that the CAS cooperatives won out over the CCSs, but ultimately the conflict resulted in a shift towards the UNAG-Bukharin model, with a reduction in large units directly controlled by the state. The war was intensifying in the border area with Honduras, a mountainous area ideal for insurgency. Between 1981 and 1985 the Contras carried out a reported 133 attacks in this area, leaving 242 dead, 49 wounded and 44 abducted, limited to cooperative members and workers on state farms only.[39] The FSLN responded by introducing the draft, which it dubbed Patriotic Military Service (SMP), and by changing its agrarian policy. The goal was to regain the political initiative and promote the defence of territory adjacent to the cooperatives' lands.[40] The need was particularly acute because worsening economic conditions were creating support for the Contras.[41] Farmers whose land had been confiscated, and those who thought their land might be expropriated, were especially disaffected. Most of the Contra leaders were farmers from Matagalpa and Jinotega who saw the revolution as a threat. Their dissatisfaction had to be allayed.

The state's new policy on land tenure was designed, in simple terms, to confiscate land from ten people and hand it over to one hundred. The high point of the agrarian reform was 1984, when 37 per cent of the 2.7 million hectares ultimately affected by the agrarian reform was given out in the form of 'special titles'. In reality, these titles simply recognised families' legal right to occupy small plots that they had been farming for decades, but the issuing of this type of title was also due to the war: 66 per cent of the special titles were 'granted' in 1984, and only 13.57 per cent had been issued prior to that. The reform that benefited cooperatives was similar: 86 per cent of the land granted to cooperatives was received between 1983 and 1987, whereas only 10 per cent of the total land ultimately allocated was distributed between 1979 and 1982.[42]

Strengthening a peasant front that would be loyal to the revolution and that would hold back the advance of the counterrevolutionaries was a matter of urgency. A tight network of individual FSLN sympathisers and cooperatives was built, all of them beneficiaries of land reform. The land was taken from recently

---

38   A. Grigsby, 'Nicaragua: conflicto armado y políticas económicas y sociales', Mimeo, 2001.
39   Wheelock, *La reforma agraria*, 127.
40   D. Kaimowitz, 'La planificación agropecuaria en Nicaragua, 70.
41   CIERA, *La reforma agraria*, 414.
42   CIERA, *La reforma agraria*, vol. IX, 39–44.

confiscated farms or from former state farms.[43] Some 39 per cent of the land allocated in 1986–7 came from confiscated farms of over 350 hectares and only 8 per cent came from farms smaller in size. The remaining land was formerly state-controlled.[44] The war meant the growth of the Bukharin-UNAG model marked a rupture with the blueprint that had, until then, guided land distribution policies. The war laid the groundwork for an exceptionalism that had not featured in the FSLN's original plans.

The redistribution that took place in those years changed the structure of land tenure in Nicaragua, creating a greater proportion of small farms. This shift in tenure patterns created the conditions for different kinds of innovation and facilitated later experiments with organic production and participation in fair trade networks. These far-reaching achievements might have gone even further, but the FSLN never wholeheartedly embraced the UNAG-Bukharin model. Michel Merlet, an agroeconomy expert who worked with INRA throughout most of the 1980s and now directs AGTER, an association for the improved governance of natural resources, notes that,

> between 1985 and 1987, almost half the state sector was redistributed to cooperatives or peasants. These measures helped the government regain control of the situation: production of basic grains increased, the Contra advance was halted, but an indisputable division persisted, a real schism at the heart of the peasantry. A more flexible agrarian reform from 1984 on did not lead to a radical review. No sooner had the country emerged from the emergency situation than the FSLN stopped expanding and intensifying the agrarian reform.[45]

The last line is discouraging. According to Merlet's figures, the transformation of the land tenure structure was significant, but still only partial, in 1988:

> The large holdings (more than 350 hectares) only represented 19 per cent of all farmland (7 per cent private and 12 per cent state farms) compared to 36 per cent in 1978. Production cooperatives were working 12 per cent of the land and the rest was in the hands of individual peasant farmers and strata of rural petty bourgeoisie. Some 70,000 peasant families received land: almost one out of every two peasant families. But the area redistributed for individual usage only represented 5 per cent of all farmland.[46]

The Sandinista land reform repeated all the errors and abuses of the reform undertaken by Mexico's Lázaro Cárdenas 50 years previously: a slow start to redistribution, successive debt pardons, a prohibition on selling or inheriting

---

43 The FSLN granted some 383,600 hectares between 1984 and 1987. Eduardo Baumeister, 'Transformaciones agrarias y revolución en Nicaragua'. Paper presented at the LASA conference, New Orleans, 17–19 Mar. 1988.

44 Ibid.

45 M. Merlet, 'Fragilidad y límites de las reformas agrarias en América Central. Las enseñanzas de dos países: Honduras y Nicaragua'. Course for 'Gestión y Tenencia de la Tierra en Centroamérica', BIVICAT- RECCAT, FAUSAC, URACCAN, IRAM, París, Francia, from 1 July to 30 Sept. 2004.

46 Ibid.

land, the under-utilisation of plots, a fall in production and productivity, a mix of paternalism and subjection, and investment wasted on extravagant projects.[47]

The Sandinista piñata and the neoliberal turn

The 1990s brought an abrupt change in approach. Violeta Chamorro's electoral victory meant that the government cabinet was largely made up of a group of technocrats educated in US universities, well-versed in theories of monetarism and neoliberal ideology. Sharing the business sector's faith in the market's invisible hand, they implemented a series of policies aimed at dismantling state controls, privatising state-owned land and lowering taxes. The General Board of National Public Sector Corporations (CORNAP) was created in 1990 to take over the state's business functions. It was effectively a holding company responsible for offloading state enterprises.

However, even before CORNAP had gestated in the neoliberal womb, the Sandinista regime had begun privatising state assets. In the two-month transition period between the FSLN's electoral defeat in February and Violeta Chamorro's inauguration in April, the Sandinista leadership implemented the swiftest transfer of goods in national history: farms, houses, buildings, factories, vehicles, tractors, small islands and millions of dollars in cash were taken from the state and given to the Sandinista elite. Compared to the Sandinista 'piñata', as it came to be known, the other redistribution programmes of the 1980s pale into insignificance. The piñata contributed to a rollback of agrarian reform that has never been fully examined. Leading Sandinistas, including the agrarian reform minister and deputy ministers, ended up with some of the country's best farms, with the result that CORNAP started operating with what remained after the Sandinista piñata. Most of the properties bestowed by CORNAP – 52 per cent of transfers, accounting for 59 per cent of their value – went to private buyers or tenants. Only after a major battle did the new government reluctantly reward workers of the former state-owned entities with 23 per cent of the properties, representing 30 per cent of the total value. The percentage of former combatants who gained from the privatisation process, either from the Sandinista Popular Army or the National Resistance, was tiny.[48] Former combatants were beneficiaries of just 241 of the 1,532 transactions carried out by CORNAP between 1991 and 1994, but the value of the property given to them – a little over 15 million córdobas – represented less than 1.4 per cent of the total value of the property transferred.[49] They made their dissatisfaction felt immediately.

47　E. Krauze, *Biografía del poder. Caudillos de la revolución mexicana (1910–1940)*, 458–60.

48　National Resistance is what all armed counterrevolutionary groups called themselves. It included the Nicaraguan Democratic Force (FDN, in Spanish) in the north, the Democratic Revolutionary Alliance (ARDE) in the south and MISURASATA, from the Miskito, Sumo and Rama Amerindian peoples of Nicaragua's Atlantic coast.

49　D. Close, *Los años de Doña Violeta*, 214.

Meanwhile the US government, which had generously disbursed millions to keep the armed counterrevolution in weaponry, refused to have anything to do with the now retired 'freedom fighters' and pressured the Chamorro government into reducing the Sandinista Popular Army to a bare minimum. Troops plunged from 86,810 in January 1990 to 16,200 in 1992 and then to 14,553 by 1994, making the recently renamed Army of Nicaragua the smallest in Central America. It was reduced by 86 per cent overall, at a rate of 21.5 per cent per year. According to Nicaraguan military expert Roberto Cajina, the scale of demobilisation that took place in Nicaragua is unprecedented – we might say exceptional – in contemporary military history.

The process was hastily implemented and chaotic, with benefits unfairly skewed towards the more senior ranks. For the most part, the thousands of two-year conscripts were simply happy to return home, but for those of all ranks who had made the army their career and had committed to revolution, there were various plans, some of which stressed seniority criteria and others the rank reached. They also had diverse compensation methods such as houses, land, money or staggered disbursements. Worst of all, the seemingly political criteria for deciding who would remain in active service and who would retire were never made clear. Even more so than the unequal compensation and subsequent lack of government compliance due to insufficient resources, the emotions related to being summarily dismissed from the herd after all the sacrifice and danger, without any clear and understandable explanation, fuelled resentment.

'Recompas' and 'recontras': together for land

Between April and December 1992 many demobilised soldiers, fed up with broken promises, led a series of protests and hunger strikes to spotlight the government's failure to implement signed agreements corresponding to the three discharge plans. They sought proper titles to their lands and access to loans and technical assistance. They argued that grants of land to demobilised army personnel had been based on elitist criteria that favoured high-ranking officers – the total of 582 officers (2 colonels, 25 lieutenant colonels, 97 majors and 458 captains), represented just 5.8 per cent of all demobilised officers. Many of the latter were also adversely affected by the mechanism of compensation payments disbursed over a long period. Many dissenters organised into groups, rearming themselves: some to get the government's attention, some to carry on the war and others to engage in low-level banditry.

Ex-National Resistance members were also dissatisfied. In their case the main problem was the chaos in the land titling process and facilitation of repayments or compensation prioritised in agreement two of the disarmament protocol. Meagre resources were meted out to provide for the war wounded, orphans and widows, resulting in miserable pensions. Talk began to be heard of a social divide that did not allow services to get through to the regions where settlements of demobilised Resistance fighters were situated.

Bands of armed army veterans ('Recompas') and Resistance veterans ('Recontras') turned their rearmament and rebellion into a means of demanding land and forcing the government to keep other unmet promises. At first some Recompa groups reactivated to respond to Recontras' revenge abuses, but more often than not, the two formerly adversarial groups discovered they had shared interests and united in bands under separate commands known as 'Rejuntos', or a joint command known as 'Revueltos', to engage in publicity-seeking actions such as taking over a city or stretch of highway.[50]

The Chamorro land reform was mostly an instrument for awarding severance pay and unemployment benefit to Army and Resistance veterans, and an attempt to pacify the rearmed groups. Although the government did not always keep its promises, some land distribution took place on the agricultural frontier, sometimes fanning the flames of ethnic conflicts with indigenous peoples on the Caribbean side of the country, and sometimes being drawn from privatised state properties. Of the 22,000 demobilised Contras, 11,385 had received a total of 231,000 hectares of land by 1992.[51] Some of these together with certain land grants conflicted with other state programmes. For example, the Chamorro government granted land in areas later demarcated as forestry reserves, generating conflict in both directions. The presence of settlers had the demonstrable effect of attracting new invaders to the reserve areas, so the army would carry out evictions that were legitimate according to one law but in violation of another. In spite of these short circuits, possibly expressions of the diverse interests at play, the post-1990 reform – which was meant to strengthen the peace process – was in many ways a continuation of the Sandinista agrarian reform. Both were shaped by a combination of peasant demands and the consequences of the war itself. This new distribution of land, in significant if not enormous quantities, was an exceptional policy within Central America. Demobilised soldiers in other Central American countries did not receive the same benefits and, as a result, went on to form organised crime groups or to carry out contract killings for drug cartels, as happened with the Guatemalan *kaibiles*.[52]

Better a hired hand on another's farm than the boss of one's own

At the end of the 1980s the ATC, with its 65,000 members, had grouped together union branches according to the kind of crop or enterprises their workers were involved in. For the branches related to coffee production, the ATC guaranteed workers' participation, putting its money into a 'deprofessionalisation' of the organisation to rid it of bureaucrats and allow greater union participation in

50 These names are an emblematic example of Nicaraguan humour in adversity: permutations on the well-known phrase 'juntos pero no revueltos' – together but not mixed – referring to generations of families forced to live under the same roof due to poverty rather than choice.
51 E. Baumeister and A. Fauné, 'Elementos para una nueva estrategia gremial de la UNAG'. Paper presented at a seminar to Junta Directiva Nacional of UNAG, Managua, 8 June 1992.
52 A. Hernández, *Los señores del narco*, 399.

the economic management of the enterprises within it. This process accelerated with the privatisation of state enterprises in the 1990s, especially following farm seizures. The ATC promoted these to upset the Chamorro government's privatisation plans, which were designed to favour business owners with which it was connected. The ATC was thus finally able to achieve the objective pursued in training received in the 1980s: worker-managed state enterprises.[53] The workers thus became owners too, a situation unforeseen in the revolutionary government's early plans.

The farm workers organised in the ATC managed to acquire a coffee-processing operation and nine coffee estates, covering a combined area of 16,670 hectares, scattered across Matagalpa, Jinotega, Carazo and Managua. In 1999 these properties were combined to form a coffee company, AGROCAFE S.A., with 2,032 members, 98 per cent of whom were workers on the farms, which also grew basic grains and managed cattle ranches and a large area of forest. According to AGROCAFE, the estates belonging to the Workers' Property Area (APT), the new name for these lands, were responsible for 7 per cent of the country's coffee production, which was, and still is, the country's most important export.[54]

By 1994 the situation for the worker/entrepreneurs on these farms was already looking unpromising. In one of them, the Adolfo García, covering 255 hectares in El Crucero, only 16 out of 165 members knew how to read and write. School dropout rates did not augur a better future for them: only half of 250 farmworkers' children managed to finish the 1993 academic year. They were acutely aware of their limitations in managing their own businesses. Furthermore, they were being strangled by a financial debt of 583,000 córdobas and a dearth of agricultural inputs. The migration of some members to other farms, the cities and Costa Rica started undermining their capacity for self-management. The ten córdobas a day they could get as hired hands on other farms was almost double the income they received working for themselves.[55] Some of their farms were sold or rendered unproductive due to lack of credit.

A range of circumstances conspired against worker management. Merlet points to 'economic insecurity' as a big factor, explaining that structural adjustment policies brutally changed the rules of the game by getting rid of the various subsidies that benefited farmers. The new small farmers and the former state enterprises, now managed by workers, were subjected to pressure from former owners and the police, who were able to justify their interference because of various unresolved legal problems with property titles. The new owners were also economically asphyxiated by a drastic reduction in access to credit and little or no renegotiation of the debts previously acquired by their cooperatives or enterprises. According to Merlet, who has followed the fate of the agrarian

53 CIERA, *La reforma agraria*, vol. VI, 101.
54 M. González, 'Worker-owned coffee farms: the bitter and the sweet,' *Envío*, no. 154, May 1994.
55 Ibid.

reform through all the years since it began, a considerable portion of the land awarded was sold at prices way below its market value. This was partly because of the lack of adequate title deeds, especially in the case of the best lands or those with urban development or tourism potential. If a balance sheet were drawn up of the gains (land given to former combatants, for example) and losses (sales of land and land returned to former owners), beneficiaries of the reformed sector would have a net loss of some 400,000 hectares between 1990 and 2000. And the process is not yet over.[56]

Forty years later?

It has often been said that a return to extreme inequality in land tenure has occurred in the last decade, an agrarian counter-reform spurred on by elites, old and new, grabbing farms of all sizes. Eduardo Baumeister charts the state of land tenure to four milestones in Nicaraguan history which fall close to census dates: the start of Somoza's decline, the end of the Somoza dynasty, the end of Sandinista agrarian reform and the end of two neoliberal governments (those of Violeta Chamorro and Arnoldo Alemán).[57]

Between 1963 and 1978 there were no significant changes in landholdings. The relative drop in the area of farms larger than 350 hectares is a result of the division of farms between multiple heirs. This stratum was transformed, although not as much as some desired, between 1978 and 1988. Collectives absorbed 25.5 per cent of the farmland, while holdings of 140 hectares or more dropped precipitously, from just over 52 per cent of total landholdings to just over 26 per cent: basically, the big farms fed the collectives. The most significant increase in the number of small farms took place between 1988 and 2001: the proportion of land held in units of 140 hectares or less grew by almost 13 percentage points, partly due to the breaking up of cooperative land and state farms into individual plots, and partly due to the land being given to veterans of both sides and to returning exiles. The fact that collectives shrank by more than 20 per cent does not just reflect their being parcelled out to farm workers and cooperative members. A large part of this land was returned to former owners or acquired by old or new large-scale owners, which accounts for the number of farms over 140 hectares having also increased in the same period.

It should be noted that the increase in the number of smallholdings does not necessarily imply a rise in the number of smallholders. Some of the change is due to members of the middle class having acquired many small farms to diversify their sources of income. There is also a risk that the governing party could use the current situation, in which the Nicaraguan is described – according to current propaganda – as 'Christian, socialist and in solidarity', to bring back the methods of the outmoded paternalist state to engage in new expropriations and distribute

---

56 Merlet, 'Fragilidad y límites'.
57 E. Baumeister, 'Treinta años de agricultura nicaragüense (1978–2008)', 400.

properties among the 'good'. The later in this 'second stage of the revolution' are submissive yes-men.

Range (Hectares)	1963	1978	1988	2001
Up to 7	3.5	2.1	3.1	4.5
From more than 7 to 35	11.2	15.4	16.7	20
From more than 35 to 141	26.5	30.1	28.4	36.6
From more than 141 to 352	17.6	16.2	12.8	18
More than 352	41.2	36.2	13.5	16.5
State land	0	0	11.7	0.4
Collective property	0	0	13.8	4
Total	100	100	100	100

Figure 5.1. Evolution in the size of farms by range (in percentages of land used for agriculture).
Source: CIERA and agricultural census of 1963, 1978, and 2001.[58]

Without doubt, a fresh attempt at redistribution would be welcomed by the many who are again landless, from the recipients of freebies and by those who benefit from troubled waters. The passage of time is a great fragmenter of smallholdings. It is inevitable that any such project would necessarily ignore the burden of unresolved conflict that Nicaraguans still carry as a result of the agrarian reform of the 1980s. This time redistribution would be implemented without the legitimacy the FSLN once enjoyed and abused, and it would ignore the fact that property rights are not the only – or even the most important – reason for the struggle around land, its use and the distribution of its benefits.

New struggles could be more aligned to common interests and the common good, and they might include other components, provide more options, adopt new strategies and diversify demands and approaches. This could happen, if, as Merlet suggests, instead of talking about 'land,' we talked about 'rights to land'; if we understood that a title or deed covers different rights, but not all rights; and if we talked about 'land tenure regimes' instead of 'terms of ownership'.[59]

Another factor might come into play which could have the opposite effect, as it tends towards the rolling back of the agrarian reform: the expropriation of small- and medium-sized properties along the possible route of the interoceanic canal which is unlikely to be constructed. This *coup de main* would result in the concentration of farms and residential properties in the hands of the

---

58 E. Baumeister, 'Treinta años de agricultura nicaragüense (1978-2008)', in *Nicaragua y el FSLN [1979-2009] ¿Qué queda de la revolución?* (Barcelona, 2009): 400.

59 M. Merlet, 'Regímenes de tenencia de la tierra, sistemas financieros y construcción de nuevas modalidades de gobernanza'. Paper presented at the international seminar 'Economías campesinas y sistemas financieros rurales', Foro latinoamericano y del Caribe sobre finanzas rurales (FOROLACFR), La Paz, Bolivia, July 2007.

canal company and its shareholders.[60] Considerable resistance has been made against the expropriations of the canal project, in the form of four protest marches, all led principally by medium and small-scale farmers.[61] So far, the government has reacted with indifference and repression: the authorities have not passed judgement on the matter and the police have turned a blind eye when government sympathisers attack the demonstrators. At the same time, the government cannot feign indifference in the face of the peasants' ability to communicate their complaints to various national stakeholders and international fora. Government apathy on this matter is a result of the fact that the FSLN wins far more votes in urban areas, which is where most of Nicaragua's population is now concentrated.[62]

This indifference is built upon a sense of contempt for some of the most lasting achievements of the agrarian reform – achievements which have survived for 40 years. The Nicaraguan peasantry has shown itself to be organised and conscious of its interests, even though it was required to subordinate them to the directives of the revolutionary government in the 1980s, when urban-focused policies that were harmful to peasant interests were emphasised.[63] Since 'consciousness' is an intangible benefit, the exact scope of which is not easily measured, I will mention a more concrete and tangible achievement: in the 2002/2003 cycle Nicaragua sold 3,925,364 kilograms of coffee through Fair Trade channels, which was 6.12 per cent of Fair Trade coffee originating from Latin America, and 3.45 per cent of the global output, making it the fifth largest producer in Latin America.[64] The democratisation of coffee cultivation in Nicaragua has created the right conditions for Fair Trade. Its cooperatives and small-scale farmers are highly attractive partners for institutions that promote this alternative to the conventional market, including Espanica, a Fair Trade organisation that distributes coffee in Spain, sourced from farmers in Matagalpa and Condega who are organised in cooperatives that own lands from the old APP.

Some agrarian reform cooperatives continue to stand out in Fair Trade circles. The Promoter for Cooperative Development in Las Segovias (PRODECOOP) is one of the most successful examples of coffee-producing cooperatives in the Fair Trade market. Founded in 1993, it brings together more than 2,000 small farmers who are members of 40 different cooperatives. In 2002 it controlled

---

60 M. López Baltodano, 'Truths about the canal concession all Nicaraguans should know', *Envío*, no. 390, Jan. 2014.
61 E. Romero, 'Campesinos marcharon contra el canal', *La Prensa*, 22 Apr. 2016.
62 J.L. Rocha and T. Martínez, 'A country divided: relative defeats and victories', *Envío*, no. 232, Nov. 2000.
63 R. Mendoza Vidaurre, 'We erred to win...', *Envío*, no. 111, Oct. 1990.
64 J. Vieto, 'Foro Internacional. El café sostenible en América Latina. Situación actual de la oferta y tendencias', Centro de Inteligencia sobre Mercados Sostenibles, 25 Nov. 2003, Lima, Perú.

assets worth more than a million dollars.⁶⁵ The Centre for Coffee Cooperatives of the North (CECOCAFEN) comprises 12 organisations which have 2,637 members (709 women and 1,928 men). Both of these cooperatives have gained in strength because Fair Trade prices are considerably higher than the price on the New York exchange. For example, in the 2002/2003 cycle, when the average price of coffee in Nicaragua was US$68.93 dollars per *quintal*, CECOCAFEN and PRODECOOP paid US$110 and 104.76 per *quintal* respectively. The average prices paid by the commercial giants CISA and Atlantic were US$71.15 and 64.94 dollars per *quintal* respectively.⁶⁶ In times of crisis, thanks to Fair Trade's relatively captive customers, the difference between the Fair Trade price and the price on the New York exchange increases. In 2001, when the average price of coffee in Nicaragua was US$60.22 per *quintal* and CISA and Atlantic paid no more than US$56, the Union of Agricultural Cooperatives (UCA) paid US$87.15, PRODECOOP paid US$80.25, while CECOCAFEN averaged US$99.61 and COSATIN – a cooperative in Boaco – paid more than US$104.⁶⁷

To a great extent Nicaragua's participation in the Fair Trade and organic markets is rooted in the legacy of the two models of cooperativism. It is not just that farmers with small/medium holdings are obvious targets for Fair Trade, but rather that a series of ideological affinities has ensured that cooperativists, organised peasants and NGOs promoting them have worked together to boost Fair Trade – and this situation is clear in the case of coffee.⁶⁸ However, huge gaps in knowledge exist in other areas where the likelihood of the positive impact of agrarian reform is also detectable. That impact makes Nicaragua an exceptional case in Central America. It remains for future studies to investigate whether the diversification of agricultural production and the incursion into less conventional products for export – mangoes, pineapples, yucca – is also, at least partially, rooted in the legacy of the agrarian reform. With the onslaught of Monsanto and its control over seeds, as well as the importation of corn and other basic products for which national demand used to be satisfied with domestic production, another question is raised: to what extent has food sovereignty and the food security crisis been halted as a result of the structure of land tenure which in turn is a result of the agrarian reform?

There is no doubt that the trend towards inequality in land tenure and the threat of an abrupt seizure of large amounts of land to benefit the canal owners are threats to this more democratic system of land use. The banks and the local loan sharks are the principal agents of this move towards concentration. Their daily work takes place silently but constantly. In contrast, the business of the interoceanic canal, including the highly probable fact that in the end there will be no canal, would be a more sudden blow and of greater concern: it affects

65   PRODECOOP, 'Quinta asamblea de delegados. Informa a la Asamblea General', Nov. 2002.
66   Datos del Centro de Trámites de las Exportaciones (CETREX), Exportaciones de café por empresa. Cosecha 2002/2003.
67   Ibid., Cosecha 2001/2002.
68   R. Mendoza Vidaurre, 'La paradoja del café.

27 per cent of the territory of 13 municipalities and 23,847 farmers, most of them small or medium producers.[69] This tour de force of the counterreform would establish a perverse symmetry with the reform of the 1980s: while in the past the process of granting land was accelerated for military reasons, here the expropriations would be carried out for economic reasons. Land tenure would again be a dependent variable shaped by the macropolitics of a state that has another goal in mind. The peasants who were sacrificed on the altar of the revolution are now being asked to make another sacrifice in the name of progress or, more probably, for the sake of the greed of a group of politicians and investors. It is, at the very least, disconcerting and disheartening that the same organisation – the FSLN – is the one that has always demanded and still does, the one that gave and now seeks to take away. Nevertheless, the FSLN's actions make sense: to a great extent land tenure will again be determined by the requirements of geopolitics.

In the past, the progress that the FSLN had in mind revolved around one great landowner who guaranteed greater productivity and cohesion: the state. In the present, progress consists of ceding control of the area to large private landowners, a project that resembles the model developed by liberals in the 19th century. In both cases, the final results do not match the original plans. In the 1980s, peasant resistance and the war itself – which was fought by a discontented peasantry – were the real drivers of Nicaraguan exceptionalism, because they accelerated agrarian reform, pushing it closer to the Bukharin model and prolonging it beyond the revolutionary decade. This culminated in the Chamorro government's post-1990 reform, which was necessary to secure a lasting peace. Peasant actions made agrarian reform exceptional in terms of both infrastructure and superstructure, shaping land ownership and ideology. Nicaragua's participation in Fair Trade networks is built upon these achievements. At the time of writing, as the spectre of the interoceanic canal threatens to prompt a massive reconcentration of land ownership, it is once again the strength of peasant activism that has halted the trend towards greater inequality.

Bibliography

Baumeister, E. (1988) 'Transformaciones agrarias y revolución en Nicaragua', paper presented at the LASA conference, New Orleans, 17–19 Mar.

—— (2009) 'Treinta años de agricultura nicaragüense (1978–2008)', in S. Marti i Puig and D.W. Close (eds.), *Nicaragua y el FSLN [1979–2009] ¿Qué queda de la revolución?* (Barcelona).

Baumeister, E. and A. Fauné (1992) 'Elementos para una nueva estrategia gremial de la UNAG', paper presented at a seminar to Junta Directiva Nacional of UNAG, Managua, 8 June.

69 Network for Democracy and Local Development, 'What territories will the canal divide and what populations will be displaced?', *Envío*, no. 408, July 2015.

Centro de Investigaciones y Estudios de la Reforma Agraria (CIERA) (1989) *La reforma agraria en Nicaragua 1979–1989. Estrategia y políticas* (Managua).

— (1981) *Las clases sociales en el campo de Jinotega* (Managua).

Castoriadis, C. (1976) *La sociedad burocrática* (Barcelona).

Close, D. (2005) *Los años de Doña Violeta* (Managua).

Envío (1981) 'The Agrarian Reform Law in Nicaragua', (Aug.).

Fitzgerald, V. and A. Chamorro (1987) 'Las cooperativas en el proyecto de transición en Nicaragua', *Encuentro*, 30.

Grigsby, A. (2001)'Nicaragua: conflicto armado y políticas económicas y sociales', *Mimeo*.

González, M., (1994) 'Worker-owned coffee farms: the bitter and the sweet,' *Envío*, 154 (May).

Hernández, A. (2010) *Los señores del narco* (Grijalbo, México).

Kaimowitz, D. (1989) 'La planificación agropecuaria en Nicaragua: de un proceso de acumulación basado en el estado a la alianza estratégica con el campesino', in *El debate sobre la reforma agraria en Nicaragua. Transformación agraria y atención al campesinado en nueve años de reforma agraria (1979–1988)* (Managua).

Krauze, E. (2006) *Biografía del poder. Caudillos de la revolución mexicana (1910–1940)* (Barcelona).

Ley de Reforma Agraria, Decreto no. 782, Junta de Gobierno de Reconstrucción Nacional de la República de Nicaragua, 16 Oct. 1981.

López Baltodano, M. (2014) 'Truths about the canal concession all Nicaraguans should know', *Envío*, 390 (Jan.), www.envio.org.ni/articulo/4805 (accessed 28 Apr. 2019).

Maldidier, C. and P. Marchetti (1996) *El Campesino-Finquero y el potencial económico del campesinado nicaragüense* (Managua).

Marchetti, P. (1989) 'Semejanzas y diferencias en dos debates sobre el campesinado: la economía mixta y la vía al socialismo', *Encuentro*, 37/38: 35–45.

Mendoza Vidaurre, R. (1990) 'We erred to win…', *Envío*, 111 (Oct.), www.envio.org.ni/articulo/2637 (accessed 28 Apr. 2019).

— (2002) 'La paradoja del café: el gran negocio mundial y la peor crisis campesina: un estudio comparativo de la producción de las cadena del café en Nicaragua y en el Reino Unido', Instituto de Investigación y Desarrollo NITLAPAN (Managua).

Merlet, M. (2004) 'Fragilidad y límites de las reformas agrarias en América Central. Las enseñanzas de dos países: Honduras y Nicaragua', course for

'Gestión y Tenencia de la Tierra en Centroamérica', BIVICAT-RECCAT, FAUSAC, URACCAN, IRAM, París, Francia, 1 July–30 Sept.

— (2007) 'Regímenes de tenencia de la tierra, sistemas financieros y construcción de nuevas modalidades de gobernanza', paper presented at the international seminar 'Economías campesinas y sistemas financieros rurales', Foro latinoamericano y del Caribe sobre finanzas rurales (FOROLACFR), La Paz, Bolivia, July.

Merlet, M. and C. Maldidier (1987) 'El movimiento cooperativo, eje de la sobrevivencia de la revolución', *Encuentro*, 30.

Network for Democracy and Local Development (2015) 'What Territories will the canal divide and what populations will be displaced?', *Envío*, 408 (July), www.envio.org.ni/articulo/5052 (accessed 28 Apr. 2019)

PRODECOOP (2002) 'Quinta asamblea de delegados. Informa a la Asamblea General' (Nov.).

Rocha, J.L. and T. Martínez (2000) 'A country divided: relative defeats and victories', *Envío*, 232 (Nov.), http://www.envio.org.ni/articulo/1462 (accessed 28 Apr. 2019).

Romero, R. (2016) 'Campesinos marcharon contra el canal', *La Prensa*, 22 Apr., www.laprensa.com.ni/2016/04/22/nacionales/2022805-en-vivo-marcha-anticanal (accessed 28 Apr. 2019).

Saravia-Matus, S. and J. Saravia-Matus (2009) 'Agrarian reform: theory and practice. the Nicaraguan experience', *Encuentro*, 84.

Spoor, M. (1990) 'Rural employment and agrarian markets in transition: Nicaragua (1979–89)', *The Journal of Peasant Studies*, 17 (4).

Vieto, J., (2003) 'Foro Internacional. El café sostenible en América Latina. Situación actual de la oferta y tendencias', Centro de Inteligencia sobre Mercados Sostenibles, 25 Nov. (Lima, Perú).

Vilas, C. (1987) *Perfiles de la revolución sandinista* (Managua).

Viola, L. (1989(*The Best Sons of the Fatherland: Workers in the Vanguard of Soviet Collectivization* (Oxford).

— (1999) *Peasants Rebels under Stalin: Collectivization and the Culture of Peasant Resistance* (Oxford).

Wheelock, J. (1990) *La reforma agraria sandinista: 10 años de revolución en el campo* (Managua).

6. The difference the revolution made: decision-making in Liberal and Sandinista communities

Hilary Francis

On returning to office in 2007, the FSLN introduced a range of social programmes, which provided farm animals, roofing and other goods to poor rural families. At the local level these schemes were initially administered by the Consejos de Poder Ciudadano (Citizen Power Councils, or CPCs), community-level committees made up of local residents. Opponents allege that the CPCs brought centralisation, politicisation and unprecedented interference into Nicaraguans' daily lives.[1] Most commonly, the CPCs have been described as a means of establishing a clientelistic relationship between poor Nicaraguans and the FSLN.[2]

This chapter provides a detailed account of decision-making structures in two rural communities, where the evidence bears out many of the critics' charges. In both the communities surveyed here, social programmes have been specifically targeted at non-Sandinistas, and this targeting has led some traditional Liberal voters to vote Sandinista for the first time. (Historically most of the right-wing vote in Nicaragua has belonged to parties which identify as Liberal, so the word has a distinct connotation in the Nicaraguan context.) But while the poaching of Liberal voters occurred in both the communities described here, the FSLN's social programmes worked differently in the two villages. FSLN officials confronted two very different sets of social and political structures, a product of the two communities' diverse experience of Nicaragua's recent past. The revolution did make a difference, in the sense that the present is not the same as the past because of the events of 1979–90. It also created difference, in the sense that it caused previously similar communities to take very different ideological paths, and develop very different cultures of community decision-making.

1 S. Prado, 'The mettle of our civil society is going to be put to the test', *Envío*, no. 307, Feb. 2007; W. Miranda, 'Aprueban los gabinetes de Rosario Murillo', *Confidencial*, 21 Feb. 2013, R. Montoya, 'Contradiction and struggle under the leftist phoenix: rural Nicaragua at the thirtieth anniversary of the Revolution'.
2 K. Bay-Meyer, 'Do Ortega's citizen power councils empower the poor in Nicaragua?'; S. Prado, *Entre los CDM y los CPC*; J. Howard and L. Serra Vasquez, 'The changing spaces of local governance in Nicaragua'.

H. Francis, 'The difference the revolution made: decision-making in liberal and Sandinista communities', in H. Francis (ed.), *A Nicaraguan Exceptionalism? Debating the Legacy of the Sandinista Revolution* (London: University of London Press, 2019), pp. 127–44. License: CC-BY-NC-ND.

This chapter looks at two rural communities in the north of Nicaragua, less than 40 kilometres apart. One, here called 'El Junco', was a bastion of support for the Sandinista government during the 1980s. The other, 'Potrero', was a stronghold for the anti-Sandinista Contra forces. This chapter shows that the legacy of the revolution means that El Junco has a far stronger tradition of community decision-making than Potrero. However, the effect of this revolutionary legacy is not wholly positive. El Junco's stronger ties with the FSLN have meant that central government interference and control has been felt more keenly in El Junco than Potrero in the years since 2007.

Revolution, war and neoliberalism in El Junco and Potrero, 1979–2007

The inhabitants of El Junco first made contact with the Sandinistas in the late 1970s. Some community members were involved with progressive elements in the Catholic Church, and they attended religious retreats which led to their increased politicisation and opposition to the Somoza dictatorship. As a result of these contacts, religious meetings (with some political content) began to take place in the community. These were dangerous because they were forbidden by the Jueces de Mesta, which represented the Somoza state in the community. Nonetheless, those who were involved in this clandestine activity believe that this early organisation actually kept the community safe from harm:

> There were places where the Guardia carried out massacres because people hadn't been properly warned about what was going to happen ... and we were, because of the church. [We knew] that these weren't things you talk about with just anyone. We already knew ... if the Guardia came and asked about something [to say] 'we don't know anything about what's happening'.[3]

These religious meetings were regularly attended by 35 to 45 community members and on occasion passing Sandinista guerrillas also came to observe. This early activism provided a reference point for community activism after the revolution, and a foundation for the belief that, despite apparent difficulties and dangers, being organised actually kept the community safe. Much of the land in El Junco belonged to a single landowner who was a supporter of the Somoza regime. After the triumph of the revolution in July 1979, these lands were expropriated and a state farm was established there. In addition, a local Sandinista Defence Committee was formed. El Junco's current community leader remembers the work of organisation during the 1980s in glowing terms: 'We were united, with a single purpose: production and defence. At that time we were more organised than now ... there was more political consciousness.'[4] For others more actively involved in those first years, however, the picture was not so rosy: 'At the beginning it was difficult, because people were afraid. And

---

3 Interview, Juan Carlos Centeno, July 2015. All names have been changed.
4 Interview, Augusto Zeledón, July 2015.

then when rumours about the counterrevolution started, it was worse. The whole thing nearly fell apart because people were scared.'⁵

In spite of these difficulties, a strong tradition of local decision-making was forged in El Junco. In 1984 the state farm was made into a cooperative, which led to more support for devolved community decision-making. Training was provided in the theory and practice of democratic structures: how to hold a meeting and a vote; the standard roles and responsibilities for a committee's secretary, treasurer and chair. Most importantly, consistent financial support allowed community members the space and time to develop these structures. The new cooperative had a full time adviser from UNAG (Union Nacional de Agricultores y Ganaderos, a farmers' union) and the state also paid cooperative members' full-time salaries.⁶

In Potrero, the history of community decision-making in the 1970s and 1980s is harder to reconstruct. Those members who have lived in the village since the 1970s tend to be virulently anti-Sandinista and reluctant to recognise any benefit at all that might be associated with the revolution. This position was not always so entrenched: the village was home to a Sandinista 'political school' in the early 1960s, shortly after the FSLN was formed, and one of the village's more prominent families was actively involved in supporting the Sandinista guerrillas in the 1970s.⁷ In the period immediately after the revolution, local ties with the Sandinistas were broken. The reasons for this are complex, but the change was in part a result of anger about some of the land confiscations that took place in the area, as well as a feeling that local support for the Sandinistas had not been adequately repaid.⁸ As early as 1980 some community members had begun to support the fledgling Contra movement.⁹

In Potrero, as in El Junco, a cooperative was established in 1984. However, this new structure did nothing to embed a local commitment to community decision-making. Community member Alejandro Palacios explains:

> In 1984, 1985 there was an armed collective here. They grabbed people from different places and they put them in there, armed, to protect themselves ... The government just said to the evacuees that came from other communities 'here's the farm, get in there'. And that's how it happened, but there wasn't any kind of concretely delegated organisation there, no. 'Get in there' and that was it. And that's why there were problems with the agrarian reform, things weren't organised well ... Then when the war got more intense they left the land. Nobody stayed there. [They were] a bit scared.¹⁰

---

5   Interview, Juan Carlos Centeno, July 2015.
6   Interview, Augusto Zeledón, July 2015.
7   Interview, Gregorio Flores, May 2012. The information about the Sandinista political school comes from a secondary source, but citing it here would reveal the location of 'Potrero'.
8   Ibid.
9   Ibid.
10 Interview, Alejandro Palacios, July 2015.

Palacios was imprisoned by the Sandinistas for several years in the 1980s because of his support for the Contras in Potrero, so his testimony is in some ways problematic, since he was probably involved in organising the violence that made the settlers 'a bit scared'. It may be that the cooperative in Potrero had more government support than this account suggests. Even if it did, it is clear that no tradition of community organisation was established, because the settlers came from elsewhere and were quickly forced to leave the area. The Contras and their supporters had their own clandestine organisation in the community, but these structures were more hierarchical and solely concerned with the organisation of the war effort. After 1990, the community began to organise and a committee was established to manage the maintenance of the water supply, a new initiative supported by a US charity. Still, there was nothing in this post-war experience equivalent to the time and space residents of El Junco had gained from the revolution – time and space that allowed them to develop their own tradition of community organisation.

In El Junco, the community's decision-making structures were challenged by the transition which followed the Sandinistas' defeat in the 1990 elections. These structures were now charged with working with, and for, a right-wing, anti-Sandinista government. El Junco resident Famnuel Centeno explains:

> It was a bit difficult, because of the stress of the transition ... 1990–6
> was a moment of pressure, of nerves because people didn't know what was
> going to happen ... people wanted to leave, to distance themselves from
> [the community structures] because they said 'if I take part they're going to
> say I'm a Liberal and I'll put myself in danger, they're going to mark me out'.[11]

Despite these fears, the community in El Junco started to organise again from about 1993. The new effort was prompted by intervention from the (Sandinista) municipal government, which was trying to revive the cooperative movement. As for so many Sandinista-allied movements in these years, the end to the war removed the need for absolute unquestioning unity, and multiple fault lines and divisions began to appear. In the 1980s El Junco had one cooperative, but in the organisational revival of the mid 1990s three different cooperatives were formed. One comprised native-born community members, another was for settlers who had arrived in the 1980s. A third cooperative for women was subsequently formed, because they felt their voices were not being heard in either of the existing structures. These divisions notwithstanding, the community remained overwhelmingly Sandinista, and this shaped local decision-making even after the Sandinistas lost the 1990 elections:

> During the 16 years of neoliberalism they tried to involve more Liberals,
> rather than Sandinistas [in decision-making]. [But] there's very few of them
> [in the community], so in the end they included one or two Liberals in these
> bodies, but the rest were Sandinistas. So the Sandinistas always dominated.[12]

---

11 Interview, Famnuel Centeno, July 2015.
12 Interview, Famnuel Centeno, July 2015.

This dominance at the community level was facilitated by the fact that El Junco was part of a municipality which voted Sandinista; in fact, the municipal government has always been Sandinista. Similarly, Liberal Potrero was part of a municipality that voted Liberal at every election from 1990 (when municipal elections were first introduced) until 2012, when the FSLN achieved an unprecedented dominance in the municipal elections (amid allegations of widespread fraud).[13] This changing relationship with their respective municipal authorities would become crucial for both communities when the FSLN returned to power.

'They don't think any of it's important': community organisation in Potrero since 2007

When Daniel Ortega and the FSLN returned to government in January 2007, the new administration made community organisation an absolute priority. The third decree issued by Ortega on his first day in office made sweeping changes to Nicaragua's structures for local governance. Decree 03-2007 announced the government's intention to 'facilitate genuine participation of citizens and citizen democracy via direct democracy'.[14] This participation would be organised by the CPCs which comprised 16 members, each with a particular responsibility. As well as providing a focus for community deliberations, the councils were to oversee the management of the FSLN's social programmes. A key component of these was the Bono Productivo Alimentario (or the Productive Food Bonus), known colloquially in Nicaragua as the '*bono*'. It comprised a grant of a pig or cow, chickens and seeds. It has been an important component in the FSLN government's attempts to reduce poverty in Nicaragua, but it is also a tool for winning over anti-Sandinistas and increasing support for the FSLN.[15]

From the outset, this effort to change Nicaragua's political landscape was vigorously resisted by the Sandinistas' opponents. In 2008, before beginning research in Potrero for the first time, I visited the Liberal mayor who led the municipal government that governs the town. Press articles about the failure of the CPCs were prominently displayed his office walls. I was given the name of the 'coordinator' in Potrero, Alejandro Palacios, who was in fact the coordinator of the Junta Comunal (or community council) which had operated in the village before the Sandinistas returned to power. Palacios told me himself that there was no CPC in Potrero, but it subsequently transpired this was not the case, but that its coordinator was a Sandinista from another community who rarely visited Potrero. In 2009 I carried out interviews with every household in Potrero, but found only one person who would admit to being part of the 16-member CPC.[16]

13 'La violencia electoral en Nicaragua empezó en 2012', *La Prensa*, 19 Nov. 2017.
14 *La Gaceta: Diario Oficial*, no. 7, 10 Jan. 2007, 246.
15 P. Kester, *Informe evaluativo (2007–2008): Programa Productivo Alimentario (PPA) Hambre Cero*.
16 Interview, Marvin Talavera, Mar. 2009. This does not mean that no one else had agreed to be listed a member of the CPC, at least on paper. Rather, it is indicative of the stigma attached

There was considerable underlying tension in the community because of the strength of anti-Sandinista feeling, and for that reason the FSLN's political structures were practically non-existent. Despite this, the FSLN's social programmes functioned reasonably well. In 2009 five women from the community benefited from the *bono*. The programme requires that participants have at least one *manzana* of their own land where they can keep the animals, which excludes the poorest.[17] In general, therefore, the beneficiaries were certainly not well off, but equally not the poorest in the community either: one ran a small shop and another had some support from relatives resident in the United States. The considerable stigma attached to cooperation with the Sandinistas meant that only the more confident community members felt able to take advantage of the programme in its early years. The reluctance of the community also meant that benefits often passed through familial networks – one of the first beneficiaries was a Liberal from a Liberal family, but she was also the niece by marriage of the Sandinistas' municipal political secretary.

Although control of these social programmes fell to the Sandinistas, it was clear that political control in the community still remained in the hands of the Liberals in 2007–12. In rural Nicaragua, community leaders have significant power, because a letter with their signature is required for all kinds of contacts with the municipal government, including requests for funds or for permission to chop down trees for construction. As long as the municipal government remained Liberal, these kinds of requests continued to go to Palacios, rather than to the CPC coordinator. In 2009, Palacios made it clear to me that he would take immediate (unspecified) action if the CPC coordinator 'presumed' to give anyone permission to chop down trees in Potrero.[18] Such fears were certainly misplaced, since the Liberal municipal government had no intention of dealing with the CPC.

According to the leaders of the Junta Comunal (the Liberal-era community council which remained the de facto authority until the Sandinistas took the municipality in the elections of 2012), the decision-making structures of Potrero were fully democratic between 1990 and 2012: the committee was elected by the whole community and regular meetings were held. In reality though, community participation was of a limited and particular kind. In the house-to-house survey I carried out in 2009, respondents were asked how community leaders were chosen, and whether regular meetings took place. These questions were most often met with blank stares and professions of ignorance, sometimes coupled with the response that the Junta Comunal handled those things.

---

to being associated with Sandinista programmes in Potrero. Gladys Hernández, who is cited below, was also involved briefly in the first iteration of the CPC, but she did not admit this to me until 2015.

17 Kester, *Informe evaluativo*, 15. A manzana is equal to 6987.4 square metres.
18 Informal conversation, Alejandro Palacios, Mar. 2009.

Despite this weak democratic structure, the community was more than capable of acting together in pursuit of shared goals. One evening in 2009, I happened to mention to Palacios that I was using a GPS to make a map of the community. He asked if it could be used to measure the pipes used for the community's water supply as the municipality had asked the Junta to supply information about the exact quantity of pipe needed for a replacement. I said it could and we agreed to take measurements the next day. At 7.30 am the next morning I woke up to find that most of Potrero's male population had assembled, with machetes, ready to help clear the brush that had grown around the pipes so that we could take accurate measurements. The efficiency of the operation was particularly surprising to me: I was more accustomed to the community structures of El Junco, which were certainly more democratic, but where a similar water project had been held up for years, in part because of a lack of action from some community members. Many of the men from Potrero fought with the Contras during the war, and the Contra forces were subject to a strict disciplinary regime, far more absolute and hierarchical than the equivalent structures of the Sandinista army.[19] It seems likely, therefore, that the legacy of that experience partially explains this greater level of hierarchy – and efficiency – in community activity in Potrero.

In 2012 the uneasy coexistence of CPC-led social programmes and political control by the Liberal Junta Comunal came to an abrupt end. The Sandinistas won the municipal government elections in the municipality for the first time since 1990. Potrero is one of the most Liberal communities in this predominantly Liberal municipality, and on the day of the elections there was substantial conflict. A dispute arose because some of the ballot boxes containing Liberal votes were allegedly discarded in the community before the rest of the boxes had been taken to the municipal centre. There was little doubt in Potrero that the ballot boxes had been dumped. One resident who sympathised with the Sandinistas conceded that this had happened, but argued that it did not matter, because the count took place in Potrero before the votes were taken into town.[20] Community members forcibly tried to prevent the ballot boxes from leaving and the electoral officials had to be escorted away by riot police.

For Alejandro Palacios the presence of riot police is clear proof that the election itself was fraudulent:

> They put the riot police onto us ... to intimidate us. They didn't actually hit us – you can't say things happened if they didn't – but they intimidated people ... And when people see these guys in uniform, it makes them nervous

---

19 This difference is frequently noted by former Contra combatants. In an interview for a different study one combatant recalled that during the war 'we heard on the radio the way a [Sandinista] subaltern would respond with swear words to his superior – "why don't you go in yourself you son of whatever" – when he told him to go ... When he said to him "go through the entrance, Franco" [the response would be] "why don't you come here and go through yourself?" In the Contra you didn't see that.' Interview, Santiago Estrada, May 2012.

20 Nora Rodríguez, informal conversation, July 2015.

> ... this type of repression. Why did we see repression? Because when things are legal it doesn't have to be like that ... if they won they won, but they won legally, and there's nothing to do about it. We weren't very happy about it, because they snatched the election from us.[21]

One might expect to see even greater levels of conflict and polarisation in Potrero as a result of the conflict over the election – but this is not quite what happened. A new community leader was named: Efraín Flores, a Sandinista who had recently moved to the village. Now that the municipality head was Sandinista, Flores became the key conduit between the community and the municipal government, taking on the role previously occupied by Palacios. Although the stalwart anti-Sandinistas were further alienated by the events of 2012, others were won over by the Sandinistas' ongoing social programmes. At the same time, the climate of fear and stigma that prevented many from cooperating with the Sandinista programmes began to abate a little. Gladys Hernández, who had briefly been a member of the CPC back in 2007, began to participate in the FSLN's structures again in 2015. She reflected on the change:

> [In 2007] it scared me. I did it for a bit, but it scared me. Sometimes you take part not because you're a member of that party [the Sandinistas], but so you can help the community, but they got me scared and they said this, that and the other ... But no, thank god ... it's not like that anymore. People have got used to the government that's in power and you don't hear that sort of talk any more.[22]

Of course, tensions have not disappeared completely: the continuing delicacy of such matters is evident in the lengths to which Hernández goes to avoid using the word 'Sandinista' in her account of her involvement. But even the hard-core Liberals concede that the Sandinista programmes have led some people in Potrero to change their political allegiance. For the stalwarts the shift is difficult to comprehend:

> It's something I don't understand. Because I've always been a Liberal and I'm still a Liberal because I don't see the sense in changing ... it makes no sense, to change yourself to support a man because of something that isn't real, that they give you from other countries. He [the Sandinista leader] is just the conduit, he just signs off on it.[23]

In Potrero it is clear that Sandinista social programmes have been used as a political tool – and a very effective one – to win support for the FSLN. But what of the critics' other charges?[24] Is there a greater level of top-down control

---

21 Interview, Alejandro Palacios, July 2015.
22 Interview, Gladys Hernández, July 2015.
23 Interview, Ernesto Rugama, July 2015.
24 I am referring here to the criticisms of the CPC cited in the introduction to this chapter: Prado, 'The mettle of our civil society'; Miranda, 'Aprueban los gabinetes de Rosario Murillo'; Montoya, 'Contradiction and struggle'; Bay-Meyer, 'Do Ortega's citizen power councils empower the poor in Nicaragua?'; Prado, *Entre los CDM y los CPC*; Howard and Serra Vasquez, 'The changing spaces of local governance'.

in community level governance? Are decision-making structures interfering in people's daily lives in an unprecedented way?

In Potrero, the answer is mainly no. This is partly because the government has changed the format of community structures so many times. In 2013 the CPCs were discarded in favour of the Gabinetes de la Familia, Comunidad y Vida (or Cabinets for the Family, Community and Life).[25] Critics have voiced a particular concern that the new Gabinetes would have the power to interfere in private family life.[26] In both Potrero and El Junco this fear was misplaced because by 2015 the Gabinetes existed in name only and had little or no impact on how the communities were governed. In fact, at that stage, decision-making in both communities was in practice coordinated by the Comités de Liderazgo Sandinista (or Sandinista Leadership Committees, CLS). These committees have existed since 2007, but in both communities by 2015 they had taken on the functions originally charged to the CPCs: they allocated the *bono* and the zinc roofing distributed by the government, and they acted as intermediaries between the communities and the municipal government. Although the CPCs were always dominated by Sandinistas in both communities, the government was at least rhetorically committed to promoting the CPCs as apolitical organisations which valued the participation of all.[27] By 2015, the de facto situation was that all key decisions were made by an openly and exclusively Sandinista body.

Nonetheless, in Potrero in 2015 there was little evidence of absolute Sandinista control. The existence of a strong anti-Sandinista constituency meant that even though the political secretary of the CLS controlled the flow of goods and services to the community, he still remained extremely cautious in his dealings with community members. All other interviewees in Potrero and El Junco had a litany of complaints about the nature of local governance structures, the inadequacy of other community members' participation and the mistakes made by regional and national government officials. In contrast, Potero's political secretary, Efraín Flores, displayed a tight-lipped, forced enthusiasm for everything and everybody. 'To do this work here you have to be everyone's friend,' he explained. 'I have to make little jokes, all that, these people like me a lot.'[28] As both a newcomer and a Sandinista, Flores' position was tenuous. During moments of crisis, like the elections of November 2012, his power could be backed up by riot police and the Sandinista state's monopoly of violence. Most of the time, however, Flores was on his own, and the precariousness of Sandinista control meant that he had to tread very carefully.

---

25 'Gabinetes de la Familia, la Comunidad y la Vida profundizarán protagonismo y productividad de la Persona'.
26 J. Jiménez, 'El Código de la Familia es el último eslabón de un proyecto de control social', *Envío*, no. 398, May 2015.
27 Héctor M. Cruz, 'Los CPC en Nicaragua: un análisis sobre la articulación, el diseño y la implementación del Poder Ciudadano'..
28 Interview, Efraín Flores, July 2015.

The Sandinistas' tenuous control was partly a result of the persistence of anti-Sandinista feeling in Potrero. It also had to do with the community's limited interest in, and experience of, democratic decision-making and participation. In the 2009 house-to-house survey, questions about community-wide meetings prompted more blank stares. The Junta Comunal was in charge at the time and Alejandro Palacios insisted that meetings did take place, just as Efraín Flores was adamant that they were happening under the Sandinistas in 2015.[29] The problem was that, in the main, community members had little interest in such activities. Gladys Hernández feels the fault lies with the community itself:

> They do invite the whole community [to meetings], but it's difficult to get the whole community together ... They say it's a vice of Nicaraguans, that they invite us to something and we don't consider it important. We don't take things seriously. I'm a health *brigadista* and it's the same ... they tell me to call a meeting of the community, because they're going to come and give a talk on health and the same happens. There's no support from people, they don't think any of it's important.[30]

This lack of participation makes it difficult for decision-making structures in Potrero to have much power. Equally, though, there is no real expectation that community members have a right to be consulted. This lack of a democratic tradition perhaps partially explains the surprisingly muted reaction to power shifts in the community since 2012. In El Junco, in contrast, the revolution left a legacy of democratic participation and community decision-making, and as a result, the community's interaction with the FSLN government since 2007 has been very different indeed.

'The day the *asambleas* are lost, it will be the end of the world': community organisation in El Junco since 2007

In 2015 interviewees in both El Junco and Potrero had a strong perception that their communities were apathetic and participation in decision-making was dwindling. For Augusto Zeledón, the political secretary in El Junco, the change was obvious but the cause was obscure:

> I ask myself 'what's happening?' There's a decline in the social programmes and everything. The cooperatives too. They invite all 20 members [to a meeting] and 10 or 11 come. The other [cooperative] has 40 members, so 18 or 20 come.[31]

There was an acute sense in El Junco that participation was falling and people did not care, but in relative terms the tradition of community decision-making was still extremely strong. By most standards the 50 per cent attendance rate that Zeledón reports is not at all bad, particularly since the large number of

---

29   Interview, Alejandro Palacios, July 2015. Interview, Efraín Flores, July 2015.
30   Interview, Gladys Hernández, July 2015.
31   Interview, Augusto Zeledón, July 2015.

organisations in the community meant that meetings were frequent and the burden of participation was high:

> [People] don't participate like they did before. Because there are lots of meetings, that's the issue. There are meetings of the cooperative, meetings for the school, meetings for community work, to deal with problems with the water supply ... and in the end it's the same people in the community who are going to meetings two or three times a week. So it doesn't work, people get sick of it and they have lots of farm work to do. Immigration is affecting this too. Because of the [coffee] rust problem a huge number of people are going to work in Managua or abroad.[32]

Growing apathy was also related to the passage of time. For the older generation of community leaders, all of whom are devout Sandinistas who lived through the war in El Junco, the experience of the 1980s created an unshakeable commitment to community work and to the FSLN, one that is not always shared by their sons and daughters. In recent years, the FSLN has tried to ensure that the younger generation takes up positions of leadership at the local level, but this policy has failed. This is partly because most young people do not have the time nor the financial resources to carry out this voluntary work. Community members in El Junco, however, believe that it is also because younger people don't have the same commitment to political work, because they did not live through the revolution and the war.

> The government wanted to revoke the community structures and put in young people. It didn't work out for them. Young people have a different way of thinking. [They care about] fun, discos. And that doesn't leave time for community work. It didn't work out for them. So who was left? The leaders are all about 50, I'm 52 for example. For a young leader it's difficult, much too difficult. They don't have that revolutionary consciousness. That revolutionary *mística* that one gets, once it's got you, you never get rid of it ... It's a consciousness that's born in the trenches, born from the war.[33]

The younger people agreed with this assessment. Rafaela Castillo, who is a member of the CLS and coordinator of the Sandinista Youth in the community, explained that 'We've tried to involve more young people, but the young people like having fun rather than serious things.'[34] Nonetheless, for a significant minority of this younger generation, community activism continued to matter, and the legacy of the revolution informed and shaped their involvement too:

> At the beginning I was scared to work ... in this kind of organisation, because I was working with people who had lived it [the revolution], who had felt it, and I didn't, I was someone who had just heard about it second hand. But we started working, and I would ask questions about what happened, and I got more involved that way ... all the things that they lived through, I made them my own. Made it so it was as though I had lived it too.[35]

32 Interview, Famnuel Centeno, July 2015.
33 Interview, Augusto Zeledón, July 2015.
34 Interview, Rafaela Castillo, July 2015.
35 Ibid.

The importance of this legacy, even for the younger generation, is clear in the community's attitude to *asambleas*, or community-wide meetings. In spite of widespread concern about declining participation, and multiple problems related to the practical functioning of decision-making structures, all members considered the *asambleas* to be extremely important. Famnuel Centeno was not directly involved in the CLS and he was a child during the 1980s. Nonetheless, he considers the survival of the *asambleas* to be paramount:

> The *asambleas* have a massive impact in the community. Because it's the only way that people get information, it's the only means we have to identify or discuss problems in the community. Or [talk] about new projects, about new initiatives. Imagine a community where there are no *asambleas*, or where there are no meetings, how would the people of the community get information? They're indispensable, I think the *asambleas* will never never ... the day the *asambleas* are lost it will be the end of the world.[36]

Because of this deeper engagement with politics, the actions of the FSLN government have had a much greater impact in El Junco, not all of it positive. Greater community activity means that government directives can have a considerable, often unforeseen, effect on the delicate political balance within the community. In July 2015, shortly before the interviews for this study were carried out, the FSLN government distributed the latest tranche of zinc roofing and *bono* in El Junco and Potrero. In both communities a list of beneficiaries was drawn up by the political secretary of the CLS – and in both places officials from Managua came to check their choices and made changes to those lists. In Potrero this led to some grumbling about the fact that the Sandinistas 'lied', and political secretary Efrain Flores conceded (in a characteristically mild way) that the changes had caused him some problems.[37] In El Junco, in contrast, the changes prompted open warfare between CLS members.

In El Junco the CLS political secretaries are the aforementioned Zeledón and Amada Acuña.[38] Acuña and Zeledón had a considerable disagreement over the changes to the list. Zeledón suspected that Acuña had helped the visitors from Managua make the changes, a charge she vehemently denied:

> None of them listened to me, not the ones from the mayor's office or the ones from Managua ... They didn't use guides ... So one day I went to the mayor's office and I said to them 'please explain to the political secretary [Zeledón] that it wasn't me who accompanied you, that I didn't have anything to do with the plan techo stuff, or the *bono* ... it's not my fault'.[39]

In fact, for Acuña, the changes made were perfectly logical. The beneficiaries on the new list 'are poorer, and there are some people who have too many animals ... maybe they saw they were a bit thin and so they think if they can't even look

---

36 Interview, Famnuel Centeno, July 2015.
37 Interview, Efraín Flores, July 2015. Interview, Ernesto Rugama, July 2015.
38 Each CLS has one male and one female secretary, although in both El Junco and Potrero it is the male political secretary who is the overall coordinator on the committee.
39 Interview, Amada Acuña, July 2015.

after those ones ...'⁴⁰ Zeledón rejects this, but the conflict is not really about the specific beneficiaries. Rather, it has to do with the question of who has the power to make these decisions. For Zeledón, the incident was a violation of his local authority, one that has affected his relationship with the local community and the FSLN officials he reports to:

> I've questioned this a lot with the *compañeros* from the government in [local town] who coordinate my work. Because if I go to my community and I make a list and a certain *compañero* appears, that *compañero* trusts that I'm going to sort it out, but those that have a say after me are going over my head. I'm asking for leadership. I end up looking like a liar. If they're going to do it, let them do it but don't involve me. [The community] blames me and it's not my fault.⁴¹

Acuña has attempted to get Zeledón removed from his position, but she was told that unless he chooses to leave he cannot be removed before the end of his term. Clearly, such open conflict within the community's key governance structure is problematic. Substantial concern also exists in the wider community that the CLS is running things, rather than the Gabinete, which ostensibly replaced the CPC:

> They haven't let the *Gabinete de la Familia* work in the way it really should ... I think they're politicising the whole situation. So that information from the Sandinista party is passed directly to the CLS, and it isn't passed to the Gabinete. So it's the CLS that acts, and not the Gabinete. Even though they say that the Sandinista structure, the structure for the CLS, is only for political matters and the other is for community projects, information from the party is always passed to the CLS and not the Gabinete, so they haven't really given them the opportunity to take control. Because the water project shouldn't be ... it's a community project ... so it should be managed by the Gabinete. The solar panels project, the electricity project, the road repairs ... the CLS shouldn't have anything to do with it, it should be the responsibility of the Gabinete.⁴²

Famnuel Centeno sees this structural change as evidence of a wider, creeping politicisation of community decision-making, and believes that this shift has caused increasing apathy more widely:

> I think it's because in every meeting they bring politics into it ... at the moment everything comes via the CLS and the CLS is required to bring it up in every *asamblea* ... do an introduction on what the FSLN is, the projects of the FSLN ... If I put myself in the shoes of a Liberal ... if I was a Liberal and I'm in an *asamblea* I'm not going to like it that they keep going on about the Frente.⁴³

It may be that the present government's approach alienates Liberal voters, but it is also true that these divisions are deep-seated and that Liberals have never

40 Ibid.
41 Interview, Augusto Zeledón, July 2015.
42 Interview, Famnuel Centeno, July 2015.
43 Ibid.

participated much in El Junco's community structures. In 2009, when I was making a map of El Junco, I discovered that there was a whole (Liberal) sector of the community that I had never heard of or visited, despite living there for a year in 2004–5. A friend, born in 1976, gave me directions for the route down a particular lane. He got this information second-hand: even though he had lived in the community his entire life, and the path was less than half a mile from his house, he had never walked that way because it was adjacent to the property of a prominent anti-Sandinista landowner. Just as the tradition of participation in Junco is a legacy of the revolution, so too are these extremely entrenched divisions. Just as the passage of time has diminished political commitment in the area, it has also gradually reduced this political polarisation. Nonetheless, participation in community decision-making is so intimately connected with the legacy of the revolution and the war that it is difficult to see how a truly apolitical structure could exist, regardless of the central government's approach.

The strength of local decision-making in El Junco is a result of the community's long experience of organising, and a widespread recognition that this kind of work is valuable and important. Critics of FSLN policies since 2007 have characterised the new social programmes and community committees as an attempt to build a clientelist state, and it is clear that the diffusion of benefits has won the Sandinistas some new supporters. However, it is also clear that the real backbone of the system – and the reason for its relative success in El Junco – was the work of particular individuals with a long-standing commitment to the revolution. The national government relied upon the voluntary work of committed individuals who were not paid for their contributions. That reliance has limited the government's ability to run a truly centralised, top-down system of governance: any attempt to overrule local leaders results in considerable disagreement and pushback, as it did in El Junco in 2015.

The mechanisms of government control were starker, and more sinister, in relation to individuals who were directly employed by the state. One close friend in El Junco refused to talk on tape about the village's governance structures, even though he knew that all names and locations would be changed. He was employed as a teacher in the village and he was afraid he might lose his job if it was discovered he had said anything negative about Zeledón. While the community's volunteer leaders were more than happy to criticise their superiors and each other, those directly employed by the state have to be much more cautious. Alejandra Martínez ran a nursery school in the village; 20 children attend, the minimum number required for a nursery to qualify for state support. When another community member attempted to start another nursery school, thereby threatening Martínez's quota, Zeledón vetoed the new nursery, thereby protecting Martínez's income. Understandably, Martínez was thus reluctant to say anything against the political secretary. The caution demonstrated by state employees is amply justified: some individuals have been penalised for disagreeing with government policy. 'Not long ago a teacher lost her job [in a nearby town] because she spoke out, brought up situations where she didn't agree with the government. And her criticisms made sense, but they were complaints and so ... [she was fired].'⁴⁴

There were several different dynamics at play in the relationship between the Sandinista government and the residents of El Junco. Some villagers, previously Liberal voters, had begun to vote for the FSLN as a result of the current government's social programmes. This alliance is a clear example of a clientelistic relationship, but not all the links between El Junco and the FSLN government can be understood in terms of pure clientelism. For state employees, the restrictions on freedom of expression suggest a relationship that is too coercive to be described as mere clientelism. On the other hand, the community's many committed Sandinistas have a relationship with the state that is as much ideological as it is material. Community members in El Junco have contributed considerable time and effort to organisation because of a sense of civic duty, ideological commitment and a desire to continue the revolutionary project.⁴⁵ This kind of commitment is particularly notable among the older generation. Famnuel Centeno is one of six children, all of whom are professionals and university graduates. His parents, who did not learn to read and write until after the revolution, are stalwart Sandinistas:

> My parents will never change [their support for the FSLN]. Never ever, whatever happens. And up to a point I think that maybe they are right. Because if the FSLN had not existed, none of their children would have gone to school. I don't know what would have happened. We would be peasants or working on a hacienda somewhere, but we wouldn't have been able to go to school. We wouldn't have a house either because we wouldn't have anywhere to build it. I don't know what would have happened.⁴⁶

As Rocha and Soto's contributions to this volume attest, the revolution failed to provide permanent access to land and opportunities for many of the desperately poor Nicaraguans who needed it. Even in El Junco this process was by no means as clear-cut as local collective memory might imply: community members only gained individual plots when the revolutionary-era cooperative was broken up in 1990. There is no doubt that it is the granting of individual plots, rather than participation in the collective, which is the pivotal moment celebrated in local memories. The actual chronology is elided so that land ownership is seen as the primary benefit of the revolution, as a reward given for the community members' many sacrifices during the years of war. Even as local memory rewrites some of the crucial elements of this recent past, this constructed ideal of the FSLN's role belies a deeper truth. For many Sandinistas in El Junco, their experience of the revolution was transformative. It forged an unshakeable commitment to the

---

44 Interview, Famnuel Centeno, July 2015.
45 Scholars focusing on other regions in Latin America have debated the relationship between clientelism and ideology, and the question of whether these dynamics are always mutually exclusive, but the scholarship on Nicaragua has not yet addressed such questions. D.J. Epstein, 'Clientelism versus ideology: problems of party development in Brazil'; M. Coppedge, 'The dynamic diversity of Latin American party systems'.
46 Interview, Famnuel Centeno, July 2015.

FSLN. The very strength of this commitment is a cause for concern: it allows the FSLN government to become increasingly autocratic without any fear of reproach from their core supporters.

This revolutionary legacy also powers a robust tradition of community organisation, although it could certainly be argued that this tradition has its limits. One standard measure of community democracy, Arnstein's ladder of citizen participation, ranks such structures according to the amount of power they have: are they truly autonomous? Do they have the capacity to make their decisions felt at higher levels of authority?[47] In El Junco, the answer to these questions has always been a resounding 'no'. In both the first and second stages of the revolution, being organised never meant genuine, bottom-up democracy. That state of affairs continues. In 2017, as a result of a decision reached in an *asamblea*, the community sent a united plea to the municipal government for much-needed improvements to the only access road, but the request went unheeded. And as the conflict over the distribution of the *bono* in 2015 clearly shows, there is little that the community can do when the central authorities choose to overrule local decisions.

Why, then, does the community place so much value on the *asambleas* and other aspects of this culture of participation and 'being organised'? These attitudes are certainly not universal. In 2012 Birgit Kvernflaten noted the lacklustre approach of local residents towards a municipal *cabildo* (or municipal assembly) in rural Matagalpa. The event was poorly attended and nobody asked questions. 'Some sit in the front and applaud hard', one of her informants told her, 'but only because they got their project funded.'[48] El Junco residents' commitment to being organised is driven partly by the fact that it brings clear benefits not directly related to the state. As Rocha notes, a capacity for participation and organisation makes it much easier to integrate into global Fair Trade networks,[49] and El Junco's cooperatives have strong links with national and international buyers for their Fair Trade, organic coffee. Equally, as Cooper argues, being organised brings benefits in the form of links with national and international NGOs.[50] Compared to Potrero, El Junco has a much broader range of links to such organisations, which have brought a variety of projects to the community.

Although local community members certainly recognise the material benefits that being organised provides, it would be a mistake to reduce these traditions to some kind of rational choice or profit-seeking urge. The generational divide which exists in community work, and the greater involvement of the generation that lived through the revolution and the Contra War, makes it clear that this particular heritage has created a particular way of doing things in El Junco. That

47 S. Arnstein, 'A ladder of citizen participation', 216–24.
48 B. Kvernflaten, 'Conflicting health interventions: participation in health in rural Nicaragua', 308.
49 See the chapter by Jose Luis Rocha in this book.
50 See the chapter by David Cooper in this book.

same generational divide makes it difficult to predict how these local traditions will fare with the passing of time – it is certainly possible that community participation is dependent upon the activism of the revolutionary generation. With its endless meetings, petty fiefdoms and often-vicious infighting, El Junco is no revolutionary utopia. Nevertheless, a commitment to local democracy has survived here, despite the upheaval of the war, the uncertainty and poverty of the neoliberal years and the multiple interventions of the FSLN. This culture of participation is far from perfect but, for now, it does deserve to be called exceptional.

Bibliography

Arnstein, S. (1969) 'A ladder of citizen participation', *Journal of the American Institute of Planners*, 35 (4): 216–24.

Bay-Meyer, K. (2013) 'Do Ortega's Citizen Power Councils empower the poor in Nicaragua?', *Polity*, 45 (3).

Coppedge, M. (1998) 'The dynamic diversity of Latin American party systems', *Party Politics*, 4 (4).

Cruz, H.M. (2009) 'Los CPC en Nicaragua: un análisis sobre la articulación, el diseño y la implementación del Poder Ciudadano'. Paper prepared for delivery at the 2009 Congress of the Latin American Studies Association, Rio de Janeiro, Brazil, 11–14 June (available at http://hemcruz.googlepages.com/LosCPCsenNicaragua-workingdoc.docx).

El 19 Digital (2013) 'Gabinetes de la Familia, la Comunidad y la Vida profundizarán protagonismo y productividad de la Persona', *El 19 Digital*, 5 Jan., www.el19digital.com/articulos/ver/titulo:7414-organizan-gabinetes-comunitarios-en-nicaragua (accessed 29 Apr. 2019).

Epstein, D.J. (2009), 'Clientelism versus ideology: problems of party development in Brazil', *Party Politics*, 15 (3).

La Gaceta (2007) *Diario Oficial*, 7, 10 Jan.

Howard, J., and L. Serra Vasquez (2011) 'The changing spaces of local governance in Nicaragua', *Bulletin of Latin American Research*, 30 (1).

Jiménez, J. (2015) 'El Código de la Familia es el último eslabón de un proyecto de control social', *Envío*, 398 (May), www.envio.org.ni/articulo/4993 (accessed 29 Apr. 2019).

Kester, P. (2009) *Informe evaluativo (2007–2008): Programa Productivo Alimentario (PPA) Hambre Cero* (Embajada del Reino de los Países Bajos).

Kvernflaten, B. (2012) 'Conflicting health interventions: participation in health in rural Nicaragua', *Forum for Development Studies*, 44 (2): 301–22.

La Prensa (2017) 'La violencia electoral en Nicaragua empezó en 2012', 19 Nov., https://www.laprensa.com.ni/2017/11/19/politica/2333211-la-violencia-electoral-nicaragua-empezo-2008 (accessed 29 Apr. 2019).

Miranda, W. (2013) 'Aprueban los gabinetes de Rosario Murillo', *Confidencial*, 21 Feb., www.confidencial.com.ni/archivos/articulo/10385/aprueban-los-gabinetes-de-rosario-murillo (accessed 29 Apr. 2019).

Montoya, R. (2013) 'Contradiction and struggle under the leftist phoenix: rural Nicaragua at the thirtieth anniversary of the Revolution', in J.L. Burrell and E. Moodie (eds.), *Central America in the New Millennium: Living Transition and Reimagining Democracy* (New York).

Prado, S. (2007) 'The mettle of our civil society is going to be put to the test', *Envío*, 307 (Feb.), www.envio.org.ni/articulo/3461 (accessed 29 Apr. 2019).

— (2008) *Entre los CDM y los CPC: modelos de participación ciudadana y presupuestos municipales* (Managua).

7. Grassroots verticalism? A Comunidad Eclesial de Base in rural Nicaragua*

David Cooper

How do we come to form judgements about the way something so intangible as a nation, or a society, might change or remain the same? If a society is understood to have changed, what values or images do we refer to in order to gauge whether that change is for the better or for the worse? If a process of social change is thought to have rendered a nation *exceptional*, then on what conceptual basis are comparisons made? In the case of Nicaragua, and in relation to the question of how, and whether, the Sandinista Revolution gave rise to a state of exceptionality – in comparison both with its neighbours and its own pre-revolutionary past – a central analytical imagery has been an orthogonal opposition between the 'vertical' and the 'horizontal'. This chapter delves in detail into a highly localised ethnographic scenario – examining the continuing activity of a liberation theology group in rural Nicaragua – and aims to draw insight from that scenario for these larger questions of political and historical evaluation. While forming broad comparative judgements about Nicaraguan society by reference to an opposition between the vertical and the horizontal has been of central importance for scholars – and, indeed, for liberation theologians – the case explored here suggests that this potent evaluative framework is not necessarily the most pertinent one for some of those whose lives have been most profoundly affected by the revolution.

For the Nicaraguan *campesinos* (or farmers) among whom I conducted ethnographic fieldwork, the movement of socio-political history was often gauged by a different measure. Rather than referring to a diagrammatic opposition between vertical and horizontal social or political forms, they focused upon the difference between a politics characterised by inclusion and care, and a politics of abandonment. The contrast carries concrete political implications.

---

*   This chapter is based upon ethnographic fieldwork conducted in Gualiqueme and neighbouring villages from Nov. 2011–July 2012 and Jan. 2013–July 2013. A return visit was made in Nov.–Dec. 2015. Names of individuals and those of some locations and organisations have been changed. This work was supported by the Economic and Social Research Council under Grant ES/H012478/1, and by the European Research Council (ERC) under Grant ERC-2013-CoG, 617970, CARP.

D. Cooper, 'Grassroots verticalism? A Comunidad Eclesial de Base in rural Nicaragua', in H. Francis (ed.), *A Nicaraguan Exceptionalism? Debating the Legacy of the Sandinista Revolution* (London: University of London Press, 2019), pp. 145–64. License: CC-BY-NC-ND.

The notion that desirable social change amounts to an elimination of the vertical – as the ethnography explored below makes clear – can easily translate into a sense that the minds of *campesinos* require structural adjustment through the inculcation of a culture of horizontalism. But the *campesinos* I came to know attributed their ongoing economic struggle not to flaws in their own way of understanding the world, but instead to the degree to which the moral behaviour of those in positions of power facilitated the kinds of inclusion that were desired. They focused their energies, correspondingly, upon the effort to elicit an appropriate ethical orientation, as they understood it, from powerholders. The basic aim of this chapter is to explore the ways in which these contrasting models of socio-political transformation found expression in one particular ethnographic scenario, but then to think through the implications of that discussion for scholarly debates about Nicaragua's broad trajectory of change, the kind of difference the revolution is taken to have made, and the implications of established perspectives in those debates for our understanding of *campesino* political culture.

Grassroots verticalism

'Just "Ricardo"', requested the priest leading the proceedings, as he was once again addressed honorifically as 'don Ricardo'. During the 2012 annual meeting of PROOR (Proyecto Oscar Romero), a development initiative established by liberation theologians in northern Nicaragua, the tensions underlying this minor exchange emerged time and again. When I spoke to Ricardo about the PROOR project, he expressed his pride in what had been achieved by participants over the years. The organisation had been established after a small group of Spanish priests, Ricardo among them, secured a generous donation from Germany to provide emergency relief in the wake of Hurricane Mitch in 1991. Wishing to ensure that the money was used wisely, PROOR was established to give beneficiaries a say in how funds would be administered. Developments since then had been entirely in the hands of participants, Ricardo stressed. They took the initiative themselves to propose and establish a mutual savings and credit organisation. The structure of meetings, and the concrete form the project had eventually taken, had all been directed by participants' own suggestions and ideas. His role has always been merely one of facilitator, he emphasised, taking on such minor responsibilities as arranging for the rental of chairs for the meetings.

During the meeting, however, Ricardo encountered some starkly contrasting readings of his own role in the organisation. The honorific 'don' persistently prefixed his name, despite his repeated requests, as speakers apparently insisted upon placing him in a position of seniority and status. When he announced that this was to be the last meeting for which he would be convener, a series of individuals proceeded to stand up and make impromptu, celebratory speeches of gratitude, each commending him for his commitment to the project and praising him for the successes that had come as a result. The majority of these improvised contributions emphasised the benefits of having participated in the project in highly personalised terms, constructing their own lives as having been positively improved due to Ricardo's transformative assistance. Ricardo's discomfort with the hagiographic tones of these homilies was all too clear – one speaker even suggested that he would go down in local memory alongside Oscar Romero himself.

The central ethnographic focus of this chapter is an active Comunidad Eclesial de Base (CEB) in the village of Gualiqueme, in the Segovian mountains, and their regional network based in the city of Estelí. As we shall see, the tension in PROOR's meeting described above encapsulates a substantive disagreement regarding the form of the forces underpinning relevant social and historical change which runs through liberation theology activities. Among CEB participants and their neighbours, the prospects and possibilities of CEB activity are frequently discussed in relation to a set of social and political assumptions which I will tentatively term 'grassroots verticalism'; tentatively, because the discussion below ultimately leads me to reject the concept. I use the phrase to point to understandings of political possibility which view apparently vertical – even hierarchical – social relations as a source of potential and as a viable target of political activity. Ricardo's discomfort, however, points to the way in which grassroots verticalism shows up as problematic from the perspective of liberation theology itself. At issue in PROOR's meeting were two competing readings of the productive, transformative potentials enabled by participation in the project. Ricardo emphasised the extent to which transformative possibilities were enabled by the horizontal, self-organising capabilities of participants, while many of the latter put forward an image which construed Ricardo himself as a transformative figure, whose personal input and capacity as an intermediary was the crucial factor in the project's value. For Gualiqueme residents, as we shall see, CEB activity is shot through with such tensions. Participants often speak about the value of taking part in terms of the possibilities it opens up of gaining access to the valued 'help' of liberation theologians themselves – assistance which is viewed as an instance of a broader developmental force associated with Sandinismo and the revolution – while liberation theologians understand themselves to be working to dislodge and combat hierarchical social and religious thinking.

In viewing moments of apparent preference for vertical political forms as disturbing – and, as we shall see, something to be combated – liberation theologians draw upon a set of assumptions about the shape of political history that is often shared by scholarly analysts of Nicaragua's post-revolutionary situation. Indeed, evaluations of Nicaragua's trajectory since 1990 make frequent recourse to an analytic which constructs the vertical as corresponding to a process of historical regression. On this analysis, the revolution's 'progressive' advances are viewed as having been overturned to the extent that horizontal political forms and intra-class solidarities have been eroded, with a resurgent and disempowering verticalism taking their place. Here progress is viewed as coterminous with a diagrammatic shift from the vertical to the horizontal.[1] Drawing upon concepts such as clientelism, populism and *caudillismo* to describe these developments, scholars work to construct Nicaragua's political trajectory as veering tragically *backwards*, towards a standardised Latin American form.[2] If the revolution's transformations once rendered Nicaragua exceptional insofar as the nation made concrete 'advances' towards a horizontal social order, these analyses amount to the claim that Nicaragua's exceptionalism has been slipping away.

My aim in this chapter will be to use an exploration of one community's involvement with CEB activity to think through the implications of this depiction of verticalist politics. Though the orthogonal imagery I chart is central to a critique of trends towards authoritarianism, corruption and *caudillismo* at Nicaragua's political centre, it is important to ensure that this potent line of political polemic does not eclipse the possibility of perceiving ways in which hierarchy may be drawn upon as an active political resource by subaltern populations. In interrogating – and finally rejecting – the notion of grassroots verticalism, I point towards aspects of the political thought of Nicaraguan *campesinos* that risks being obscured by a model of political change founded upon horizonal-vertical oppositions. If constituencies of present-day Sandinista supporters are not to be dismissed as the mere dupes of populist strategies deployed by political elites, or as helplessly caught up in overarching processes of political regression, attending to the specific contours of the political imaginaries which inform continuing commitment to the FSLN is crucial. The broader

---

1   It should also be noted that, during the 1980s, Sandinista governance was explicitly tied to theories of revolutionary vanguardism that have themselves been described in terms of 'verticalist' politics. Indeed, a central line of analysis in diagnoses of the problems faced by the revolutionary government in the 1980s has been grounded in critique of such verticalist tendencies: see, e.g., R. Montoya, *Gendered Scenarios of Revolution*.

2   E.g., Hoyt warned us that the Ortega-Alemán pact 'returned Nicaragua to the old days of *caudilllismo*': K. Hoyt 'Parties and pacts in contemporary Nicaragua', 18. A recent analysis by Close and Martí í Puig, 'The Scandinistas and Nicaragua since 1977', 9, views Alemán's politics as 'the perfect adaptation of classical Latin American caudillo politics to the demands of electoral democracy. Rosario Montoya, 'Contradiction and struggle under the leftist phoenix', 46, views Ortega's incumbency as characterised by 'assistentialism', and suggests that the 'caciquismo [...], familialism, and exclusion of women' evident in recent state and NGO projects stands as a *return* of 'familiar rural forms' that worked to undermine revolutionary practice in the 1980s. And Dennis Rodgers, 'Searching for the time of beautiful madness', 84, portrays the 'social atomisation' of the neoliberal present as standing in stark contrast with the 'pervasive solidarity and collective support' of the 1980s. This line of analysis resonates with a key argument regarding the development of rural political support for the FSLN in first place. Pre-revolutionary rural politics is widely understood to have been founded upon patron-client ties: J. Gould, *To Lead as Equals: Rural Protest and Political Consciousness in Chinandega, Nicaragua, 1912–1979*; V. González-Rivera, *Before the Revolution: Women's Rights and Right-Wing Politics in Nicaragua, 1821–1979*; M. Gobat, *Confronting the American Dream: Nicaragua under US Imperial Rule*. Revolutionary political mobilisation, correspondingly, has been viewed as having been possible where sociological shifts undermined that hierarchical social pact; see, e.g., L.R. Horton, *Peasants in Arms: War and Peace in the Mountains of Nicaragua, 1979–1994*, 55–61. To the extent that revolutionary political practice has been understood to depend upon the erosion of clientelism, recent vertical trends come to appear as primarily a step *backwards*.

intention here, then, is to use the ethnographic tension identified in one local CEB to open up analytical space for comprehending grassroots participation in Ortega's 'assistentialism' in a way that does not cast rural people as simply responding mechanically, inevitably and predictably to political distribution.

After providing a brief historical account of Gualiqueme's history, the chapter will describe the nature of CEB activity both in village meetings and in the regional meetings periodically held in the city of Estelí. An exploration will follow of the view of hierarchical thinking that emerges from the theoretical perspective of liberation theology itself. This perspective – in common with many critical commentaries on the clientelism of Ortega's recent governance – mobilises a strong historical narrative in which hierarchy is rendered coterminous with an oppressive past. Hierarchy is constructed as integral to a traditional Latin American culture, and CEB activity is theorised as offering the possibility of leaving that culture behind and achieving authentic subaltern political agency. If apparently vertical thinking persists among CEB participants, this perspective takes it as evidence of an incomplete process of cultural change. The chapter will proceed, however, to explore the practical activities of the CEB group. By examining the practical engagement of Gualiqueme residents with their CEB, and exploring the parallels villagers draw between CEB participation and a range of other institutional experiences, it will argue that the ideas we provisionally termed grassroots verticalism are, in fact, bound up with a view of political possibility which an orthogonal imagery fails to adequately illuminate. Revolving around a sense that crucial prerequisites for political and economic progress are located elsewhere, this view implicitly contests the notion that social change should be sought by modifying *campesino* culture or social practice. Instead, it is the moral orientations of elites that are presumed to stand as the most coherent target for transformative endeavour.

CEBs in Gualiqueme

The village of Gualiqueme was established in 1984, in the middle of the Contra War and in the midst of Contra activity in the northern mountains near Honduras. It was created as an *asentamiento* as part of the creation of a Cooperativa de Autodefensa (CAD), a militarised and collectivised agricultural organisation, the founding members of which comprised displaced *campesinos* whose previous villages had been attacked by the Contras.[3] After the Sandinista victory in 1979, the land later granted to the cooperative had initially been established as a state farm. Comprising areas formerly belonging to three large haciendas, the farm had been well endowed with a substantial dairy herd, a coffee farm and a commercially exploited pine forest. As FSLN agrarian policy shifted over the course of the 1980s, an initial preference for state farms gave way and the formation of cooperatives became a priority. In war-torn regions, granting

3 On the creation of *asentamientos* during the Contra War, see J. Ercoreca Bilbao, et al., 'Reforma agraria, migraciones y guerra: asentamientos en Nicaragua'; J.L. Hammond, 'Resettlement and rural development in Nicaragua'.

land to agrarian cooperatives came to be viewed as offering the possibility of creating outposts of loyal Sandinistas capable of defending vulnerable territories against Contra incursions.[4] The formation of the Rigoberto Cruz cooperative, then, was intended to meet a range of goals: resettlement, military defence and rural development.

For several years after it was established, the cooperative functioned collectively, with members assigned work responsibilities by an elected leadership and receiving a salary. Ultimately, however, amid the economic turbulence caused by the Contra War – and subsequently, with the complete withdrawal of state support for agricultural cooperatives once the Sandinistas were voted out of office in 1990 – the members ended up dividing the land out among themselves and working individually. Today the cooperative still exists as an institution, and the land is still legally owned by the cooperative, although land sales to non-residents are an increasing problem. Residents speak about the history of their cooperative in a range of ways: they often readily acknowledge the difficulties the institution experienced and are sometimes critical of the poor performance of some leaders, but mostly they emphasise the tremendous value of the cooperative as an organisation. Local accounts of the village's early years, however, tend to be overwhelmingly focused upon the difficulties and suffering of the war. These difficulties have done nothing to dent the loyalty of villagers to the FSLN, however. Gualiqueme residents describe themselves as Sandinistas through and through, and many proudly affirmed that every single person in the village voted for the FSLN in the 2011 elections.

The close relationship of liberation theologians to the revolutionary process in Nicaragua has been well-documented, and activists within the popular church have become personally known to Gualiqueme residents over the years.[5] For example, narratives of the community's history invariably emphasise the fact that when people arrived at the village site, the area was just *puro monte* (wilderness), and initially people had to live collectively in old hacienda buildings. They were able to build their own houses, people explained, when Padre Bonifacio, the director of an organisation known as the Escuela Radiofonica Nicaragua, established a project which provided them with the materials to do so. This historic involvement continues to the present day. Several villagers are involved with PROOR, the organisation whose meeting I described at the start of

---

4   The changing priorities in Sandinista agrarian policy in the 1980s have been well-discussed in the literature, with many scholars viewing rural discontent with FSLN governance as the result of a refusal to grant land to individuals until late in the revolutionary decade. M.J. Saldaña-Portillo, *The Revolutionary Imagination in the Americas and the Age of Development* offers one of the more recent overviews of these debates.

5   J. Kirk, *Politics and the Catholic Church in Nicaragua*; M. Foroohar, *The Catholic Church and Social Change in Nicaragua*; D. Sabia, *Contradiction and Conflict: The Popular Church in Nicaragua*; and P.J. Williams, *The Catholic Church and Politics in Nicaragua and Costa Rica* provide historical accounts of the development of the liberation theology movement in Nicaragua and its relationship with the Sandinista Revolution.

the chapter. Considerably more active within the everyday life of the village, however, were the activities of the Comunidad Eclesial de Base.

Theology and practicality in CEB activity

Village meetings

The CEB group in Gualiqueme meets each week, on a Sunday, at around 11am. They own a small adobe building, purchased in recent years in order to have a dedicated space to hold their activities, which generally remains locked and unused for the rest of the week. As some other villagers make their way to the Catholic chapel for their regular Sunday service, CEB members assemble in their modest building. The timing means that participants face a clear choice: they cannot attend the conventional Catholic service in addition to the CEB celebration. If a female participant arrives early, she might quickly sweep the floor, as the men remove the heavy wooden stakes blocking the windows to let in the light. The walls are decorated with posters of Óscar Romero, one displaying a montage of dozens of photos of the martyred Salvadoran priest at different stages of his life. Plastic chairs are unstacked and placed optimistically at the front of the room – as other participants arrive, they will usually be repositioned towards the back when people take their places. Well-worn books containing hymns in the liberation theology tradition, photocopied and bound by hand, are handed around. There are rarely enough for a copy each. Once a reasonable number of people have assembled, the celebration will begin.

The group comprises a small number of core members, who take responsibility for proceedings, undertake to lead or contribute to these weekly sessions, and frequently attend the regional meetings which are occasionally held in the city of Estelí. In addition, a number of villagers are associated with the group to a degree, but do not attend as frequently. Always present, however, are a group of seven or eight teenage girls, sometimes referred to as *las becadas* – those who are receiving *becas* (studentships for secondary study) from the CEB – who sit right at the back of the room and firmly resist the attempts of more senior participants to encourage them to contribute to discussions. After a request has been made for a volunteer, and following a long silence, one or two of these apparently reluctant participants will be made to stand up and give a scripture reading.

Proceedings always follow a regular structure. Meetings open with a prayer, followed by several hymns. Perhaps surprisingly, the opening prayer in meetings I attended was frequently the *Novus Ordo*, or 'Yo Confieso' (I confess), containing the strong emphasis of personal sin; 'Yo confieso ante dios todopoderoso … que he pecado mucho … por mi culpa, por mi culpa, por mi gran culpa.'[6] The hymnbooks, however, contained songs from the *Misa Campesina Nicaragüense*, such as '*vos sos el dios de los pobres*', and '*vamos a la milpa del señor*', which would

---

6   'I confess before God almighty … that I have sinned greatly … I am to blame, I am to blame, I am truly to blame.'

be accompanied by guitar on those occasions when a musician had brought an instrument along.[7]

Following printed guidelines for scriptural readings and themes to explore, the proceedings attended were generally led by don Lucas, sometimes by Samuel, another leading member of the group. After the opening prayer and songs, a reading of a selected biblical passage is made. Subsequently the person leading the proceedings offers a commentary on the text and invites participants to contribute to the discussions. Contributions I witnessed were frequently striking in their stark conjunction of themes; participants occasionally referred to ideas that drew very clearly from a liberationist tradition, but it was also common for discussion to centre upon more conventional Catholic questions of personal sin or prospects of salvation and damnation in the afterlife.

Once the discussion of the weekly scriptural reading draws to a close, the meeting shifts to administrative and organisational concerns. Upcoming financial requirements of the group are discussed – for example, the need for everyone to contribute to pay for the meeting house's electricity bill. Arrangements for any upcoming events being held by the regional group are discussed. On occasions when there are plans for other members of the regional group to visit Gualiqueme for a celebration, for example, such discussions might revolve around who will contribute food or make a financial contribution, who will cook, and who will be able to offer accommodation to visiting members of other groups – commitments which place considerable demands upon participants. An offering of a few córdobas will generally be placed on a table at the front, which will be used to cover the basic running costs of the group itself, before people make their way home.

Regional meetings

Central to the activities of the group are monthly regional meetings, which are conducted in a sizeable CEB building in Estelí. These being together leading members of local groups from a number of villages surrounding the city, as well as some members based in Estelí itself. It is significant that several practising Evangelicals are among those who attend.[8] The regional group is overseen and administered by Camila, a liberation theologian of Spanish origin, who has lived for many years in the village of one of the member groups. Participants described her to me as a former nun, and when speaking about the activities of the CEB, active participants and other villagers almost always emphasised her central

---

7   'You are the God of the poor', and 'Let's go to the Lord's cornfield'.
8   In meetings I attended participants openly discussed some of the difficulties potentially faced by Evangelicals who involved themselves in CEB activities. E.g. one woman described how her pastor had subjected her to sanctions within her church as a consequence of having been involved. The pastor imposed the standard disciplinary procedure of withdrawing 'privileges' such as the right to read or sing in services for a fixed period, in her case two months. This form of punishment might also be directed at those who have 'sinned' by committing adultery, drinking or smoking.

organising role and her Spanish origins. As well as meeting in Estelí, the groups that are linked together through the regional nucleus occasionally assemble in meeting houses within particular villages.

The participants I knew in Gualiqueme looked forward to regional meetings as an exciting event, as it can be a somewhat rare opportunity to visit the city.[9] They take place over a weekend, beginning at around lunchtime on Saturday, and finishing in the early afternoon the following day. Members who have travelled from rural areas sleep in the building, for which purpose the group has a supply of mattresses and pillows which are spread out on the floors of back rooms as people arrive. Travel costs are reimbursed from the group's funds and meals are provided. These, which include meat and cheese, especially in months when cash is in short supply, and when many weeks may have passed with no alteration in the boiled beans and tortilla eaten daily at home, are a real attraction.

As with those at village-level, regional meetings were generally organised around a dual structure. First, a scriptural session which might involve a reading and discussion of particular biblical passages, lessons on elements of liberation theology's history and thought given by Camila, and extended presentations or performances on a prepared theme given by leading members of the group, interspersed with liberation theology hymns. First thing on a Sunday, a mass might be performed, with one of the group's lay leaders or Camila leading proceedings, and using tortilla as Communion bread. Subsequently, however, attention would be turned to more practical matters and the group would discuss financial issues, organisational requirements for upcoming activities, and ideas for new projects.

Both village and regional meetings, then, exhibit a clear organisational distinction between theological matters and practical concerns. Though liberation theology itself generally insists that theology and praxis are inseparable, and is committed to the idea that praxis is closely informed by theology, and vice versa, my suggestion here is that my provisional term 'grassroots verticalism' shows up in a different light in relation to each key segment of CEB activity. The theological component completely works to construct verticalism as an entrenched idea that needs to be examined and confronted. Within the domain of the practical organisation of CEB projects, however, a focus on hierarchy and personalised assistance can be understood as a pragmatic engagement with organisational structures related to forms of top-down funding and the channelling of social provision through local leaders, something common to CEB activity, NGO practice and state social projects alike.

---

9   During the main periods of fieldwork in 2011–13, return bus fares to Estelí from Gualiqueme cost 80 córdobas (or 110 if an 'express' bus was taken between Condega and Estelí). No CEB participants had access to any other means of transport. During the same period, a day labourer might have been paid between 60 and 120 córdobas per day, depending on the nature of the work and whether or not food was provided by the employer; 80 córdobas without food was the most common arrangement. At the time, US$1 was worth approximately 22 córdobas.

Theological intervention: confronting entrenched ideas

A critical element of the theological component of the CEB endeavour is the injunction to rework forms of thought inherited from the Catholic tradition, which are viewed as antithetical to liberation. Liberation theologians and critical scholars frequently emphasise this model of cultural re-examination. Through the encounter with scripture facilitated by CEB activity, religious assumptions, cosmological ideas or ethical norms, viewed as working to foster the forms of dependency and hierarchy that characterise the traditional Catholic Church and the social order of the past, can be examined alongside their possible role in reproducing the present-day social conditions underpinning poverty. Through this process, it is assumed, authentic political agency among the poor can be awakened, precisely to the degree that those old, disempowering forms of thought can be confronted, challenged and changed.[10]

This model of theological-cultural change was also particularly evident in the regional meetings in Estelí attended by Gualiqueme residents. Indeed, Camila, the group's coordinator, was at times clearly conscious of needing to temper her explicit evaluations of participants' thinking as part of what she understood as a slow, long-term project of cultural change. One regional meeting activity I participated in, for example, involved discussing the scientific account of the world's origin in the 'Latin American bible'. Camila had prepared a handout which conveyed a 'creation' narrative: modelled upon the biblical creation story, it described the origins of the world and the genesis of human life on earth in terms drawn from modern science and made reference to biological evolution. Camila herself was keenly aware that this modern account stood in stark contrast to deeply held understandings among the group's participants. She commented, however, that the biblical stories were just that, stories, and what the scientists said about these things were true. She knew that it was difficult for people to get their heads around, she said. The biblical stories are of great value, they are sacred, she affirmed – but they aren't true. However, she said, she had no intention of pressing that point, because she knew that it would take a long time for people's thinking on those matters to change.

Discussion of the handout was subsequently undertaken in smaller groups, with responses fed back to the whole group afterwards. The conversations elicited by this activity revealed considerable diversity in the participants' evaluation of this putatively scientific account of creation. In the group I joined, several people observed that the narrative in the handout could not possibly be accurate, given that it contradicted starkly the account of creation given in the bible. Rosa disagreed, arguing that the bible story was itself simply a lie foisted upon people by 'power', and that it had to do with the 'God of Fear'. With most participants

---

10 See A. Dawson 'The origins and character of the base ecclesial community: a Brazilian perspective'. In the Nicaraguanist literature, Montoya shows how mainstream liberation theology's effort to forge a society without hierarchy sits at odds with the thinking of one *campesino* intellectual. R. Montoya, 'Liberation theology and the socialist utopia of a Nicaraguan shoemaker'.

in my group, however, this radical interpretation – placing the biblical and scientific narratives in stark opposition – did not appear to resonate. Most discussants found much more persuasive the idea that, despite the superficial differences between the scientific story and biblical creation, they exhibited an underlying compatibility. This, they argued, was because it was evidently the case that scientists have themselves learned from the bible (*se han preparado de la biblia*) in developing their knowledge. The text in question involved the explicit literary device of rewriting the biblical creation story with a scientific account. Rather than simply misunderstanding this device, though, it appeared to me that, in concluding that science is grounded in biblical insight, the discussants worked quite specifically to *avoid* a stark oppositional framing such as that articulated by Camila or by Rosa's reference to the God of Fear.

Despite acknowledging that transforming long-standing religious thinking would be a slow process, sometimes Camila was less forgiving in her evaluation of the ideas articulated by participants. In the subsequent month's regional meeting, the group was reading a handout about the 2012 'Integral Law against Violence Towards Women', a new law which had strengthened legal protections for women in circumstances of domestic violence.[11] In the course of discussion, one participant made reference to the idea that 'we're all born in sin', an idea that many conventional Catholics would consider unproblematic – and which was also a frequent theme in village CEB meetings where Camila had not been present. Camila's response to the comment was unequivocal; 'No, no, no!' she insisted. 'Nobody, ever, is born already in sin! Not even somebody who had been born of a prostitute, a mother living the worst kind of life, no matter what the conditions, that baby would be born clean, absolutely clean!' These kinds of ideas, Camila argued throughout the session, were integral to the old 'Church of Power' to which the liberation theology tradition was opposed, the Church that the conservative hierarchy still fought to sustain. She argued that it cultivated fear specifically in order to instil passivity among the people and a consequent dependency upon the Church itself for the promise of otherworldly salvation.

A clear dynamic was established, then, by this kind of exchange. Certain ideas needed to be combated, some of them slowly and gradually, and some of them immediately and with force. The project of social transformation promised by the popular Church – and the enabling of subaltern political agency that Camila presumed it to produce – necessarily depended upon this project of introspective examination and religious transformation. The promise it offered depended upon participants working to examine these old, entrenched assumptions in the light of scripture, investigate their implications and develop a new perspective on their old theological commitments. Social change required a change of *campesino* minds still in the grip of the Church of Power.

It is certainly the case that this model of liberationist thinking, which stands at odds with entrenched theological assumptions, can find plenty of supporting

---

11 For a critical discussion of this law, see A.Z. Miklos, 'Mediated intimacies: state intervention and gender violence in Nicaragua'.

material within the dynamic of CEB meetings. The striking difference in theological tone between village meetings at which Camila was not present, and regional meetings where she was able to guide discussions, certainly resonates with this model. However, I do not want to focus here on the extent to which CEB activity has, so far, succeeded or failed in a project to instil ideological and theological change among participants, however that might be understood. While this model is very much part of liberation theology's own theorisation of what CEB participation *should* involve, my argument here is that in evaluating verticalist thought among CEB participants, this model potentially obscures as much as it reveals. In constructing the aim of CEB activity as overcoming 'traditional' theological ideas – ideas which themselves contribute to social inequality and the condition of poverty by cultivating passivity and dependency – liberation theology evaluates verticalist thinking within a paradigm that opposes conservative tradition to liberatory change.

Grassroots verticalism of the kind articulated by CEB participants in Gualiqueme, then, shows up in the light of liberation theology's *own* theorisation of its activities as exactly this kind of phenomon: the heavy weight of cultural baggage. The argument I wish to develop here is that this view of verticalist thinking does not correspond to the way Gualiqueme residents themselves thought about politics. To do so, I will focus in particular upon one crucial aspect of liberation theology's theorisation of CEB activity. As mentioned previously, CEBs are viewed as enabling scripture to become relevant by allowing it to be read in the light of everyday problems, thereby facilitating a scripturally informed critique of those problems. Critical here is the assumption that the problems in question exist *apart from* and *external to* the activities of the group itself. That problems will need to be confronted goes without saying – this is a simple implication of the defining commitment of liberation theology to work with 'the poor'. Liberation theology's (uncontentious) understanding of poverty as a condition of struggle and suffering is integral to this orientation. Poor people's lives are difficult by definition, it is assumed. It is this integral difficulty of impoverished existence which is taken to be the vital context – the relevant domain of the actual and everyday – which CEB discussions are committed to acknowledging, engaging with and confronting.

The radical nature of this commitment in relation to Catholic theology prior to Vatican II and Medellín is clear, and is well-appreciated in the literature. Vitally important as a critical acknowledgement of the struggles of poverty may be, I would argue that in developing an ethnographic analysis of grassroots hierarchy, positing the problems of life as an a priori background condition of poverty risks passing over the ways in which involvement with CEB activity itself has come to be closely bound up with one of the most critical problems faced by rural people in Nicaragua in grappling with their conditions of existence. A simple observation guides this statement: poverty as a condition of life in rural Nicaragua at present cannot be understood separately from the interventions which aim to grapple with that condition. Rural Nicaraguans, as the ongoing targets of varied interventions intended to overcome their economic plight – interventions themselves premised on a broad range of analyses regarding the causes and dynamics of poverty itself – now confront their own conditions in a context itself thoroughly conditioned by these interventions.[12] CEB institutional arrangements, in their close mirroring of NGO methods of distributing and administering aid funds, are viewed by participants as one among a range of possibilities for gaining distributive material support by performing the requirements of being 'organised'. Examining the social projects integral to CEB activity will clarify this point.

CEB social projects

If, for Camila, CEB activity was viewed as facilitating a process of reflection whereby hierarchical thinking – assumed to be traditional and politically regressive – might be left behind, residents of Gualiqueme participating in the group appeared to work from somewhat different assumptions. Indeed, while religious interest in the theological and spiritual components of CEB activity was clear, these group members primarily described the value of participation in material terms, which was closely related to the idea that Camila herself stood as a valuable intermediary. The first thing that don Lucas, a senior member of the group, mentioned to me about their activities was that their leader, a dynamic Spaniard, had access to significant international funds for social projects. Time and again, participants pointed out that the group provides a number of Gualiqueme youths with scholarships to pursue their secondary studies. As with the ovations to 'don' Ricardo's activities in PROOR and the historical narratives which imputed the infrastructural development of the village itself to the personal benevolence of a liberation theologian priest, discussion of the material prospects attendant upon CEB participation were strongly personalised. Camila's work, I was often told, was to go around Spain looking for funding, which would go towards the projects that the group arranged. The value of CEB activity was frequently depicted as a product of Camila's own *ayuda* (help), assistance which derived from her position as a foreigner with ties to wealthy church organisations abroad.

Central to CEB activity for participants in Gualiqueme are the economic and social projects undertaken and funded by the group. The regional group has access to a considerable stream of international financing which is deployed in a variety of different endeavours, each aimed at providing economic opportunities and the possibility of income and security for participants. Decisions about how to allocate and spend this money are taken in regional meetings, and Camila ensures that participants play a central role in proposing, designing and

---

12 A number of studies examine the way in which development discourse has constructed the Nicaraguan peasantry as a target for intervention in recent history. See, e.g., Saldaña-Portillo, *The Revolutionary Imagination in the Americas*; S. Langley, 'Revisiting "resistance", "the peasantry", and liberation/development: the case of Sandinismo in the 1980s'; and Montoya, *Gendered Scenarios of Revolution*.

implementing the projects in question. At the time of research, active projects included natural medicine workshops, in which participants received a wage to provide training sessions for other members of the community; the maintenance of several cows which had been purchased from the funds and were to be raised and sold at a profit; and the provision of secondary-school scholarships. Though the aim of projects was generally economic or educational, some projects had cultural goals. A series of painting workshops, for example, were also being conducted at the time of research.

Initiatives frequently took forms that were familiar to participants both from NGO activity and from state programmes. Another project active at the time of research was a *fondo revolvente* (revolving fund), a micro-credit scheme which theoretically should have been self-sustaining. Small loans were offered to members of the group for a variety of purposes, to be repaid at low interest. This kind of community savings scheme was frequently a component of both development projects and government programmes. Participants in the Bono Productivo, for example, have been required to make contributions that in theory will be used in a similar way.

Participants in CEB were able to propose projects of their own design. Many of the active projects had emerged from a collaborative decision-making process in regional meetings. In line with a commitment to the horizontal, group consultation and deliberative decision-making regarding the allocation of funds was strongly emphasised, although decisions were not always taken collectively. During the period of research, a new project was proposed by several of the more senior CEB participants from Gualiqueme. At that time, a severe coffee rust epidemic was just beginning to take hold across Central America.[13] In the face of potentially severe threats to their income should their own coffee fall victim to the disease, and alert to the possibility that many farmers in the region might need to replant areas of their plantations completely, don Lucas and Samuel suggested that it would be an opportune time to undertake a *vivero* (nursery) project in order to grow coffee saplings. On this occasion, the idea was not discussed among the group as a whole; Samuel took Camila aside during one of the breaks to discuss the idea privately. The group's plan for Gualiqueme was to solicit a loan from the CEB, via Camila, in order to fund the equipment needed for the endeavour. The loan (eventually agreed at 6,000 córdobas) would cover the cost of purchasing 20,000 plastic bags required for the plants as well as the cost of labour needed for the project.[14] The original loan would eventually be repaid from the profits made from the *vivero* sales. Coffee plants might sell for anywhere between 4 and 10 córdobas, and so if the project were to realise its full potential, a decent profit could be achieved. As with the revolving credit

---

13 See M. Vidaurre, 'El café en los tiempos de la roya', *Envío*, no. 372.

14 Though there are a range of methods for planting coffee, nursery cultivation has become standard. Earth first needs to be dug up and prepared to a fine tilth, which is used to fill plastic planting bags. In 2012 a *tarea* (requirements for a day's work) generally stood at 500 bags and would be paid at 100 córdobas. Achieving that many was a full day's work for a skilled worker.

scheme, the design of this nursery project was strongly reminiscent of many NGO projects experienced by the residents of Gualiqueme and with its design the group was following a familiar institutional model.[15]

Being organised

The parallels between CEB activity and the organisational structures of NGOs and state projects were by no means overlooked by Gualiqueme residents. Indeed, the notion of being organised and its implications and potentials were a constant topic of discussion and a central point of reference in local analyses of political life. When a Sandinista official stated in a local Comite de Liderazgo Sandinista meeting – while discussing upcoming government projects – that '*todo viene por medio de organización*' (everything comes through organisation), he echoed a sentiment I had heard articulated innumerable times among the villagers. The official in question intended this statement to dissuade attendees from applying themselves to getting personally involved in the projects. He was asserting that everything would be delivered through the proper institutional channels, making clear the extent to which direct solicitation is, in fact, employed as a strategy.[16] For Gualiqueme residents, however, being organised had come to represent a key political status, upon which viable citizenship was, to a large extent, understood to depend. Beneficial forms of political incorporation, and associated material support, were broadly understood to be contingent upon this status of being organised. Personal and collective advancement were conceptualised as requiring the successful achievement of this status. CEB activity was depicted as part and parcel of this broad range of distributive political possibility and viewed as just one of many ways of realising the state of organisation that might render flows of enabling assistance possible.[17]

Intensive NGO activity in Nicaragua has been central to the emergence of this set of associations. Horton informs us that 'in the post-1990 era, access to development aid and projects is often conditioned on demonstrating at least

---

15   The literature makes clear that Nicaragua is one of the Latin American countries with the highest density of active NGOs. See, e.g., R.N. Gwynne and C. Kay, *Latin America Transformed: Globalization and Modernity*, 205.

16   The proper channels in question were the Gabinetes de Familia, Salud y Vida as well as the various agricultural cooperatives active in the area, the institutions of an 'organised' citizenry as defined by the FSLN. Established in 2013, Gabinetes replaced the earlier form of local organisation, the Consejo de Poder Cindadano (Citizen's Power Council, CPC).

17   Indeed, one village resident, Wilber, noting the social projects available to participants, was led to conclude that the CEB was not really a religious group at all. The group was in fact an '*organismo*', he said, using the term by which NGOs are known. Furthermore, Mauricio, a senior member of one of Gualiqueme's Pentecostal congregations, spoke critically of CEB activity by comparing it with that of NGOs. 'Christian' groups should not involve themselves in such mundane matters, he insisted, drawing on a definition of Christian which excludes all non-Evangelicals. However, CEB participants made similar comparisons with a positive ethical valence, asserting that CEB activity was equal in value.

minimal forms of community organization'.[18] And indeed, Gualiqueme has been the location of a long series of development projects exhibiting precisely these demands. Perhaps most significantly, Ortega's flagship social programmes since 2007, such as Plan Techo and the Bono Productivo, have been integral to further amplifying associations between the imperative of being organised, a demand for subjective transformation and the prospect of accessing social projects. Residents of Gualiqueme were intensely interested in these programmes, particularly those who sensed they were being excluded from their benefits. Many residents perceived these projects to be administered unfairly, and felt the only people able to secure any kind of benefit were those directly organised in the local Gabinetes de la Familia, formerly CPCs.[19]

Don Lucas and Samuel, leading participants in the Gualiqueme CEB, were deeply concerned about the accessibility of the distributive resources associated with Ortega's post-2007 welfare programmes. At the time of research, they were also important members of a group that had caused a political stir locally by registering to vote in the adjacent municipality of Telpaneca, despite being resident in an area officially part of the territory of Condega. This move was motivated by profound discontent both with the leadership of the cooperative and the way it had previously administered government programmes such as Plan Techo and with the role of the mayor of Condega as an intermediary capable of properly channelling the distributive resources of Ortega's 'assistentialist' regime. Telpaneca's mayoress was described as being willing to work hard and continuously attract projects for her constituents. It is worth noting that this evaluation closely parallels the qualities emphasised in their descriptions of Camila's role as head of the regional CEB grouping. By realigning with Telpaneca, this group aimed to overcome the frustrations they had experienced in realising the local ideal of being organised as a form of political incorporation.

It is in this context, I suggest, that Gualiqueme residents' emphasis of the value of personalised assistance in relation to CEB activity needs to be understood. With Ortega's distributive politics comprising a central point of political reference – and yet with everyday political life frequently characterised by an effort to negotiate and overcome obstacles to fully realising the promise of incorporation projects such as Plan Techo – CEB activity offers a scenario in which the local vision of being organised might be viably fulfilled. In this vision social hierarchy stands as a target of solicitation, the exploitation of which offers a possibility of security and development. Far from being viewed as antithetical to progress, proper negotiation of vertical social forms is held to be integral to the possibility of advance. In being receptive to petitioning, and in placing resources in the hands of participants to administer as they deemed most appropriate,

---

18 L.R. Horton, 'From collectivism to capitalism: neoliberalism and rural mobilization in Nicaragua', 132. See also D. Chahim and A. Prakash, 'NGOization, foreign funding, and the Nicaraguan civil society'.

19 Among Gualiqueme residents these were mostly perceived to be the same organisation and were mostly referred to as 'CPCs' rather than the new name.

Camila – and other liberation theologians active in the area such as Ricardo in PROOR – came to stand as model intermediaries of the kind Gualiqueme residents like don Lucas and Samuel were striving to secure in relation to state projects.

The idea that the value of being organised amounted to the creation of a horizontal political culture was therefore far from being what Gualiqueme residents meant when they embraced FSLN rhetoric emphasising the importance of organisation. The notion that developing peer-to-peer organisational ties among fellow *campesinos* was enough to deal with the problem of poverty seemed implausible. Rural Nicaraguans in this relatively well-connected part of the country have had abundant exposure to the ways in which foreigners – whether NGO staff, *internationalistas* or liberation theologians – appear able to tap into and marshal economic wellsprings deriving from elsewhere. This luxury is unimaginable for smallholding farmers and landless rural labourers. For Gualiqueme residents, the idea that the most viable solution to local economic problems might derive from reforming the immanent structures of *campesino* organisational or cultural life therefore seemed to ignore the developmental possibilities of participating in a range of redistributive flows quite evidently coming from *outside*. But likewise, any sense that the hierarchical, vertical quality of relationships with figures like Camila was what mattered does not seem to capture the sentiments documented here. Rather than an orthogonal model depicting elites as standing vertically 'above', Gualiqueme residents understood Camila and others to offer the prospect of binding them into crucial redistributive flows originating *elsewhere*. The prospect of development here was imagined to be possible – not as the product of a shift from the vertical to the horizontal – but through the connective work that moral appeals to elites promised to perform. If the possibility of development lay elsewhere, the value of being organised was taken to lie in organisational methods which served to open up channels of involvement with distant, otherwise disconnected, sources of economic abundance.

Conclusion

to return to the opening questions of this chapter, it would appear that an imagery of verticality, while neatly mapping a view of political transformation shared by liberation theologians and many scholarly critics of the FSLN's recent political trajectory, fails to capture an important analytical model, that drawn upon when rural supporters of the FSLN discuss current political possibilities. Rather than viewing the basic trajectory of desirable political change as being a transition from the vertical to the horizontal, Gualiqueme residents cultivated a potent sense that abundant developmental resources lay beyond local boundaries. In the light of that image, desirable political change appeared to be connected with the work of establishing the right kinds of connection with these abundant resources. Instead of verticalism, it might be more appropriate to refer to this as a desire for inclusion.

When compared with the orthogonal analytic described above, this imagery led to a completely different view of the kind of work that would need to be done in order to actively propel desirable change. Liberation theology's tradition of social analysis, in conversation with Latin American dependency theory, posits hierarchical thinking as part of an oppressive cultural tradition which renders subaltern populations passive and dependent, and which the vital encounter with scripture enabled by CEBs promises to challenge and gradually overturn. In addition, critical commentaries on Nicaragua's political trajectory since 1990 frequently mobilise an evaluative model of history which draws on comparable associations, casting desirable progress and the possibility of popular political agency as coterminous with the elimination of social hierarchy. When assessing the revolution's legacy in the light of this model, scholars are led to the conclusion that Nicaragua's revolutionary exceptionality has been lost. For Gualiqueme's Sandinista supporters, however, a central change effected by the revolution is understood to be connected with how much those in positions of influence and power are able to bind *campesino* lives into broader national and international redistributive flows. If anything needs to be worked upon in order to effect such change, it is the moral orientation of elites, intermediaries and powerholders. As the material above makes clear, the association of vertical thinking with the passivity and dependency of a benighted past fails to do justice to how the relationships which might realise this connective vision stand as a target of active political effort among Gualiqueme residents. Daniel Ortega's increasing support among rural people – and the plausibility for many of them of his claim that Nicaragua's revolutionary exceptionality continues in full force – might therefore be understood to reflect a successful effort to play into this desire for inclusion in material flows which offer a sense of connection to an abundant elsewhere.

Bibliography

Bilbao Ercoreca, J. A., A. Belli and E. Rivas (1989) 'Reforma agraria, migraciones y guerra: asentamientos en Nicaragua', *Encuentro: Revista Académica de la Universidad Centroamericana*, 37–8: 97–113.

Chahim, D. and A. Prakash (2014) 'NGOization, foreign funding, and the Nicaraguan civil society', *VOLUNTAS: International Journal of Voluntary and Nonprofit Organizations*, 25 (2): 487–513.

Close, D. and S. Martí i Puig (2011) 'The Sandinistas and Nicaragua since 1979', in D. Close, S. Martí i Puig and S.A. McConnell (eds.), *The Sandinistas and Nicaragua since 1979* (Boulder, CO), pp. 1–20.

Dawson, A. (2007) 'The origins and character of the Base Ecclesial Community: a Brazilian perspective', in C. Rowland (ed.), *The Cambridge Companion to Liberation Theology* (Cambridge, 2007), pp. 139–58.

Foroohar, M. (1989) *The Catholic Church and Social Change in Nicaragua* (New York).

Gobat, M. (2005) *Confronting the American Dream: Nicaragua under US Imperial Rule* (Durham, NC).

González-Rivera, V. (2011) *Before the Revolution: Women's Rights and Right-Wing Politics in Nicaragua, 1821–1979* (University Park, PA).

Gould, J. (1990) *To Lead as Equals: Rural Protest and Political Consciousness in Chinandega, Nicaragua, 1912–1979* (Chapel Hill, NC).

Gwynne, R.N. and C. Kay (2004) *Latin America Transformed: Globalization and Modernity*, 2nd edn., (London).

Hammond, J.L. (1989) 'Resettlement and rural development in Nicaragua', *Monthly Review*, 41 (5): 22–35.

Horton, L.R. (1998) *Peasants in Arms: War and Peace in the Mountains of Nicaragua, 1979–1994* (Athens, OH).

— (2013) 'From collectivism to capitalism: neoliberalism and rural mobilization in Nicaragua', *Latin American Politics and Society*, 55 (1): 119–40.

Hoyt, K. (2004) 'Parties and pacts in contemporary Nicaragua', in D. Close and K. Deonandan (eds.), *Undoing Democracy: The Politics of Electoral Caudillismo* (Oxford, 2004), pp. 17–42.

Kirk, J.M. (1992) *Politics and the Catholic Church in Nicaragua* (Gainesville, FL).

Langley, S. (2004) 'Revisiting "resistance", "the peasantry", and liberation/development: the case of Sandinismo in the 1980s', *Social Analysis*, 48 (1): 179–95.

Mendoza Vidaurre, R. (2013) 'El café en los tiempos de la roya', *Envío*, 372 (March), www.envio.org.ni/articulo/4653 (accessed 30 Apr. 2019).

Miklos, A.Z. (2014) 'Mediated intimacies: state intervention and gender violence in Nicaragua', *Encuentro*, 100: 6–37.

Montoya, R. (1995) 'Liberation theology and the socialist utopia of a Nicaraguan shoemaker', *Social History*, 20 (1): 23–43.

— (2012) 'Contradiction and struggle under the leftist phoenix: rural Nicaragua at the thirtieth anniversary of the Revolution', in J.L. Burrell and E. Moodie (eds.), *Central America in the New Millennium: Living Transition and Reimagining Democracy* (Oxford, 2012), pp. 33–48.

— (2012) *Gendered Scenarios of Revolution: Making New Men and New Women in Nicaragua, 1975–2000* (Tucson, AZ).

Rodgers, D. (2009) 'Searching for the time of beautiful madness: of ruins and revolution in post-Sandinista Nicaragua', in H.G. West and P. Raman (eds.), *Enduring Socialism: Explorations of Revolution and Transformation, Restoration and Continuation* (Oxford, 2009), pp. 77–102.

Sabia, D. (1997) *Contradiction and Conflict: The Popular Church in Nicaragua* (Tuscaloosa, AL).

Saldaña-Portillo, M.J. (2003), *The Revolutionary Imagination in the Americas and the Age of Development* (Durham, NC).

Spalding, R.J. (2012) 'Poverty politics', in D. Close, S. Martí i Puig and S.A. McConnell, *The Sandinistas and Nicaragua since 1979* (Boulder, CO).

Williams, P. (1989) *The Catholic Church and Politics in Nicaragua and Costa Rica* (Pittsburgh, PA).

8. Nicaraguan legacies: advances and setbacks in feminist and LGBTQ activism*

Florence E. Babb

Following the 1979 Sandinista Revolution, Nicaragua became known around the world as a small Central American nation that had risen up against a long-entrenched dictatorship and the US imperialism that supported it. The 1980s began with high hopes and notable accomplishments, including in women's rights, but later in the decade the US-funded Contra War divided the country and eroded the gains of the revolution. During this period, lesbian and gay Nicaraguans made their first public appearance after clandestine meetings and a brief, but notable, Sandinista effort to stifle their political organising. As a number of writers have assessed the meaning of the revolution's legacy for feminism in Nicaragua, my main focus will be on its meaning for the LGBTQ community.[1] Most analysts agree that the revolution had both enabling and limiting effects. It is credited for such advances as having mobilised the population to halt the spread of HIV/AIDS, for enabling greater

---

* An earlier version of this work was presented as 'Salir del clóset en Nicaragua: Identidades y políticas LGBT durante la revolución' (Coming out in Nicaragua: LGBT identities and politics during the Revolution), Congreso Internacional, 'Diversidad sexual en contextos de guerra', Dirección de Diversidad Sexual, Secretaria Distrital de Planeación, Bogotá, Colombia, Sept. 2015. I am grateful to José Fernando Serrano Amaya and Cristina Rojas Tello for their invitation and commentaries. I also wish to thank Karen Kampwirth and Victoria González-Rivera for allowing me to read chapters from their manuscript in preparation, *One Hundred Years of LGBT History in Nicaragua*, a much-anticipated history of LGBT Nicaraguans over the past century. Shannon Walsh and Karen Kampwirth offered their much-appreciated comments on a draft of this work. For the research I conducted in Nicaragua from 1990 through to 2010, I received generous support from the Wenner-Gren Foundation for Anthropological Research, the Fulbright Foundation, the University of Iowa and the University of Florida. Finally, I thank Hilary Francis for her invitation and encouragement to contribute to this volume.

1 LGBTQ refers to lesbians, gay men, bisexuals, transgender and queer. Although 'queer' has only recently come into wider use in Nicaragua, later in this chapter I discuss the appearance of Operación Queer in Managua. Among those who examine feminism and the legacy of the Nicaraguan revolution, see especially K. Kampwirth, *Feminism and the Legacy of Revolution: Nicaragua, El Salvador, Chiapas*, and S. Heumann, 'The challenge of inclusive identities and solidarities: discourses on gender and sexuality in the Nicaraguan women's movement and the legacy of Sandinismo'.

F.E. Babb, 'Nicaraguan legacies: advances and setbacks in feminist and LGBTQ activism', in H. Francis (ed.), *A Nicaraguan Exceptionalism? Debating the Legacy of the Sandinista Revolution* (London: University of London Press, 2019), pp. 165–78. License: CC-BY-NC-ND.

security through community support and the creation of women's police stations, and for reducing crime so that we now see far fewer Nicaraguans than other Central Americans fleeing north.[2] Nonetheless, the Sandinista insistence on state-led development resulted in restrictions placed on autonomous initiatives for change, including those of gay men, lesbians and other sexual minorities.

This chapter will examine the particular ways in which LGBTQ Nicaraguans have mobilised during the last three decades and suggest that Nicaraguan 'exceptionalism' may account for both the positive formation of this social movement and for the ambivalence expressed by the Sandinista leadership when that movement emerged. Based on my ethnographic research spanning from 1989 through to the first decade of the new millennium, as well as the rich scholarly literature, I trace the way in which Nicaragua broke from its past as a Central American 'backwater' to play an active part in both national and regional LGBTQ culture and politics. Important to this development was the solidarity of feminists based in NGOs and social movements that supported sexual rights and AIDS education.

Notwithstanding the advances for gender rights, and (to a lesser degree) sexual diversity, during the decade when the Sandinistas first came to power, setbacks also arose during that time. Indeed, the florescence of civil society organisations and autonomous social movements found greater space for development in the neoliberal 1990s, though still more challenges have emerged in the post-2007 period since Daniel Ortega returned to power. During the past decade, the FSLN government has targeted feminists and other left groups that are critical of the government's anti-democratic actions to quell dissent. Interestingly, transgender groups and NGOs received somewhat greater government support just as women's rights were diminishing; still, LGBTQ Nicaraguans in general have continued to experience persistent homophobia and social exclusion. This chapter asks what the legacy of Nicaraguan exceptionalism should be considered to be when inconsistent practices and ambivalent outcomes around gender and sexual rights are observed in present-day Nicaragua.

The chapter will then consider the experiences of lesbian and gay and other sexual minorities in Nicaragua during the time of the Sandinista Revolution, with an emphasis on lesbian feminist centrality. It focuses on the war years, from the Sandinista mobilisation through the decade of revolutionary government and Contra War (pre-1979 to 1990). The chapter then outlines the background of the period during which I conducted research, 1989–2010, a particularly robust time for feminist and LGBTQ organising. The third section examines what the return of the FSLN government and of Daniel Ortega has meant in relation to the LGBTQ community since 2007, with commentary on some recent developments. The conclusion compares remarks on Nicaraguan and Cuban exceptionalism in relation to LGBTQ populations, and offers a brief assessment of how the LGBTQ experience provides a useful lens for illuminating national-

2   For an assessment of women's police stations and human security in Nicaragua, see S.D. Walsh, 'Advances and limits of policing'.

level dimensions of change. Ultimately, I hope to shed light on the question of Nicaraguan exceptionalism by asking to what degree these recent developments may (or may not) be considered legacies of the Sandinista Revolution.³

The emergence of LGBTQ culture and politics in the Sandinista Revolution decade, 1979–90

The FSLN (Frente Sandinista de Liberación Nacional) formed in 1961 to confront the long legacy of the Somoza family dictatorship in Nicaragua. The Somozas were notorious for their cruel practices, backed by force over decades. Surprisingly enough, their politics around women and sexual minorities would be rather more liberal. As historian Victoria González-Rivera has shown, the years of dictatorship provided some space for an early women's movement to emerge and for gay men and lesbians and others deemed sexually different to live their lives.⁴ After the FSLN had built a mass movement and triumphed in 1979, the new Sandinista government's outlook on sexual difference or diversity was that it formed part of the decadent past represented by the Somoza dictatorship, in much the same way that homosexuality in Cuba was associated with the Batista dictatorship's bourgeois past. While the new revolutionary leadership quickly carried out reforms to benefit women, they did not view sexual minorities as worthy of the same attention.

During the time of the guerrilla movement, awareness existed of gay and lesbian participants in the armed struggle, even if this was not spoken of publicly. The Sandinistas had built up a mass movement across diverse sectors of the population by the late 1970s and their attitude appeared to be that as long as gay men and lesbians supported the revolution, their private lives were tolerated. I have argued elsewhere that the revolution itself provided the opportunity for young people away from family to discover their sexual difference and to act on new desires.⁵ Still, they had to prove their commitment to Sandinismo and to keep their sexual orientation to themselves. This policy of 'Don't ask, don't tell', which mirrored the general expectation in Nicaraguan society, continued into the 1980s when the Sandinista government was introducing a series of

---

3   There are far too many contributions to the literature on feminist and LGBTQ politics, culture and history in Nicaragua to do justice to them here. I rely on my own past writing on the subject – F.E. Babb, *After Revolution: Mapping Gender and Cultural Politics in Neoliberal Nicaragua*; 'Out in Nicaragua: local and transnational desires after the revolution'; *The Tourism Encounter: Fashioning Latin American Nations and Histories* – as well as other recent writings: V. González-Rivera, *Before the Revolution: Women's Rights and Right-Wing Politics in Nicaragua, 1821–1979*; Heumann, 'The challenge of inclusive identities and solidarities'; E.K. Hobson, '"Si Nicaragua Venció": lesbian and gay solidarity with the revolution'; C. Howe, *Intimate Activism: The Struggle for Sexual Rights in Postrevolutionary Nicaragua*; K. Kampwirth, 'Organizing the Hombre Nuevo gay: LGBT politics and the second Sandinista Revolution'.

4   See González-Rivera, *Before the Revolution*, and V. González-Rivera, 'The alligator woman's tale: remembering Nicaragua's "first self-declared lesbian"'.

5   See Babb, *After Revolution*; and Babb, 'Out in Nicaragua'.

progressive reforms in the areas of the economy (land reform and state sector employment), popular political participation, education and healthcare. Lesbian and gay Sandinistas had to be satisfied with keeping a low profile in relation to their sexuality – and, in any event, their 'personal' and 'private' matters were viewed as secondary to, and a distraction from, the broad revolutionary struggle.

During the first years of the Sandinista revolutionary government, health and literacy brigades, as well as brigades working in the coffee and cotton harvests, offered more opportunities for gay men and lesbians to find one another and, freed of family obligations, to explore their sexuality. Thus I contend that although Nicaraguans often live in large families with little privacy, revolutionary participation gave Sandinista supporters new opportunities for self-discovery and sexual awakening. Whereas gay historian John D'Emilio has written that in western capitalist societies it was the transition from agricultural economies to urban, industrial economies that freed young men and women to self-identify as gay or lesbian,[6] I argue that revolutionary Nicaragua offered a very different context for the same sort of self-discovery. In both capitalist societies like the United States and socialist-oriented Nicaragua, a key element was that of newfound independence and the freedom to escape the prying eyes of family and traditional social norms. Testimonies of participants in the revolution relate that individuals would find moments in the fields during a cotton harvest or evenings free from duties with a literacy brigade to socialise and form romantic relationships.[7]

By the mid 1980s, a group of lesbians and gay men began gathering together in private homes to talk for the first time about their own interests and their experiences of discrimination and social injustice. At times more than 60 women and men gathered, and, significantly, women often outnumbered men. In 1987, the government became aware of their organising activities and a number of gay men and lesbians were called in for questioning by Sandinista State Security. Some 30 of them were briefly detained in prison but they were soon released as the Sandinista government sought to avoid the international disapproval that would surely follow should it come to light that they were denying rights to LGBTQ Nicaraguans. While state intervention quelled gay and lesbian political organising in the short term, it was not long before a number of individuals were becoming more brazen and coming out publicly.[8]

One way in which space was opening up for gay and lesbian activism came via the state as the government charged the health ministry, then headed by Dora

6   J. D'Emilio, 'Capitalism and gay identity'.
7   V. González-Rivera and K. Kampwirth, *One Hundred Years of LGBT History in Nicaragua* (manuscript in progress). See also Thayer's discussion of lesbian movements in Central America, where she notes the space for intimacy created within the context of revolution: M. Thayer, 'Identity, revolution, and democracy: lesbian movements in Central America'.
8   See Babb, 'Out in Nicaragua', for more discussion, including references to other sources relating to these developments. Note that while I generally refer to LGBTQ Nicaraguans in order to be inclusive of diversity, I sometimes refer to gay men and lesbians when the historical record suggests that these two groups were most prominently involved.

María Téllez, a highly respected *comandante* of the revolution and understood by many to be a lesbian, with working to prevent the spread of HIV/AIDS. Nicaragua's model of mass mobilisation around healthcare and education facilitated its success in containing the spread of HIV, and several NGOs with international funding (including CEPSIDA and Nimehuatzín) began developing popular education programmes and workshops on safer sex alongside legal and psychological services. Condoms were distributed in gay men's cruising areas and among students and sex workers, and publications addressed a host of issues around health and wellbeing.

In 1989, some 50 gay and lesbian Sandinistas, along with their international allies, marched openly in Managua's tenth anniversary celebration of the Nicaragua revolution. Gathering together at the Plaza of the Revolution, they wore black T-shirts with pink triangles, signalling their readiness to make their identities known within the FSLN and the wider society. On that landmark date they were empowered to call for recognition of their rights to self-expression and to lives free of prejudice. That summer, when I made my first trip to Nicaragua, was a momentous time for LGBTQ organising in Nicaragua. Still, the broader context of the 1980s in Sandinista Nicaragua needs to be considered. Increasingly during that decade, the US-sponsored Contra War was dividing the country and undermining efforts to further the revolution's ambitions to transform the society. More resources were devoted to defence rather than to social spending and families were torn apart by the ravages of the conflict and the loss of life. As pressure built and people longed for the fighting to stop, there was little opportunity or will to address social change in terms of the LGBTQ population. With the coming of the 1990 elections, most observers expected the re-election of Daniel Ortega as president; in retrospect, it was not so surprising that he lost to Violeta Barrios de Chamorro of the UNO coalition. The nation's prolonged conflict caused many voters to choose peace, which would come only when the United States let up its war of aggression against the Sandinistas, expressed through the Contra War.

Postrevolutionary neoliberalism and the rise of civil society, 1990–2006

The 1990 election ushered in peace but it also brought a turn to neoliberalism, and the harsh structural adjustment measures that came along with it. For many Nicaraguans the changes that were introduced produced greater hardship and despair.[9] With the Sandinistas out of government, civil society and NGOs began offering services that were no longer provided by the state. The women's movement, formerly organised through AMNLAE, the 'women's branch' of the FSLN, began to establish organisations that were autonomous from the state and the LGBTQ community found a space as well, with the two often overlapping. Lesbians had a public and well-received 'coming out' at the autonomous women's

---

9   See Babb, *After Revolution* on discourses of development, neoliberalism and the body.

movement's 'Festival of the 52 Percent' in Managua in 1991. Although this was a difficult time of transition in the country, important political openings occurred for social movements that were no longer tied to the interests of the FSLN. Notably, the NGOs Nimehuatzín and Xochiquetzal were founded by lesbian feminists who were devoted to addressing HIV/AIDS and the gay and lesbian community, though these NGOs were careful to state publicly that they served a broad and diverse clientele of those seeking sex education and sexual rights, not just the LGBTQ community.

During my many return trips to Nicaragua in the 1990s, I was fortunate to observe and participate in the growing LGBTQ presence in Managua and a few other cities in the country.[10] In the new neoliberal context, and with the rolling back of the progressive reforms of the Sandinista Revolution, a draconian sodomy law (Law 204) was instituted in 1992, with the result that Nicaragua was subject to the wholesale criminalisation of both gay men and lesbians. This repressive move by the government served to galvanise LGBTQ political activism and give it international exposure, even as activists needed to exercise caution lest they violate the new law. Beginning in 1991, Nicaragua began celebrating Gay Pride annually in late June, with a *jornada* (fortnight) of events, including talks and workshops, social events, and often a drag performance and 'Miss Gay' pageant. That same year, the feminist NGO Puntos de Encuentro began publishing *La Boletina*, which gave regular attention to gay pride and politics. Women continued to play a leadership role in the NGOs, in organising events and in attracting international funding. In 1993, the NGO Xochiquetzal launched the magazine *Fuera del Closet*, with articles on health, the body and LGBTQ lives, to coincide with Gay Pride events.

The distance that lesbians had come in gaining visibility was clear in 1996 during Gay Pride events. Psychologist and lesbian feminist Mary Bolt González's book *Sencillamente Diferentes…* had a launch to discuss its theme of lesbian self-esteem in urban Nicaragua, which drew a large audience.[11] The panellists included the lesbian feminist co-director (with Bolt) of Xochiquetzal, Hazel Fonseca and the famed comandante Dora María Téllez, and the festive evening closed with music by leading singer-songwriter Norma Elena Gadea.

While women have been the protagonists in much LGBTQ organising in Nicaragua, they have nonetheless continued to experience exclusionary practices in a *machista* society. Whereas gay bars attract men and offer them public areas in which to socialise, women have few such spaces. In one successful effort to correct the absence of women and lesbians in much of popular culture, Puntos de Encuentro produced a highly regarded and much-watched television series, *Sexto*

---

10 My own coming out during those years coincided with the developments in Nicaragua, and I followed them with keen interest.

11 M. Bolt González, *Sencillamente diferentes… La autoestima de las mujeres lesbianas en los sectores urbanos de Nicaragua*.

Sentido, with both gay and lesbian characters.[12] In 1999, a new (though short-lived) lesbian magazine, *Humanas: Por la visibilidad de lesbianas y sus derechos humanos*, was launched, with the objective of reaching out to Nicaraguan lesbians.

Lesbians in Nicaragua throughout the years of the Sandinista revolutionary government (and into the new millennium) have benefited from coordination with international feminist delegations to the country. As activist Rita Arauz expressed during the 1990s, 'We would always tell our foreign sisters, "Ask about the lesbians. Ask for us by name – my name, the names of the others. Remind them that we exist, that we're here and we're not going away"'.[13] Thus sexual orientation was identified as a feminist issue, making the Sandinista leadership and other Nicaraguans better aware of lesbians' existence in the country. This was furthered by the formation of such lesbian organisations as Nosotras, Grupo Safo, Entre Amigas, Grupo Lesbiana por la Visibilidad and the Lesbian Feminist Collective.

Lesbian visibility increased in the 1990s, but by the end of the decade, there was backlash. In 1998, shock waves were felt throughout Nicaragua when former President Daniel Ortega was charged by his adoptive stepdaughter Zoilamérica Ortega Murillo with 20 years of sexual abuse, beginning when she was 11 years old. While Ortega remained silent and hid behind his parliamentary immunity, his wife (Zoilamérica's mother) Rosario Murillo spoke often and publicly against her daughter's allegation. Appealing to religion and the traditional nuclear family, she was quoted as alleging that Zoilamérica's supporters were motivated by their 'uncertain sexual identity' into trying to influence her daughter, as well as projecting hatred for the opposite sex, rejecting marriage and motherhood, and, in general, the values and culture of heterosexuality. This effort to discredit the charges against Ortega by implying that lesbians were to blame for influencing Zoilamérica with distorted ideas became widespread.[14]

Post-2006 gains and losses with the return of the Sandinista government

Ortega's animosity towards women who defied social convention and opposed him politically was later expressed in the form of a backlash against feminists during his electoral campaign in 2006, and into his new presidency. In order to appeal to conservative voters, he chose to ally with the conservative Catholic

12   For an extensive discussion of this television series and of the protagonism of lesbians in the struggle for sexual rights in Nicaragua, see Howe, *Intimate Activism*.
13   Randall, *Sandino's Daughters Revisited*, 277.
14   This was not the only instance of politically motivated lesbian-baiting in Nicaragua, but that goes beyond the scope of this work. See Hobson, 'Si Nicaragua Venció' for an interesting discussion of international lesbian and gay solidarity with the Nicaraguan revolution, which describes the female masculinity that emerged with the struggle. This image of lesbians in Nicaragua, while seductive for many lesbians from the north, may have fed heteronormative fears in the country.

Church and to stand against abortion rights, even in the case of 'therapeutic' abortion following rape or when a woman's life was in danger. This extreme stance was challenged by feminists, who saw Ortega as an anti-democratic opportunist masquerading as a champion of the people.

Once elected, Ortega's comeback was marked by his targeting of feminists and other progressives who stood in opposition to his *caudillo* (macho/ strongman) style of politics. Notably, while shunning feminists, he began favouring the LGBTQ community, particularly the trans community, with resources and recognition. This may have been an effort to drive a wedge between feminists and the LGBTQ community, groups that had long worked together on issues of gender and sexuality. Moreover, it seemed to be a way of deflecting unwanted national and international attention from his stance on women's reproductive rights. And finally, as argued by González-Rivera and Kampwirth, supporting the LGBTQ community was a way to appear 'modern' in the current Latin American context and in the international arena of human rights.[15] Even so, as these scholars have expressed, there was 'more circus than bread', that is, there was greater cultural support than extension of political rights, although the infamous Law 204 was repealed and some new anti-discrimination legislation introduced in the revised Penal Code in 2007.[16]

As Kampwirth notes, 'the FSLN's new sexual diversity politics is not merely a response to international trends, but is also shaped by domestic politics, in particular by the history of FSLN-feminist movement relations, and by the tradition of clientelism in Nicaraguan politics'.[17] Some positive developments in recent years include the institutionalised presence of sexual diversity groups in every office of the Juventud Sandinista around the country. Furthermore, LGBTQ groups have benefited from resources made available by the Centro de Estudios Internacionales, headed by Zoilamérica Ortega Murillo (who is estranged from her mother, the Nicaraguan first lady). President Ortega named long-time activist Samira Montiel as the Procuradora de Diversidad Sexual (ombudswoman for sexual diversity) in the office of human rights in 2009. This may all be a form of 'pink washing', that is, using a friendly stance towards LGBTQ issues to conceal other more conservative stances, such as that on therapeutic abortion rights and the persecution of civil society actors, including well-known feminists. Moreover, some activists claim that despite the showcasing of LGBTQ concerns, there is little more beyond that as few new rights have been extended. Nonetheless, as a result of receiving a degree of state support, the LGBTQ community is expected to offer patronage and has lost some credibility as an autonomous social movement.

---

15 González-Rivera and Kampwirth, *One Hundred Years of LGBT History*.

16 See K. Kampwirth 'Abortion, antifeminism, and the return of Daniel Ortega: in Nicaragua, leftist politics?'; and N. Jubb, 'Love, family values and reconciliation for all, but what about rights, justice and citizenship for women?

17 Kampwirth, 'Organizing the Hombre Nuevo gay', 320.

When Ortega's government established new policies on family rights and protections in recent years, a number of feminists and LGBTQ activists were disappointed that the right to marry was not extended to same-sex couples, a right that is now expanding in the Americas, including Argentina, Brazil, Uruguay, Canada and the United States. Others, however, were not surprised and felt that the time was not yet right. When a new Family Code was debated in 2012, it was criticised for its exclusion of single-parent households and of LGBTQ-headed families. That same year, the Miss Gay Nicaragua pageant and the demonstrations against the Family Code were followed by incidents of violence, which suggests that despite some recent political gains, there are very real limits to Nicaraguan society's understanding and acceptance of gender and sexual difference.[18]

It is worth noting that in 2013 a collective of artists, academics and activists joined together in Nicaragua as 'Operación Queer' in order to give more visibility to gender and sexual difference. The collective's impact has been both cultural and political as it takes up questions of the body and identity, and of forms of exclusion relating not only to gender and sexuality but to social class, ethnicity, age, ability and aesthetics. Those in the collective have addressed whether there is something like a community among 'queer' Nicaraguans, understood to be diverse and fluid in its formation. The intellectual sophistication and cultural emphasis of Operación Queer should not stand in the way of recognising its fundamental political potential as well. As one indication of its ability to push LGBTQ Nicaraguans further in their analysis, Operación Queer has addressed its own elitism and appears to take a highly self-critical approach; indeed the collective acknowledges that, for example, a trans sex worker in the Managua market may not be familiar with queer theory, yet nonetheless transgresses everyday norms of sexual performance.[19]

Comparative revolutions and LGBTQ political cultures: Nicaragua and Cuba

In discussions of Latin American revolutionary societies, Nicaragua has often been compared to Cuba. While their revolutions were two decades apart, triumphing in 1979 and 1959 respectively, both had aspirations for social transformation based on economic development that was oriented towards socialist principles, and both stood up to the United States in order to struggle for such an ambitious goal. The two revolutionary societies had hidden histories of same-sex sexuality, which at first were attributed to the decadent past of their dependent capitalist dictatorships.

18   Kampwirth, 'Organizing the Hombre Nuevo Gay'.
19   For the discussion of Operación Queer I consulted various websites, including www.bienalcentroamericana.com/2016/08/08/operacion-queercochona/ (accessed 30 Apr. 2019). I also wish to acknowledge helpful conversations with Nicaraguan participants at a summer school on 'The culture of Sandinismo in Nicaragua', held in Wuppertal, Germany, July 2017.

Homosexuality was repressed even among the revolutions' supporters, with Cuba going so far as to imprison gay Cubans for crimes of anti-social behaviour and to quarantine those with HIV/AIDS. In more recent decades, both Cuba and Nicaragua have introduced more progressive legislation to protect the rights of gay men and lesbians. Although Nicaragua has emulated Cuba in establishing a Family Code, it has not gone as far in recent years to assure the social inclusion of its LGBTQ citizens. Interestingly, in both nations the daughter (or stepdaughter) of the standing president – Mariela Castro Espín in Cuba and Zoilamérica Ortega Murillo in Nicaragua – has played a key part in championing the rights of sexual minorities. Cuba's government, however, has gone further in addressing the needs of these new groups, including paying for transgender individuals to have sex reassignment surgery. The neoliberal, and patriarchal, tilt of the post-2006 FSLN government makes this level of support most unlikely in Nicaragua.

Cuba and Nicaragua have often been considered exceptional cases in Latin America, as both have had 20th-century revolutions that received wide popular support and altered the course of their histories. In the case of Cuba, its reputation for exceptionalism is more clearly deserved, as the nation steadfastly maintained its political commitment even in the face of frequent attempts by the United States to destabilise the government of Fidel Castro. In contrast to Cuba's half-century of defiance, Nicaragua's revolutionary government of the 1980s lasted only a decade before it was voted out of office. The destabilisation wrought by the Contra War was in large measure the work of the United States, which achieved its goal through the illegal supplying of arms to counterrevolutionaries. Nonetheless, Nicaragua's achievements during that brief revolutionary period, as well as after it, were in a number of ways exceptional.

In the post-1979 decade, Nicaragua accomplished a great deal of progressive change on many fronts, whether because of FSLN mobilisation experience, or in spite of it. By the end of the 1980s, not only feminists but also LGBTQ activists were finding a voice and a political space. Following the Sandinista electoral defeat in 1990, autonomous organising of women, including lesbians, and of gay men took the path of further movement-building activity. By March 1991, Nicaragua played host to a historic gathering of Central American feminists at the Montelimar beach resort. Nicaragua was emerging from what many considered 'backwater' status as a small Central American nation to become a regional leader in LGBTQ activism and cultural development.

Even where political rights have not yet been extended, it is notable that Nicaraguan culture has become more accommodating of gay and lesbian lives. The Gay Pride events during the annual *jornada* and the campaign for Sexuality Free from Prejudice have had an impact, lessening the stigma associated with same-sex sexuality. The media and popular culture now reflect greater diversity in people's private lives, in part the result of the hugely successful TV series *Sexto Sentido*. Viewing audiences came to know Angel and Vicki as fully drawn characters, as human beings who were struggling to come out publicly.[20] This opportunity to 'know' gay people and talk about their lives had a profound effect on viewers in Managua and beyond. During these years, the language itself shifted from using the local and disparaging terms '*cochones*' and '*cochonas*' to homosexuals or gays and lesbians. Recognising sexual identity as diverse and not as 'unnatural' has been a big step forward in granting greater dignity to sexual minorities in Nicaragua, as elsewhere.[21]

The Nicaraguan difference? Revolutionary legacies and limitations

How do we account for these changes and what can this tell us about the wider society? The Nicaraguan experience suggests that the period of social mobilisation wrought through the revolution gave lesbians, gay men and other sexual minorities who were involved a way of finding one another, and of recognising their own sexual difference. Their involvement in the revolutionary process also gave them the strategic tools necessary to develop a way of struggling for sexual rights. Some of the lessons of the revolution were carried over into activism. For example, NGOs supporting LGBTQ rights made use of broad-based popular education to promote sexual awareness and safer sex; activists looked to the grassroots to distribute condoms; and they seized public spaces to hold demonstrations and claim visibility, as when they held festive *plantones* (monthly gatherings) in the middle of Managua's busiest traffic island at Metrocentro. Even as they may have employed mobilisation strategies developed in the revolutionary setting, however, LGBTQ activists needed to move beyond the Sandinista reductionism of inequality to social class differences, to assert their sexual, gender and cultural rights, and their demands for social justice.[22]

To be sure, activists were also influenced by – and influenced – international currents in LGBTQ culture and politics. In earlier years, they sometimes had to deflect criticism that gay identity and activism were imported from the United States or elsewhere, that these were foreign (and contaminating) and not truly 'Nica'. Now that same-sex and queer sexualities and histories are better understood in Nicaragua, as elsewhere, it is not deemed necessary to shun association with transnational currents of LGBTQ activism. It is well recognised that some of Nicaragua's activists were deeply influenced by years of living abroad

20 See Howe, *Intimate Activism*.

21 When I gave a talk at the feminist NGO Puntos de Encuentro in 2003 on the occasion of the Gay Pride *jornada*, a member of the press approached me afterwards and asked if homosexuality was 'natural'. Such uncertainty about sexual identities persists in Nicaragua, but today there is arguably greater awareness of the fluidity of sexuality and greater tolerance for sexual difference.

22 It is notable that in the discussion of gender and sexual rights in Nicaragua, the focus is on the country's dominant *mestizo* (mixed race) population, without reference to minority indigenous and Afro-descendant peoples. For a broad treatment of the cultural history of sexuality by a prominent Nicaraguan feminist, see S. Montenegro, *La cultura sexual en Nicaragua*.

and brought back with them strategies for winning cultural and political rights, and that internationalists living in Nicaragua also contributed to building the movement. No longer was this seen as being at odds with the development of specifically Nicaraguan ways of 'doing politics' and enabling cultural identities to flourish.[23]

At the present juncture, given the ambivalent and contradictory politics of the FSLN, it is unclear whether the nation will continue along this path, but the state's neoliberal recognition of individual rights, and its desire to become more 'modern', may pave the way towards further gains. Moreover, Nicaragua's long-time association with social mobilisation at the popular level suggests that it may continue to serve as an example of what can be achieved with or without state support. The Nicaraguan Revolution was exceptional in Latin America for occurring *after* the emergence of feminist and gay social movements at the international level. This helped to shape the radical change that came about, from granting women rights as beneficiaries of land reform to granting more public space to lesbians, gay men, bisexuals and, most recently, trans Nicaraguans. Lesbians, as women whose sexuality has often been rendered nearly invisible in the past, have had an especially difficult challenge to gain recognition of both their gender and sexuality, yet they have frequently been the protagonists in sexual rights activism. As a result of their social struggle, many Nicaraguans in the LGBTQ community have undergone personal transformation and have won greater acceptance in daily life, and that in itself is no small accomplishment. Nonetheless, the LGBTQ community faces numerous challenges ahead as they strive to overcome the historical legacy of a still-heteronormative and sexist postrevolutionary society. As such, their recent experience shines a light on both the advances and the limitations of this 'exceptional' Central American nation.

Bibliography

Babb, F.E. (2001) *After Revolution: Mapping Gender and Cultural Politics in Neoliberal Nicaragua* (Austin, TX).

— (2003) 'Out in Nicaragua: local and transnational desires after the Revolution', *Cultural Anthropology*, 18 (3): 304–28.

— (2011) *The Tourism Encounter: Fashioning Latin American Nations and Histories* (Stanford, CA).

---

23 For transnational currents in LGBT organising in Nicaragua, see Babb, 'Out in Nicaragua', and Howe, *Intimate Activism*. See also the earlier work of R.N. Lancaster, *Life is Hard: Machismo, Danger, and the Intimacy of Power in Nicaragua*, which argued against using western-derived terms like 'gay' and 'lesbian' to describe Nicaraguans who engage in same-sex practices, and the recent discussion by P. Welsh 'Homophobia and patriarchy in Nicaragua, pp. 39–45, which draws attention to both 'modern' gay men and lesbians as well as more 'traditional' same-sex relations in today's Nicaragua. Welsh addresses Nicaraguan exceptionalism insofar as the country has fewer hate crimes than its neighbours, but notes the persistent homophobia as well.

Bienal Centroamericana (2016) 'Operación Queer/Cochona', www.bienalcentroamericana.com/2016/08/08/operacion-queercochona/ (accessed 16 Nov. 2019).

Bolt González, M. (1996) *Sencillamente diferentes... La autoestima de las mujeres lesbianas en los sectores urbanos de Nicaragua* (Managua).

D'Emilio, J. (2007) 'Capitalism and gay identity', in R. Parker and P. Aggleton (eds.), *Culture, Society and Sexuality: A Reader* (New York), pp. 250–8.

González-Rivera, V. (2011) *Before the Revolution: Women's Rights and Right-Wing Politics in Nicaragua, 1821–1979* (University Park, PA).

— (2014) 'The Alligator Woman's Tale: remembering Nicaragua's "first self-declared lesbian"', *Journal of Lesbian Studies*, 18 (1): 75–87.

González-Rivera, V. and K. Kampwirth (forthcoming) *One Hundred Years of LGBT History in Nicaragua.*

Heumann, S. (2014) 'The challenge of inclusive identities and solidarities: discourses on gender and sexuality in the Nicaraguan women's movement and the Legacy of Sandinismo', *Bulletin of Latin American Research*, 33 (3): 334–49.

Hobson, E.K. (2012) '"Si Nicaragua Venció": lesbian and gay solidarity with the Revolution', *Journal of Transnational American Studies*, 4 (2).

Howe, C. (2013) *Intimate Activism: The Struggle for Sexual Rights in Postrevolutionary Nicaragua* (Durham, NC).

Jubb, N. (2014) 'Love, family values and reconciliation for all, but what about rights, justice and citizenship for women? The FSLN, the women's movement, and violence against women in Nicaragua', *Bulletin of Latin American Research*, 33 (3): 289–304.

Kampwirth, K. (2004) *Feminism and the Legacy of Revolution: Nicaragua, El Salvador, Chiapas* (Athens, OH).

— (2008) 'Abortion, antifeminism, and the return of Daniel Ortega: in Nicaragua, leftist politics?' *Latin American Perspectives*, 35 (6): 122–36.

— (2014) 'Organizing the Hombre Nuevo Gay: LGBT Politics and the second Sandinista Revolution', *Bulletin of Latin American Research*, 33 (3): 319–33.

Lancaster, R.N. (1992) *Life is Hard: Machismo, Danger, and the Intimacy of Power in Nicaragua* (Berkeley, CA).

Montenegro, S. (2000) *La cultura sexual en Nicaragua* (Managua).

Randall, M. (1994) *Sandino's Daughters Revisited: Feminism in Nicaragua* (New Brunswick, NJ).

Thayer, M. (1997) 'Identity, revolution, and democracy: lesbian movements in Central America', *Social Problems*, 44 (3): 386–406.

Walsh, S.D. (2007) 'Advances and limits of policing and human security for women: Nicaragua in comparative perspective', in V. Sanford, K. Stefatos and C. Salvi (eds.), *Gender Violence, Conflict, and the State* (New Brunswick, NJ).

Welsh, P. (2014) 'Homophobia and patriarchy in Nicaragua: a few ideas to start a debate', *IDS Bulletin*, 45 (1): 39–45.

9. Conclusion: exceptionalism and Nicaragua's many revolutions

Justin Wolfe

As historians, we do well to remember that what's new is invariably old. Nicaraguan exceptionalism – particularly framed around the Sandinista Revolution and its aftermath – is one in a long history of such claims. At the very least, we ought to begin with Nicaragua's early 19th-century declaration of its 'geographic destiny' – defined by the potential for an interoceanic canal across its territory – to become the world's 'New Constantinople'.[1] By the latter half of the 19th century, as Nicaraguan elites surveyed the landscape of instability and authoritarianism that had come to define Central America, they boasted of Nicaragua, with its regular elections and single-term presidencies, being the 'Switzerland of Central America'.[2] As the 20th century dawned, Nicaraguan exceptionalism shifted from something material or institutional to a quality inherent in Nicaraguans, a widespread belief in what Hilary Francis refers to as Nicaragua's 'revolutionary heritage'. The earliest version of this framed the actions of Augusto Sandino's unrelenting struggle against US military occupation. Even if the Great Depression and Roosevelt's Good Neighbour Policy combined to diminish the US appetite for such endeavours, Nicaraguans looked to Sandino's rebellion as the essential element in US withdrawal in 1933.[3] Indeed, that exceptionalism formed the foundation for the FSLN's origin story and trajectory. For, despite the diffusion of guerrilla movements throughout Latin America after Cuba's success in 1959, only the FSLN succeeded in taking power to establish a revolutionary regime.[4]

How, when and to what extent this sense of a distinct heritage radiated across Nicaragua is at the heart of the chapters that make up this book. These are not

1 F. Kinloch Tijerino, *Nicaragua, identidad y cultura política (1821–1858)*.
2 A.J. Cruz, Jr., *Nicaragua's Conservative Republic, 1858–93*; C. Cruz, *Political Culture and Institutional Development in Costa Rica and Nicaragua: World-Making in the Tropics*.
3 E. Camacho Navarro, *Los usos de Sandino*. Jaime Wheelock Román, one of the FSLN's leading intellectuals, worked to position Sandino within a longer history of Nicaraguan exceptionalism in *Raíces indígenas de la lucha anticolonialista en Nicaragua, de Gil González a Joaquín Zavala, 1523 a 1881*.
4 T.P. Wickham-Crowley, *Guerrillas and Revolution in Latin America*.

J. Wolfe, 'Conclusion: exceptionalism and Nicaragua's many revolutions', in H. Francis (ed.), *A Nicaraguan Exceptionalism? Debating the Legacy of the Sandinista Revolution* (London: University of London Press, 2019), pp. 179–84. License: CC-BY-NC-ND.

easy questions to answer, and the works in this collection remind us that the history of the Sandinista Revolution is a moving target. It is the revolutionary struggle from the founding of the Sandinista National Liberation Front (FSLN); it is the revolution in triumph from 1979 to 1990; it is the Revolution in defeat. It is even, perhaps, the FSLN in resurgent power since 2007. It is also and always, all of these 'revolutions' in memory. Moreover, despite its relatively small size, Nicaragua's geographic and social diversity suggests even more that we are walking within a garden of forking paths.

Much of the richest work published in the aftermath of the Sandinista defeat in 1990 wrestled with the Sandinista loss by delving deeper into the history of Nicaragua's social and cultural complexity, too often ignored or minimised in the class-reductive analysis of Sandinista leadership. Whether it was peasants, indigenous communities or women, scholars revealed people whose lives and politics intersected with the revolution in ways that often seemed complementary, but which ended up in conflict as these communities' agency butted heads with the FSLN's vanguardist approach.[5] The chapters by Florence Babb and José Luis Rocha are particularly apt examples, albeit for different reasons. As Babb shows, the FSLN had trouble placing LGBT identities and rights within its ideological framework. With land reform, by contrast, the FSLN claimed to know better than peasants their needs and desires. What these chapters also reveal, and what is displayed in even fuller flower in the chapters by Fernanda Soto, David Cooper, Francis and Johannes Wilm, is how the Sandinistas provided both an ideological framework and the tools for organising newly imagined selves.

In some ways, it has been taken for granted that in creating new, revolutionary subjectivities, Nicaragua's pre-revolutionary selves were more straightforward, if not static. In 1985, relying on the dossiers of participants in the fighting to oust Somoza, Argentine sociologist Carlos Vilas tried to define the 'social subject' of the Sandinista Revolution.[6] An astute observer of contemporary Nicaraguan society, Vilas recognised and engaged with the country's regional variation – for example, that students accounted for 29 per cent of the participants from Matagalpa, but only 16 per cent in Masaya. That said, his analysis of occupational categories like *gentes de oficio* and *jornaleros* suggested a fixity not matched by historical experience.[7] The departments of

---

5 See, e.g., J. Gould, *To Lead as Equals: Rural Protest and Political Consciousness in Chinandega, Nicaragua, 1912–1979*; C.R. Hale, *Resistance and Contradiction: Miskitu Indians and the Nicaraguan State, 1894–1987*; J. Charlip, *Cultivating Coffee: The Farmers of Carazo, Nicaragua, 1880–1930*; J.L. Gould, *To Die in This Way: Nicaraguan Indians and the Myth of Mestizaje, 1880–1965*; E. Dore, *Myths of Modernity: Peonage and Patriarchy in Nicaragua*; J. Wolfe, *The Everyday Nation-State: Community and Ethnicity in Nineteenth-Century Nicaragua*.

6 C.M. Vilas, 'El sujeto social de la insurrección popular: La Revolución Sandinista', 20 (1) (Jan. 1985): 119–47.

7 *Gentes de oficio* is a category which includes skilled, self-employed workers in a range of occupations, such as craftsmen, plumbers, mechanics, carpenters, tailors and barbers. *Jornaleros* means day-labourers.

Chinandega and Carazo, for example, registered the highest degree of rural proletarianisation in the 1970s and consequently, Vilas noted, emerged as 'the departments where the political work of the FSLN began earlier with agricultural workers'.[8] The histories of their proletarianisation and what these meant for their political subjectivity, however, led these departments to have distinct experiences of the revolution in power and in post-1990 politics.[9]

Even in areas that seemed more homogenous, like the 'agricultural frontier' of Nueva Segovia, a teasing out of historical details further reveals the complex dynamics of the revolution. Lynn Horton's extraordinary study of the revolution and counter-revolution in the Segovian region of Quilalí explores the diverse entanglements within the Segovias. Quilalí had a diverse, yet highly unequal, distribution of land, a reality exacerbated in the 1970s by ongoing eastward migration into a zone with little resemblance to the undeveloped frontier of the 1950s. The FSLN's failure to understand these existing divisions, and the dreams of autonomy that drove frontier migration, made it nearly impossible for them to perceive what attracted some peasants to the revolution, and what enraged those who joined the Contras.[10] As Francis, Soto and Cooper show, the intersection between agency and institutionalisation remained crucial not just in the aftermath of the FSLN's electoral loss in 1990, but even with the FSLN's return to power in 2007.

For many of the authors in this collection, new forms of political organisation and participation constitute another key legacy of the revolution. The 20th century saw a number of major developments of this kind in Nicaragua, the first under the dynastic rule of the Somoza family, the second under the FSLN – often with striking parallels. Under US occupation, the Nicaraguan military was replaced with Guardia Nacional, which not only concentrated power in the hands of the Somozas, but created a truly viable national armed force in Nicaragua for the first time, one that both forged the culture of its members and established a new regime of policing (albeit, as Robert Sierakowski notes, highly corrupt and ineffective) across the territory.[11] Sierakowski argues that an equally dramatic shift in the culture of policing attended the revolution's creation of the Sandinista Police, one that initially persisted with its transformation into the post-1990 Nicaraguan National Police.[12] Following his return to power in 2007, however, Daniel Ortega initiated a campaign of political favouritism

8 Vilas, 'El sujeto de la insurrección popular', 135.
9 See, e.g., Gould, *To Lead as Equals*, 292–6; Charlip, *Cultivating Coffee*, 220–8; Wolfe, *The Everyday Nation-State*, 205–6. See, too, Karen Kampwirth's critique of the fixity of these categories in *Women and Guerrilla Movements: Nicaragua, El Salvador, Chiapas, Cuba*, 138–45.
10 L. Horton, *Peasants in Arms: War and Peace in the Mountains of Nicaragua, 1979–1994*.
11 R. Millett, *Guardians of the Dynasty*; K. Walter, *The Regime of Anastasio Somoza, 1936–1956*; R. Grossman, '"The Blood of the People": The Guardia Nacional's Fifty-Year War against the People of Nicaragua, 1927–1979', 59–84.
12 A useful comparison ought to be made with the Sandinista Popular Army and its transition into the Nicaraguan Armed Forces.

that undermined the police's institutional independence and converted it into a partisan tool of coercion.

The leadership of Anastasio Somoza García brought other substantial changes to Nicaraguan society, notably consolidating politics within a populist framework that built upon the anti-*caudillo* campaign of the US occupation and bureaucratising the state under his leadership.[13] Together, these transformed Nicaraguan political culture, especially in coffee and cotton zones as well as in urban centres throughout the country. Recent scholarship has contended it was these that held the Somocista state together, and more so than the Guardia's repression. As Jeffrey Gould argues in his ground-breaking study of *campesinos* (farmers) in Chinandega, 'Workers and peasants largely accepted the Somozas' variant of populism and its corresponding rules of the game, but, at the same time, they shaped and transformed Somocista populism.'[14] Victoria González-Rivera's research on women's politics within the Somocista state reveals similar shifts in political culture.[15] Indeed, growing resistance to the dictatorship was frequently framed in terms of its opposition, not in the revolutionary language of the FSLN but rather in their own experience of Somocista development. The difficult road for land reform, detailed by Rocha, and in food policy, analysed by Christiane Berth, reveal the Sandinista's blind spot to the depths of Somocista political culture. That said, as Rocha's work indicates – and so, too, that of Babb, Cooper, Francis, and even Soto – the revolution provided new institutional tools and practices that have lasted long beyond the FSLN's defeat in 1990.

In his oft-cited work on the post-Second World War defeat of fascism and the collapse of Soviet communism in the late 1980s, Francis Fukuyama argued for the emergent hegemony of neoliberal republicanism.[16] Fukuyama's thesis on 'the end of history' recognised a profound shift in the global balance of power. In this shift, the United States consolidated political and economic predominance through its assumption of the role as the 'last superpower' together with the intensified position of economic organisations like the World Bank, the International Monetary Fund and the World Trade Organization in which the US held a nearly unchecked leadership role. The world has proved itself to be more complex than Fukuyama imagined. His focus on a totalising 'common ideological heritage of mankind' led him to dismiss whatever kinds of 'strange thoughts occur to people in Albania or Burkina Faso', for their failure to be of world-historical importance or influence.[17] Since the late 1990s, it has become clear that Nicaragua (and Latin America more generally) adjusted to

---

13 Walter, *The Regime of Anastasio Somoza*; M. Gobat, *Confronting the American Dream: Nicaragua under U.S. Imperial Rule*. *Caudillo* can be translated as 'strongman'.

14 J.L. Gould, *To Lead as Equals: Rural Protest and Political Consciousness in Chinandega, Nicaragua, 1912–1979*, 293.

15 V. González-Rivera, *Before the Revolution: Women's Rights and Right-Wing Politics in Nicaragua, 1821–1979*.

16 F. Fukuyama, 'The end of history?', *The National Interest*, 3–18.

17 Ibid., 9.

these dramatic changes in quite diverse ways, producing an array of left- and right-wing governments, each often responding to questions of environment, race and ethnicity, and global capitalism in ways hardly imaginable in the 1970s.

Still, Nicaragua has continued to participate as a subordinate in the global capitalist system. Its economy has grown in recent years – with higher and more consistent rates of growth than most of Latin America since 2009 – but, it is still focused on roles long familiar to the Global South: agro exports, *maquiladoras*[18] and tourism. After returning to power, the FSLN began to develop a series of social programmes framed in revolutionary rhetoric, but which are, as Francis and Berth show, more attuned to neoliberal expectations and ties of political clientelism, and far from universal. That said, rates of extreme poverty have declined considerably over the last decade, fuelled especially by increases in income among the poorest in the country, growth in the agricultural sector, robust commodity prices and foreign aid from Venezuela. Long-term instability in prices, environmental concerns and the crisis in Venezuela, however, raise serious questions about the Sandinistas' ability to sustain these economic advances. What is more, despite its ballyhoo-ed social programmes, social investments remain too low to effect meaningful redistributions of wealth or opportunity.[19]

Most of the authors in this collection argue that an exceptional sense of self-empowerment and grassroots organisational capacity represent the key legacies of the Sandinista Revolution. Since 2007, these have played out against the backdrop of growing FSLN popularity and its consolidation of power. Still, there is a fragility to the constellation of forces that have made this possible. The Sandinistas have raised expectations while also limiting dissent. How will Nicaraguans respond if meaningful social transformations fail to materialise? Will the revolution's legacy lead to greater inclusion? Or, perhaps, serve as the springboard for change when the economy inevitably stumbles.

Bibliography

Camacho Navarro, E. (1991) *Los usos de Sandino* (Mexico City).

Charlip, J. (2003) *Cultivating Coffee: The Farmers of Carazo, Nicaragua, 1880–1930* (Athens, OH).

Cruz, Jr., A.J. (2002) *Nicaragua's Conservative Republic, 1858–93* (New York).

Cruz, C. (2005) *Political Culture and Institutional Development in Costa Rica and Nicaragua: World-Making in the Tropics* (Cambridge).

Dore, E. (2006) *Myths of Modernity: Peonage and Patriarchy in Nicaragua* (Durham, NC).

Fukuyama, F. (1989) 'The end of history?', *The National Interest*, 16: 3–18.

---

18 A foreign-owned factory or workshop that assembles goods for export and is exempt from duties or tariffs.

19 World Bank, 'Nicaragua: paving the way to faster growth and inclusion', 11–13.

Gobat, M. (2005) *Confronting the American Dream: Nicaragua under U.S. Imperial Rule* (Durham, NC).

González-Rivera, V. (2011) *Before the Revolution: Women's Rights and Right-Wing Politics in Nicaragua, 1821–1979* (University Park, PA).

Gould, J. (199) *To Lead as Equals: Rural Protest and Political Consciousness in Chinandega, Nicaragua, 1912–1979* (Chapel Hill, NC).

— (1998) *To Die in This Way: Nicaraguan Indians and the Myth of Mestizaje, 1880–1965* (Durham, NC).

Grossman, R. (2005) '"The Blood of the People": the Guardia Nacional's fifty-year war against the people of Nicaragua, 1927–1979', in C. Menjívar and N. Rodríguez (eds.), *When States Kill* (Austin, TX), pp. 59–84.

Hale, C.R. (1994) *Resistance and Contradiction: Miskitu Indians and the Nicaraguan State, 1894–1987* (Stanford, CA).

Horton, L. (2014) *Peasants in Arms: War and Peace in the Mountains of Nicaragua, 1979–1994* (Athens, OH).

Kampwirth, K. (2010) *Women and Guerrilla Movements: Nicaragua, El Salvador, Chiapas, Cuba* (University Park, PA).

Kinloch Tijerino, F. (1999) *Nicaragua, identidad y cultura política (1821–1858)* (Managua).

Millett, R. (1977) *Guardians of the Dynasty* (Maryknoll, NY).

Vilas, C.M. (1985) 'El sujeto social de la insurrección popular: La Revolución Sandinista', *Latin American Research Review*, 20 (1): 119–47.

Walter, K. (1993) *The Regime of Anastasio Somoza, 1936–1956* (Chapel Hill, NC).

Wheelock Román, J. (1974) *Raíces indígenas de la lucha anticolonialista en Nicaragua, de Gil González a Joaquín Zavala, 1523 a 1881* (Mexico City).

Wickham-Crowley, T.P. (1993) *Guerrillas and Revolution in Latin America* (Princeton, NJ).

Wolfe, J. (2007) *The Everyday Nation-State: Community and Ethnicity in Nineteenth-Century Nicaragua* (Lincoln, NE).

World Bank (2017) 'Nicaragua: paving the way to faster growth and inclusion', Systematic Country Diagnostic, Washington, DC, 18 June.

Index

Adoquines, 9
Agency, of Nicaraguans, 3–4, 11–12, 15, 56, 87–8, 96–7, 149, 154–5, 162, 180–1
Agrarian Reform, 48, 61, 64–6, 68, 81, 103–25, 129
ALBA, 76, 78, 81, 182
Alemán, Arnoldo, 33, 35, 75, 119, 148
ATC, 76, 106–10, 117–18, 123
Atlantic Coast, 13, 36, 37, 38, 115

basic grains, 64, 66–9, 81, 114, 118
Belli, Gioconda, 9, 71
bono productivo, 131, 132, 135, 138, 142, 158, 160
Borge, Tomás, 10, 12, 26, 27, 32

CAFTA, 77, 81
Callahan, Robert, 38
Canal, 5, 37, 120–3, 179
Carazo, 118, 181
Catholic Church, 128, 152, 154–5
CDS, 28–30, 128
Chamorro, Violeta, 31, 75, 115, 116–18, 123, 169
CIA, 30, 96
CIERA, 64, 67–9
CLS, 135, 137–9, 159
Colombia, 24, 46
Contra War, vii, 1, 9, 12, 14, 15, 16, 30, 32, 36, 46–56, 61, 68, 109, 149, 150, 165, 166, 169, 174
Cooperatives, 48–51, 54, 66, 106–7, 109–14, 118, 121–2, 130, 136, 142, 149–50, 159

Costa Rica, 22, 34, 92, 95, 118
CPC, 127, 131–5, 139, 159–60
Credit and Saving Cooperatives, CCS, 49, 106, 109, 111–113
Cuba, 2, 23, 25, 27, 30, 76, 89–91, 95, 166, 167, 173–174, 179

DDR, 30, 91, 93, 94
DEA, 36

El Salvador, 6, 22, 32, 33, 34, 53, 95, 151
Elections, 4, 5, 24, 37, 47, 61, 71, 74, 75, 130, 131–3, 135, 150, 169, 179
ENABAS, 63, 66, 72, 75, 76, 78
EPS, 27, 32, 47
Esteli, 8, 68, 147,148, 151, 152, 153, 154
Exceptionalism, 1–17, 22–4, 40, 46, 58, 80, 95–6, 103–6, 109, 114, 116, 117, 122–3, 143, 145, 148, 162, 166–7, 174, 176, 179, 183

Fair Trade, 16, 77, 114, 121–3, 142
FAO, 61, 63, 64, 70, 81
Fonseca, Carlos, 10, 89
food aid, 61, 69, 70, 73, 75, 77, 80
food security, 64, 65, 76, 77, 79, 80, 81, 122
food sovereignty, 62, 63, 65, 76, 77, 81
FSLN, 2, 4, 5, 6, 8, 11, 12, 13, 25, 26, 32, 35–8, 40, 45, 46, 47, 54–8, 75, 79, 81, 89, 91, 93, 104, 106, 109, 114, 123, 127, 131,

132, 134, 137, 138–43, 148–50, 159, 161, 166, 169, 170, 172, 174, 176, 177, 179, 180–3

Gabinetes de la Familia, 135, 160
Gender, 35, 166, 172–6
Germany, 146
Graeber, David, 88
Granera, Aminta, 26, 29, 35, 37, 38, 39, 41
Guatemala, 22, 32, 33, 53, 95, 117

HIV/AIDS, 165, 169, 170, 174
Honduras, 22, 33, 34, 49, 50, 95, 96, 113, 149
Horton, Lynn, 56, 159, 181
Hurricane Joan, 72–5

Indio Maíz reserve, 8
INSS, 5, 8

Jinotega, 6, 9, 113, 118

liberation theology, 25, 145, 147, 149–56, 162

Managua, 5, 8, 9, 24–6, 28, 29, 32, 38, 67, 69, 71, 74, 78, 137, 138, 169, 170, 173, 175
Matagalpa, 54, 78, 108, 113, 118, 121, 142, 180
Mexico, 24, 72, 90, 92, 114
Mística, 22, 27, 32, 40, 43, 137
MIDINRA, 111
Montoya, Rosario, 7, 11, 154n10
Murillo, Rosario, 2, 36, 37, 134, 171

National Police (PN), 5, 8, 21–2, 35–40, 45, 56–7, 118, 121, 133, 135, 181–2
Northern Triangle, 22, 33, 34

Organization of American States, 5, 7, 11
Ortega, Daniel, 1, 3, 4, 5, 6–10, 12–14, 21–3, 31, 35–40, 61–2, 74–7, 81, 87, 89, 93–4, 96–8, 131, 149, 160, 162, 166, 169, 171–4, 182
Ortega, Zoilamérica, 171, 172, 174

peasants, 5, 12–16, 46–51, 54, 55–7, 62–3, 66, 68–9, 73–3, 76, 78, 80, 81, 83, 103, 105–14, 117, 121–3, 141, 157n12, 180, 181, 182
plan techo, 138, 160
protests, 5, 8, 21, 25, 31, 37, 39, 69, 110, 116

RAAN, 47
Race, 173, 175n22, 183
Ramírez, Sergio, 3, 88, 92, 93
Reagan, Ronald, 4, 30, 64, 90, 91, 92, 105
Ruiz, Henry, 7
Russia, 15, 93–8

Sandinismo, 23, 92, 97, 147, 167
Sandinista Agricultural Cooperatives (CAS), 106, 111–13
Sandinista Police, 26–35, 52–3
Sandino, 10, 110, 179
Segovias, 121, 181
Self-Defence Cooperatives, 49, 149
SMP, 49, 57, 113
Somoza Debayle, Anastasio, 9, 10, 25–7
Somoza dynasty, 4, 7, 14, 22, 28, 30, 33, 36, 39–40, 54, 65, 66, 87, 89, 90, 104, 108, 119, 128, 167, 180, 181
Somoza García, Anastasio, 23–4, 182

Soviet Union, 30, 74, 87, 89–96, 98, 110–11
Spain, 34, 121, 157
students, 8, 10, 34, 39, 57, 87, 90, 151, 169, 180
Sweden, 34

Torrijos, Omar, 27
Trump, Donald, 1

UNAG, 76, 106–11, 113, 114, 129
United Nations, 24, 39
United States, 1, 15, 23, 87–93, 95, 96, 98, 132, 168, 173, 174, 175
   emigration to, 2, 6, 33
   intervention of, 4, 70, 74, 169, 182
universities, 9, 21, 34, 57, 115, 141
UNO, 62, 75, 81, 169
UNRISD, 64

Vatican II, 156
Venezuela, 2, 6, 9, 76n70, 81, 96–7, 183
Vivas, René, 26, 27, 31

Zero Hunger Program, 61, 76, 77, 78n78

Founded in 1965, the Institute of Latin American Studies (ILAS) forms part of the University of London's School of Advanced Study, based in Senate House, London.

ILAS occupies a unique position at the core of academic study of the region in the UK. Internationally recognised as a centre of excellence for research facilitation, it serves the wider community through organising academic events, providing online research resources, publishing scholarly writings and hosting visiting fellows. It possesses a world-class library dedicated to the study of Latin America and is the administrative home of the highly respected *Journal of Latin American Studies*. The Institute supports scholarship across a wide range of subject fields in the humanities and cognate social sciences and actively maintains and builds ties with cultural, diplomatic and business organisations with interests in Latin America, including the Caribbean.

As an integral part of the School of Advanced Study, ILAS has a mission to foster scholarly initiatives and develop networks of Latin Americanists and Caribbeanists at a national level, as well as to promote the participation of UK scholars in the international study of Latin America.

The Institute currently publishes in the disciplines of history, politics, economics, sociology, anthropology, geography and environment, development, culture and literature, and on the countries and regions of Latin America and the Caribbean. Since autumn 2019, the Institute's books, together with those of the other institutes of the School, have been published under the name University of London Press.

Full details about the Institute's publications, events, postgraduate courses and other activities are available online at http://ilas.sas.ac.uk.

Institute of Latin American Studies
School of Advanced Study, University of London
Senate House, Malet Street, London WC1E 7HU

Tel 020 7862 8844, Email ilas@sas.ac.uk
http://ilas.sas.ac.uk

Recent and forthcoming titles published by the Institute of Latin American Studies:

Rethinking Past and Present: Essays in memory of Alistair Hennessy (2018)
edited by Antoni Kapcia

Shaping Migration between Europe and Latin America: New Approaches and Challenges (2018)
edited by Ana Margheritis

Brazil: Essays on History and Politics (2018)
Leslie Bethell

Creative Spaces: Urban Culture and Marginality in Latin America (2019)
edited by Niall H.D. Geraghty and Adriana Laura Massidda

Cultures of Anti-Racism in Latin America and the Caribbean (2019)
edited by Peter Wade, James Scorer and Ignacio Aguiló

Memory, Migration and (De)Colonisation in the Caribbean and Beyond (2020)
edited by Jack Webb, Roderick Westmaas, Maria del Pilar Kaladeen and Robert Tantam

Cultural Worlds of the Jesuits in Colonial Latin America (forthcoming 2020)
edited by Linda Newson

www.ingramcontent.com/pod-product-compliance
Ingram Content Group UK Ltd.
Pitfield, Milton Keynes, MK11 3LW, UK
UKHW021838210426
5322IPUK00021B/353